THE CHIAPAS REBELLION

Es necesaria una cierta dosis
de ternura para adivinar en
esta oscuridad un pedacito
de luz, para hacer del deber
y la vergüenza una orden.

EZLN

Neil Harvey

THE CHIAPAS REBELLION

The Struggle for Land and Democracy

Duke University Press   Durham and London   1998

Fifth printing, 2005

© 1998 Duke University Press

Printed in the United States of America on acid-free paper ∞

Typeset in Carter and Cohn Galliard with Gill Sans extra bold

display by Keystone Typesetting, Inc.

Library of Congress Cataloging-in-Publication Data appear on

the last printed page of this book.

Frontispiece photograph by Neil Harvey

Translation of EZLN quotation on poster:

Amid this darkness we need some tenderness to see a little light, to make

duty and responsibility the orders by which we act.

This book is dedicated to Wendy,

with love and thanks.

Hechos son amores, y no buenas

razones.

CONTENTS

LIST OF TABLES, MAPS, AND PHOTOS

Tables

Maps

Photos

ACKNOWLEDGMENTS

Many people have made this book possible. I would particularly like to thank the members of the Organización Campesina Emiliano Zapata, the Central Independiente de Obreros Agrícolas y Campesinos, and the Unión de Uniones Ejidales y Grupos Campesinos Solidarios de Chiapas for spending the time to talk with me and for offering such wonderful hospitality in their homes and communities. I would also like to thank Walda Barrios, Antonio Mosquera, Juan Balboa, María Eugenia Reyes Ramos, and Andrés Aubry for their invaluable help and encouragement during the initial stages of my research. Marisela González generously shared her knowledge, personal letters, and documents pertaining to the peasant movements in Chiapas, for which I am especially grateful. In Mexico, I also benefited greatly from the friendship, work, and support of Luis Hernández, Humberto Carton de Grammont, Armando Bartra, Sergio Zermeño, Silvia Gómez Tagle, Carlos Heredia, Antonio García de León, Julio Moguel, Enrique Semo, Aída Hernández, and Sonia Toledo. I am particularly indebted to Jan Rus and Tom Benjamin, whose comments, suggestions, and criticisms greatly improved the quality of this book. Reynolds Smith at Duke University Press has also been a constant source of encouragement and expert guidance. I also thank Sonya Manes for her excellent work in copyediting the manuscript.

My interest in Mexico and Chiapas was sparked by my undergraduate professors at Portsmouth Polytechnic, particularly Gerald Martin and Tessa Cubitt. Their enthusiasm and commitment to Latin American Studies are greatly appreciated. At the University of Essex, I was fortunate to have been a graduate student of several scholars who have influenced this work, including Joe Foweraker, Ernesto Laclau, Alan Knight, and Christian Anglade. I am especially grateful to Joe Foweraker for his enthusiastic support of my work and his stimulating graduate research seminar in 1983 to 1984, where many of the ideas contained in my work first took shape.

I acknowledge the financial support of the Economic and Social Research Council of Great Britain, which provided funding for doctoral research in 1985 to 1987 and for postdoctoral work in Mexico in 1990 to 1992. The Nuffield Foundation provided a small grant for research in the summer of 1990. I am grateful to the Institute of Latin American Studies at the University of London, particularly Leslie Bethell and Victor Bulmer-Thomas, for the opportunity to develop my work on Mexican politics as a research fellow during 1989 to 1992. I also thank Wayne Cornelius and the Center for U.S.-Mexican Studies at the University of California, San Diego, for offering me a visiting research fellowship during 1988 to 1989. The Center's Ejido Reform Research Project has also generously provided support for fieldwork in Chiapas in 1994 and 1996. Parts of this book have been presented at various seminars, workshops, and panels organized by the Center for U.S.-Mexican Studies. I am grateful to all those who participated in these meetings for their comments and suggestions, particularly David Myhre, Keith Pezzoli, Maria Lorena Cook, Ilán Semo, Jonathan Fox, Jeffrey Rubin, Paul Haber, Juan Ramírez Saíz, Gabriel Torres, Magda Villareal, Horacio Mackinley, Kevin Middlebrook, Richard Snyder, Luin Goldring, Lynn Stephen, Rosario Pisa, Pieter de Vries, Monique Nuijten, Daniel Nugent, Sergio Zendejas, Gail Mummert, John Gledhill, and Peter Ward. I also thank Michael Redclift, Jutta Blauert, Alison MacEwen Scott, Bob Jessop, Paulo Speller, Christine Eber, Charlene Floyd, and Gil Joseph for their enthusiastic support of this project at different stages.

I would also like to thank the interest shown in my work by Tom Skidmore at Brown University and Elizabeth Mahan at the University of Connecticut during 1992 to 1994 and to acknowledge the students at both universities who participated so enthusiastically in courses on social movements in Mexico and Latin America. I learned a great deal from our interaction, and many of those classroom discussions are reflected in these pages. I am also fortunate to have found a stimulating and supportive environment at New Mexico State University. I would like to thank all the faculty, staff, and students associated with the Department of Government, particularly Nancy Baker and Bill Taggart, who generously offered their advice and guidance, and the students who contributed with their comments to the revision of the first draft. My deep appreciation goes to Chris Halverson, as well, who created all the maps for the book.

Several parts of this work have been published elsewhere. A section of chapter 5 first appeared in "The New Agrarian Movement in Mexico, 1979–90," Research Paper 23 (London: Institute of Latin American Studies, 1990). Parts of chapter 7 have appeared in three separate publications: "Rebellion in Chiapas: Rural Reforms, Campesino Radicalism and the Limits to Salinismo," pp. 1–49 in *The Transformation of Rural Mexico,* No. 5, 2d ed. (La Jolla: Center for U.S.-Mexican Studies, University of California, San Diego, 1994); "Rural Reforms and the Zapatista Rebellion: Chiapas, 1988–1995," pp. 187–208 in *Neoliberalism Revisited: Economic Restructuring and Mexico's Political Future,* edited by Gerardo Otero (Boulder: Westview, 1996); "Rebellion in Chiapas: Rural Reforms and Popular Struggle" *Third World Quarterly* 16 (1) (1995): 39–73. Part of chapter 1 is also forthcoming in the journal *Social Politics* (Oxford University Press). I am grateful to the publishers of these books and journals for permission to reproduce sections of my work here.

A great deal of encouragement has also come from my family and friends. My mother, Sheila Price, has always shown a keen interest in my studies and research. Bob Curtis has been a great source of intellectual stimulation, as well as a wonderful friend. I appreciate the support of my father-in-law, Eduardo Ontiveros Soto, and the memory of María Elena Ontiveros Nevares. For my wife, Wendy, I give my very special thanks for her love, encouragement, and critical eye, which made this book more worthy of the people whose story it tells. I appreciate her accompaniment and help at different stages of the research, including the first interviews, which we did together in Chiapas in the summer of 1987. Our two daughters, Alhelí and Jazmín, have been a source of inspiration and wonder. Unfortunately, at this stage they associate Chiapas with their dad being somewhere far away. Hopefully, when they are old enough to read this, they will see why it had to be that way now and again. The writing of this book has been a rare privilege, not only for the story it tells, but also for the wonderful people I have had the pleasure of meeting and knowing on the way, many of whose names I have not been able to include in these brief acknowledgments.

GLOSSARY OF ACRONYMS

ACIEZ	Alianza Campesina Independiente Emiliano Zapata
ACR	Alianza Campesina Revolucionaria
AEDPCH	Asamblea Estatal Democrática del Pueblo Chiapaneco
ANAGSA	Aseguradora Nacional Agrícola y Ganadera
ANCIEZ	Alianza Nacional Campesina Independiente Emiliano Zapata
ANIPA	Asamblea Nacional Indígena Plural por la Autonomía
ANOCP	Asamblea Nacional Obrera Campesina Popular
ARIC	Asociación Rural de Interés Colectivo
BANRURAL	Banco Nacional de Crédito Rural
BCCH	Bloque Campesino de Chiapas
CCA	Comité Comunitario de Abasto
CCH	Comité Coordinador Huasteco
CCI	Central Campesina Independiente
CCRI	Coordinadora Campesina Revolucionaria Independiente
CCRI-CG	Comité Clandestino Revolucionario Indígena– Comandancia General
CDLI	Comité de Defensa de la Libertad Indígena
CDP (Chihuahua)	Comité de Defensa Popular (Chihuahua)
CDP (Durango)	Comité de Defensa Popular (Durango)
CECVYM	Coalición de Ejidos Colectivos de los Valles Yaqui y Mayo
CEOIC	Consejo Estatal de Organizaciones Indígenas y Campesinas
CEPAL	Comisión Económica para América Latina y el Caribe
CEPCO	Coordinadora Estatal de Productores de Café de Oaxaca
CFE	Compañía Federal de Electricidad
CIOAC	Central Independiente de Obreros Agrícolas y Campesinos

CLCH	Coordinadora de Luchas de Chiapas
CNC	Confederación Nacional Campesina
CND	Convención Nacional Democrática
CNOC	Coordinadora Nacional de Organizaciones Cafetaleras
CNPA	Coordinadora Nacional Plan de Ayala
CNPI	Coordinadora Nacional de Pueblos Indígenas
CNTE	Coordinadora Nacional de Trabajadores de la Educación
COCEI	Coalición Obrera Campesina Estudiantil del Istmo
CODECOA	Convenio de Cooperación Agrícola
COMA	Comuneros Organizados de Milpa Alta
CONACAR	Consejo Nacional Cardenista
CONASUPO	Compañía Nacional de Subsistencias Populares
COFOLASA	Compañía Forestal Lacandona, S.A.
COPARMEX	Confederación Patronal de la República Mexicana
COPLADE	Comisión de Planeación y Desarrollo del Estado
COPLAMAR	Coordinación Federal del Plan Nacional de Zonas Deprimidas y Grupos Marginados
DAAC	Departamento de Asuntos Agrarios y Colonización
DPI	Departamento de Acción Social, Cultura y Protección Indígena
EPR	Ejército Popular Revolucionario
ESPAZ	Espacio Civil para la Paz
EZLN	Ejército Zapatista de Liberación Nacional
FCI	Frente Campesino Independiente de Oaxaca
FCP	Frente Cívico Potosino
FDN	Frente Democrático Nacional
FIPI	Frente Independiente de Pueblos Indios
FLN	Fuerzas de Liberación Nacional
FNCR	Frente Nacional Contra la Represión
FNDP	Frente Nacional Democrático Popular
FOCECH	Federación de Obreros y Campesinos del Estado de Chihuahua
FOCED	Federación de Obreros y Campesinos del Estado de Durango
FROM	Frente Regional de Organizaciones de Masas
FPZ	Frente Popular de Zacatecas
FZLN	Frente Zapatista de Liberación Nacional

GNGO	governmental nongovernmental organization
IMSS	Instituto Mexicano de Seguro Social
INI	Instituto Nacional Indigenista
INMECAFE	Instituto Mexicano del Café
JLCA	Junta Local de Conciliación y Arbitraje
LP	Línea Proletaria
MLN	Movimiento de Liberación Nacional
MLR	Movimiento de Lucha Revolucionaria
MNPA	Movimiento Nacional Plan de Ayala
MOCRI	Movimiento Campesino Regional Independiente
MULT	Movimiento de Unificación y Lucha Triqui
NAFTA	North American Free Trade Agreement
NGO	nongovernmental organization
OCEZ	Organización Campesina Emiliano Zapata
OCIHV	Organización Campesina Independiente de la Huasteca Veracruzana
ODECO	Organización y Desarrollo de la Comunidad
OID	Organización Ideológica Dirigente
OIPUH	Organización Independiente de Pueblos Unidos de las Huastecas
OPA	Organización de Pueblos del Altiplano
OPL	Organización para la Liberación
ORCO	Organización Regional Campesina de Occidente
PAN	Partido de Acción Nacional
PAOM	Partido Agrario Obrero Morelense
PCM	Partido Comunista Mexicano
PECE	Pacto para la Estabilidad y el Crecimiento Económico
PEMEX	Petróleos Mexicanos
PGR	Procuraduría General de la República
PMS	Partido Mexicano Socialista
PP	Partido Popular
PP	Política Popular
PPS	Partido Popular Socialista
PRA	Programa de Rehabilitación Agraria
PRD	Partido de la Revolución Democrática
PRI	Partido Revolucionario Institucional
PRT	Partido Revolucionario de los Trabajadores
PROCAMPO	Programa de Apoyo Directo al Campo
PROCEDE	Programa de Certificación de Derechos Ejidales y Titulación de Solares Urbanos

PRONASOL	Programa Nacional de Solidaridad
PSE	Pacto de Solidaridad Económica
PSUM	Partido Socialista Unificado de México
RAN	Registro Agrario Nacional
SAM	Sistema Alimentario Mexicano
SARH	Secretaría de Agricultura y Recursos Hidráulicos
SEDESOL	Secretaría de Desarrollo Social
SEDUE	Secretaría de Desarrollo Urbano y Ecología
SOA	Sindicato de Obreros Agrícolas
SOCAMA	Solidaridad Campesina Magisterial
SPP	Secretaría de Programación y Presupuesto
SPR	Sociedad de Producción Rural
SRA	Secretaría de la Reforma Agraria
STI	Sindicato de Trabajadores Indígenas
STPS	Secretaría de Trabajo y Previsión Social
UCEZ	Unión de Comuneros Emiliano Zapata
UCI	Unión Campesina Independiente
UCIRI	Unión de Comunidades Indígenas de la Región del Istmo
UE	Unión de Ejidos
UEEZ	Unión de Ejidos Emiliano Zapata
UEIS	Unión de Ejidos Independientes de Sinaloa
UELC	Unión de Ejidos Lázaro Cárdenas
UGOCM	Unión General de Obreros y Campesinos de México
UGOCP	Unión General Obrera Campesina Popular
UNAM	Universidad Nacional Autónoma de México
UNCAFESUR	Unión de Productores de Café de la Frontera Sur
UNORCA	Unión de Organizaciones Regionales Campesinas Autónomas
UP	Unión del Pueblo
UPM	Unión de Pueblos de Morelos
URECHH	Unión Regional de Ejidos y Comunidades de Huasteca Hidalguense
USAID	United States Agency for International Development
UTC	Unión de Trabajadores del Campo
UU	Unión de Uniones Ejidales y Grupos Campesinos Solidarios de Chiapas

INTRODUCTION

This book is an account of the struggle for land and democracy in Chiapas. The Zapatista rebellion of January 1, 1994, caught international attention as it exposed the social injustices and political repression faced by the region's Mayan population. It also provided an opening for many indigenous people in Mexico to demand full participation in deciding the future of their cultures and their nation. The historical goals of land, autonomy, and dignity became part of the search for effective citizenship.

The research contained in this book draws on fieldwork carried out over a period of ten years. It was in April 1987 that I began to investigate the different histories, strategies, and forms of organization of three peasant organizations that had been formed independently of the ruling Institutional Revolutionary Party (PRI) and its affiliated National Peasant Confederation (CNC). These were the Union of Ejidal Unions and United Peasant Groups of Chiapas (UU) in the Lacandon forest and the central highlands, the Independent Confederation of Agricultural Workers and Peasants (CIOAC) in the northern municipality of Simojovel, and the Emiliano Zapata Peasant Organization (OCEZ), principally in the municipality of Venustiano Carranza. My objective was to document and compare the struggles of these organizations in terms of their impact on the political system. This impact was interpreted as the gradual erosion of corporatist and clientelistic forms of political control though an increasing insistence on respect for constitutional rights. Yet the subsequent period was one of retrenchment for many of Mexico's peasant movements. The government of Carlos Salinas de Gortari (1988–94) successfully co-opted the leaders of several national organizations, allowing it to proceed rapidly with a series of legal and institutional reforms to reduce the state's obligations to the peasantry. At the same time, local and regional movements were seriously divided by internal leadership disputes. They were also constantly undermined by acts of repression and government corruption. The liberalization of the Mexican economy further weakened the capacity of peasant organizations to meet the pressing needs of their members. Without the strength to contest the direction of government policy, peasant movements looked like marginal players in a game dominated by the new technocratic elites in government, business, and finance. Political analysts were surprised by the muted response to Salinas's controversial decision to amend Article 27 of the Constitution, one of the main gains of the agrarian movements of the 1910–17 Revolution. Their focus shifted to the economic organizations of different sectors of small producers and their ability to remain afloat within liberalized markets. The signing of the North American Free Trade Agreement (NAFTA) in the fall of 1993 appeared to mark the future terrain of struggle for all peasant movements, whether PRI affiliated or not.

The Zapatista uprising shook up this picture in several ways. In Chiapas, the independent peasant movements gained a new lease of life, occupying over 50,000 hectares of land in the first six months of 1994 and forcing the government to recognize the continued need for land redistribution. The solidarity of large sectors of civil society with the Zapatista Army of National Liberation (EZLN) began to take on an organizational structure and common platform for the democratic transformation of Mexico. At the same time, two of the most traditionally marginalized sectors of Mexican society, women and indigenous peoples, became leading protagonists in the democratization of gender and ethnic relations. Despite internal divisions and conflicts, these different movements refocused attention on the search for new forms of political representation, this time within an explicitly democratic discourse.

This book describes these shifting patterns of popular mobilization from the vantage point of peasant activism in Chiapas since the early 1970s. Its goal is to draw on my original question concerning the political significance of peasant movements, by asking the same question of the Zapatista rebellion. Does it represent a continuation of traditional forms of rural protest, or does it break with earlier patterns and open up new possibilities for political change? In short, what does this rebellion mean for our understanding of popular struggle in Mexico?

To answer this question, we have to enter the political world of peasant communities, organizations, and struggles. This is a world full of hope, stubborn resistance, and aspirations, but also of factionalism and violence. It is a world of convergence and mobilization, but also of division and repression. In Chiapas, it is also a world in which many small acts of resistance created the conditions of possibility for the Zapatista uprising. When the EZLN appeared on January 1, 1994, it was not a small band of guerrillas hoping to incite a popular uprising. Rather, it was a well-organized indigenous army with a mass base of support.

Structure of the Book

The movements that gave rise to the rebellion are not isolated phenomena. For this reason, it is useful to locate them within broader debates concerning popular mobilization and political change in Mexico and Latin America. Chapter 1 presents some of the main lines of debate within this literature and highlights the specifically *political* nature of popular movements. The definition of movements as attempts to construct "the people" as a political actor helps to focus our attention on the relations among peasant and indigenous communities, their organizations, and the state. Chapter 2 provides a historical perspective on these relations in Chiapas from the colonial period to the 1960s. In this account, the meaning of community is seen not in static, essentialist terms, but as the always contested outcome of shifting social relations. This chapter draws particular attention to the way in which new meanings of community were constructed by colonists of the Lacandon forest through their interaction with the Catholic diocese of San Cristóbal de Las Casas.

Chapters 3 and 4 focus on the origins and early development of new indigenous peasant movements in the Lacandon forest, Simojovel, and Venustiano Carranza during the 1970s and early 1980s. They document the demands and struggles of each of these movements and also reveal some of their ambiguities and contradictions, particularly concerning relations between leaders and base and between strategic choices and alliances. These dilemmas are linked in chapter 5 to the problems of constructing national networks of peasant organizations since the late 1970s. This chapter reveals how divisions at the national level were reflected in local organizations. It also shows how new linkages to federal government agencies could be exploited in regions such as Chiapas where authoritarian elites blocked the solution of agrarian and economic demands.

Internal divisions were exacerbated by the repressive actions of the state government during the administration of Absalón Castellanos Domínguez in 1983 to 1988. In this period Chiapas was defined as a problem for national security due to its proximity to the wars in Central America. It was also seen as in need of economic development and land regularization in order to overcome social instability. Chapter 6 discusses the various measures taken by federal and state government in these years and their effects on peasant organizations in the region. It also notes the conditions under which the EZLN began to develop in the Lacandon forest.

By the time Salinas assumed the presidency in December 1988 the peasant movements in Chiapas had been weakened by repression, internal divisions, and economic crisis. They were therefore unable to significantly contest the promarket thrust of the government's neoliberal policy reforms in agriculture. Chapter 7 examines the impact of these reforms in Chiapas, particularly those concerning the coffee and maize sectors, as well as the constitutional amendments to Article 27 and the new Agrarian Law of 1992. It discusses the reaction of peasant organizations to the end of land reform and focuses specifically on the deteriorating social conditions in the Lacandon forest that led to the armed rebellion.

Chapter 8 addresses the significance of the rebellion by referring to four areas of popular mobilization that were expanded by the Zapatistas. These are the struggles for indigenous peoples' rights, democratization in Mexico, land reform in Chiapas, and women's rights. This chapter shows how each of these struggles has been present in shaping the content of the peace talks in Chiapas. The chapter also discusses their potential for coalescing into a new national movement for democratic change, and it describes the nature of conflicts between and within popular organizations and the use of violence by local elites and public security forces.

The concluding chapter discusses the precariousness of the political spaces opened by the Zapatistas. It also highlights issues of power and responsibility in responding to the challenges raised by the rebellion. In order to help orient readers, appendix A provides a brief chronology of peasant movements in Chiapas between 1965 and 1997.

I am writing this at a moment of great suffering in Chiapas. On December 22, 1997, some forty-five unarmed people, mostly women and children, were killed in Acteal in the municipality of San Pedro Chenalhó. Survivors of the attack identified the assassins as belonging to a paramilitary group with links to the PRI. Thousands of Zapatista sympathizers have fled their homes in fear of more attacks. Despite their suffering, the protagonists of this struggle remain convinced of their ability to challenge and transform the system that oppresses them. With great patience and determination they continue to demand the most basic of human rights: the right to live and participate as equal and valued members of a political community.

Chapter 1

THE RIGHT TO HAVE RIGHTS

Solutions to our problems depend on the strength we achieve. The answer lies with the people, for that is where history is made.
— Member of Emiliano Zapata Peasant Organization (OCEZ), Chiapas, September 1987

The men and women of the EZLN, the faceless ones, the ones who walk in the night and who belong to the mountains, have sought words that other men and women could understand. And so they say: First. — We demand that there be free and democratic elections.
— Comité Clandestino Revolucionario Indígena–Comandancia General (CCRI-CG), Zapatista Army of National Liberation EZLN, Chiapas, February 1994 (EZLN 1994:177)

[We call for the formation of] a political force that does not aim to take power, a force that is not a political party. . . . A political force that can organize the demands and proposals of the citizens so that those who govern, govern by obeying.
— EZLN, Fourth Declaration of the Lacandon Forest, Chiapas, January 1996

Why do the Zapatistas wear ski masks? This was the question that one journalist posed on New Year's Day 1994 to the man who presented himself as *subcomandante* Marcos. On that day, San Cristóbal de Las Casas, Ocosingo, Las Margaritas, Altamirano, Chanal, Oxchuc, and Huixtán, seven towns located in the highlands of Chiapas, had been occupied by an army of over 3,000 indigenous people demanding land, jobs, housing, food, health care, education, independence, freedom, democracy, justice, and peace (map 1.1). Marcos responded to the question by invoking the novelty of the Zapatistas:

The main reason is that we have to be careful that nobody tries to be the main leader. The masks are meant to prevent this from happening. It is

Map 1.1. Area of the Zapatista Rebellion and Location of Chiapas in Mexico

about being anonymous, not because we fear for ourselves, but rather to avoid being corrupted. Nobody can then appear all the time and demand attention. Our leadership is a collective leadership and we must respect that. Even though you are listening to me now, elsewhere there are others who are masked and are also talking. So, the masked person here today is called "Marcos" and tomorrow it might be "Pedro" in Las Margaritas, or "Josué" in Ocosingo, or "Alfredo" in Altamirano, or whatever he is called.

So, the one who speaks is a more collective heart, not a single leader, or *caudillo*. That is what I want you to understand, not a caudillo in the old style and image. The only image that you will have is that those who have made this rebellion wear ski-masks. And the time will come when the people will realize that it is enough to have dignity and put on a mask and say that they too can do this. (Autonomedia 1994:62–63)

In Mexico, the term *caudillo* traditionally refers to a type of leader who exercises undisputed control within popular movements. The caudillo commands attention and promotes unconditional allegiance among his followers. The fact that the Zapatistas have sought to transcend caudillismo is, in itself, a significant development in Mexico's long history of peasant struggles. It has also revealed the potential for new forms of political organization. This book seeks to explain how it became possible to think and act in new ways. On this basis, we can better evaluate the significance of the rebellion for political life in Mexico.[1]

The Causes of the Rebellion

Many scholars and commentators have debated the causes of the rebellion. For anthropologists with long experience in the field, the uprising resulted from a combination of ecological crisis, lack of available productive land, the drying up of nonagricultural sources of income, the political and religious reorganization of indigenous communities since the 1960s, and the rearticulation of ethnic identities with emancipatory political discourses (Collier and Quaratiello 1994; Nash 1995). Rural society was seen as finally breaking under the impact of economic crisis and neoliberal reforms. Constitutional reforms affecting the status of agrarian reform and the signing of NAFTA were considered to have exacerbated long-standing grievances over unequal land distribution and rural poverty (Barry 1995; Harvey 1994; Hernández 1994a; Ross 1995; Russell 1995). The Zapatistas' communiqués tended to confirm these findings and assured that land tenure, indigenous rights, and democratization would form the central points around which their political struggle would evolve in the following two years (EZLN 1994, 1995).

Other authors were less convinced that social grievances alone were responsible for the rebellion. In an attempt to deny the authenticity of the EZLN as an indigenous rebellion, several writers argued that outside political activists, with roots in the Marxist Left of the 1970s, were manipulating the Indians for their own political objectives. They pointed to the fact that the Zapatistas' charismatic spokesperson, subcomandante Marcos, was a university-educated,

middle-class mestizo (Pazos 1994; Warman 1994). Although recognizing the existence of grave poverty and social injustice in Chiapas, Arturo Warman and other government officials argued that the
situation was improving and that there was less racism toward Indians now than in the past. In this analysis, channels for negotiation
did exist and the decision to take up arms was therefore unjustified
and motivated solely by the political ambitions of outsiders, or, in
words of then president Carlos Salinas de Gortari, "professionals of
violence."

The most complete version of this argument was provided by
Carlos Tello (1995). In his book, Tello detailed the arrival of various leftist currents in Chiapas in the 1970s and their association
with different groups of pastoral workers of the Catholic diocese of
San Cristóbal de Las Casas. In this account, the EZLN was formed
on the back of the prior organizing efforts of the diocese and its
bishop, Samuel Ruiz García. For Tello, the socialist origins of
Marcos and other Zapatista leaders overshadow their current political discourse of democracy and freedom. The shift from revolution
to democracy is portrayed by Tello as nothing more than an opportunistic reaction to the collapse of socialism in the East and the
demise of guerrilla movements (and the Sandinista government) in
Central America. The EZLN avoided a similar fate by "discovering"
the political purchase of democracy, especially when it could be
linked to a condemnation of the very real material injustices faced
by indigenous communities in Chiapas.

Tello's book appeared precisely at the same time that the Zedillo
government launched a new military offensive against the EZLN.
On February 9, 1995, under pressure from foreign investors to
resolve the Chiapas crisis once and for all, arrest orders were issued
for dozens of alleged EZLN leaders around the country. Among the
accused was Marcos, identified by the Attorney General's Office
(PGR) as Rafael Sebastián Guillén Vicente, a former university
professor from Tampico and member of an urban guerrilla organization, the National Liberation Forces (FLN), which had been
inactive since its main cells were broken up in the mid-1970s. This
official version coincided with Tello's book, which appears to have
relied on confidential police and military files, interspersed with
selective interviews of advisers of peasant organizations in the can-

yons of the Lacandon forest (Las Cañadas) who were opposed to the EZLN.[2]

If it is true (as many critics suggested) that the timing of the book's appearance was meant to justify the armed offensive and discredit the EZLN, then it failed dramatically. Large-scale demonstrations in Mexico City demanded a peaceful solution, the reopening of peace talks, and an end to the witch-hunt of Zapatista sympathizers. Protesters marched on the Zócalo declaring "Todos Somos Marcos" in clear repudiation of the government's use of the supposed identity of the subcomandante for its military offensive. When peace talks eventually resumed in April, the EZLN demanded recognition as a political force. Agreeing to negotiate with the EZLN made it increasingly difficult for the government to uphold charges of terrorism against members of an organization they had in essence acknowledged as legitimate. Gradually, in the face of constant pressure from the EZLN representatives and human rights organizations, most of those detained during 1995 were released due to lack of evidence.

Whether the PGR files are true or not, they clearly did not determine the political significance of the EZLN to the extent Tello and others supposed. Although other authors also noted the novelty of a democratic guerrilla movement, they emphasized the validity and timeliness of the new *zapatismo*. Carlos Fuentes wrote of the first "postmodern" revolution, one that escaped the ideological confines of the cold war and which pointed toward a more pluralistic future (Fuentes 1995). Jorge Castañeda, who had recently completed a major study of the decline of the Left in Latin America, saw the Zapatistas as "armed reformists." Their goal was not to take over state power, but to get basic demands met. The arms were simply necessary to gain attention and shake the complacency of a political establishment that had long ignored the social injustices faced by indigenous people (Castañeda 1993, 1994). Some academics in the United States also celebrated the postmodern qualities of the uprising, particularly the break with old forms of organization and strategy and the effective use of media exposure and new communications technologies such as the Internet (Burbach 1994; Halleck 1994).

Although these analyses are useful in exploring the causes and possible meanings of the rebellion, I believe that insufficient attention has been given to the complexity of relationships between structure and agency. Although it is true that neoliberal reforms have altered previous modes of capital accumulation and social order, their precise impact cannot be deduced from their own internal logic. Similarly, the interests of the Zapatistas are not reducible to a predetermined essence, nor to their simple manipulation by political entrepreneurs. Instead, we need to pay much closer attention to the interactive process of identity formation, political organization, and engagement with the state.

A similar set of concerns lies at the heart of recent attempts to build a "political process" model for understanding social movements (McAdam, McCarthy, and Zald 1996; Tarrow 1994; McAdam, Tarrow, and Tilly 1997). By highlighting how movements interact with changing political opportunities, mobilizing structures, and cultural framings, this approach offers a more complete view of popular mobilization than those constrained by a sole focus on movements and the participants themselves. The approach in this book shares these same concerns but adopts a different methodology. This is due to the nature of the central research question that has driven my analysis of peasant movements and the Zapatistas. The main problem the book addresses is not, therefore, how to identify the factors that facilitate or hinder popular mobilization in Mexico and other authoritarian states. Instead, its aim is to try and grasp the political significance of popular struggle in such contexts. That is, how have peasants contested the terms under which the political system has constituted them as subordinate? More precisely, how do oppressed groups create spaces for not only contesting their material conditions but also the political and cultural discourses that reproduce their subordination? This question does not obviate the need for detailed analysis of the interactions between diverse actors and structures, but it does fix our attention on a deeper and older problem, one by no means limited to Chiapas.

This problem concerns the conditions for the exercise of effective citizenship. In twentieth-century Mexico, it can be argued that a form of "corporatist citizenship" has existed, in which the state has

sought to determine and regulate acceptable forms of political behavior. This model has been partly transformed by the electoral
reforms of the past two decades and the shift to a discourse enshrined in liberal constitutionalism. However, the Chiapas rebellion can be seen not only as a clear break with the corporatist
citizenship of the Mexican state but also as a critique of narrow
versions of democratic citizenship. The Zapatistas not only exposed
the gaps between liberal ideals and daily reality for most Mexicans;
they opened up the possibility for a more radical understanding of
citizenship and democracy.

By making the *construction* of citizenship the central question for
analysis, the methodology cannot emerge from some pregiven universal definition of what citizenship entails. Instead, it must trace
the linkages people attempt to establish between particular claims
and their broader validity. In this regard, I am in agreement with
the general thrust of poststructuralist thought on identity formation and seek to advance a nonessentialist view of categories such as
class and *ethnicity, peasant* and *Indian, state* and *citizenship*. However,
I do not accept the relativist claim that all identities can be understood solely on their own terms. While rejecting the possibility of
some uncontestable ground of universal truth, I also argue that no
identity exists in isolation from other identities. In other words, in
affirming their particularity, popular movements are unavoidably
drawn into a relative universalization. As Laclau has stated, "the impossibility of a universal ground does not eliminate its need; it just
transforms the ground into an empty space which can be partially
filled in a variety of ways (the strategies of this filling is what politics
is about)" (Laclau 1995:164). This approach challenges the idea
that the definition of citizenship is dependent on some ultimate
source of authority. Instead, it allows us to assume and demand
responsibility for the political world that we alone create. My goal
in this book is not therefore to explain a causal chain of events leading to a predetermined outcome, but, on the contrary, to stress the
political construction of citizenship from the fragments of multiple
struggles against oppression. This chapter attempts a theoretical
justification for adopting this approach by discussing some of the
main contributions to recent debates on the definition, novelty, and
significance of popular movements in Mexico and Latin America.

Political Nature of Popular Movements

What is a social, or popular, movement? Do agricultural cooperatives or communal kitchens constitute social movements? Or, are
social movements only those movements that challenge the central
institutions and values of a political system? David Slater's volume
New Social Movements and the State in Latin America was one of the
first attempts to reconceptualize popular protest in Latin America
(Slater 1985b). Slater identified a diverse array of movements and
argued that they are defined by the ways they break with traditional
practices and theories of collective action. He therefore took issue
with the influential work of Alain Touraine, who reserved the category of social movements to those struggles over historicity, or "the
set of cultural models that rule social practices" (Touraine 1988:8).
Touraine based his theory on the experience of postindustrial societies of Western Europe. In this context social movements are
simply "the work that society performs on itself," that is, the struggle over cultural meanings, identities, and difference. Material demands and class divisions no longer occupy the center of social
conflict. In their place we find the critiques of modernity itself
posed by pacifists, feminists, environmentalists, ethnic minorities,
gays and lesbians, and cultural movements. Consequently, for Touraine, much of the activity that passes as "social movements" in
Latin America can best be described as "collective defensive behavior." This category refers to actions directed toward the state
that seek solutions for particularistic demands. For example, a local
peasant movement that demands access to land or credit does not
challenge the state and its mode of operation, much less the ideas
and values that underpin government policy or modernity. Some
movements, however, may develop the potential to modify decisions or even whole systems of decision making. Touraine defined
these movements as "social struggles." In this category we might
find movements that are able to transform government policies
through their mobilization and pressure. Finally, there are "social
movements" per se. In Touraine's view these are largely absent in
Latin America because the dominant modes of historicity are established by the state and the most integrated political actors, rather

than by autonomous social actors of civil society. Popular organizations must direct their demands to the state if they are to achieve solutions. They are forced to play by the state's rules and are therefore unable to challenge the "cultural models that rule social practices."

Several of the contributors to Slater's volume rejected Touraine's classification as either misleading or simply Eurocentric. Slater himself made the valuable argument that the human rights movement in Argentina, for example, may fit each of Touraine's three categories (Slater 1985b:19–20). It is a form of defensive collective behavior in that its immediate goal was to obtain the release or appearance of all political prisoners. Their struggle for an accountable justice system can also be seen as a social struggle to transform governmental structures. Finally, the invocation of ethical values challenged the highly authoritarian and patriarchal cultural models that ruled social practices in Argentina. But are we then left without any analytical distinction between an urban neighborhood association and a full-fledged national movement for far-reaching political change? Clearly we need some way of distinguishing between levels of political engagement, without assuming the rigid separation of defensive collective behavior from social struggles or social movements. Slater attempted to resolve the definitional problem by invoking the *novelty* of Latin American social movements. That is, movements are defined by their (new) *political* practices rather than by their social composition or cultural critique of modernity. We will return to the novelty question in the following section, but here it is important to note that this way of defining social movements located them more squarely in the political sphere and, as a result, marked a crucial difference from those approaches which gave primacy to noninstitutional politics.

This "political" definition guided the contributions to the volume *Popular Movements and Political Change in Mexico* edited by Joe Foweraker and Ann Craig (1990). Foweraker argued that movements are defined by their political practices rather than by their social composition. They are therefore better understood not as "social" movements, but as "popular movements," in that they seek to establish the "people" as a political actor. They are unavoidably "institutionalist" in their orientation; that is, they must engage the political system if they are to get demands met. But they also contest the terms of political representation. In the Mexican case this approach translates into a pervasive challenge to clientelism and regional or sectoral bossism (*caciquismo*). Popular movements are therefore institutionalist and nonconformist. They seek representation without sacrificing political autonomy. This goal involves them in a gradualist strategy to redefine the parameters of struggle and expand the horizons of what is politically possible. This struggle takes place in the interstices of a contested and shifting "legal and institutional terrain" (Foweraker 1990).

Novelty of New Social Movements

The problems of definition were partly resolved by referring to the novelty of contemporary social movements. Slater drew on the work of Ernesto Laclau and Chantal Mouffe (1985) in defining the novelty. In Western Europe and the United States, "new social movements" were seen as responses to new forms of subordination characteristic of postwar capitalist societies. The increasing commodification, bureaucratization, and massification of everyday life were seen by Laclau and Mouffe as generating counterhegemonic struggles to resist the impersonal power of the market and the state. Examples of such struggles included feminism, environmentalism, and pacifism. New social movements also represented a crisis of traditional paradigms of interest representation. Rather than assuming the separate location of a political level where interests rooted in the social sphere find representation, Laclau and Mouffe argued that the politicization of more and more social spaces led to the emergence of autonomous social movements, thereby dissolving the traditionally accepted division between the political and the social. The New Left slogan "the personal is political" or the student movements' struggles to democratize university education can be seen as examples of the expansion of democratic struggles to more social arenas. Finally, Slater referred to the value new social movements place on grassroots democracy, or *basismo,* in opposition to the hierarchical and patriarchal relations of centralized power that marked political parties and "old" social movements such as the labor unions. Again, new social movements were seen as promoting greater gender equality, more decentralized structures, and respect for cultural diversity.

Referring more specifically to Latin America, Slater noted some similarities and some crucial differences. New movements were also seen as resisting state power, but here state power was defined by excessive centralization and authoritarianism, rather than the massification and bureaucratization of Western liberal democracies. This kind of state power was particularly evident with the overthrow of populist regimes and the establishment of military rule in the Southern Cone and Brazil. In this new, more exclusionary political environment, social movements had to develop new strategies and practices of resistance. Second, as a result of fiscal crisis and the adoption of monetarist policies, the state in Latin America during the 1970s was unable or unwilling to meet the basic material needs of citizens. New movements responded by organizing to meet their own needs while building pressure on government agencies to modify policies that hurt the poor. These movements were particularly visible in the urban periphery of large Latin American cities, where basic services were lacking. The large proportion of female participants in these movements and the shift from workplace to community-based demands marked their novelty in the Latin American context. Finally, one of the effects of authoritarian rule and economic hardship was to generate grassroots movements that sought to maintain their autonomy from existing political parties. With the political sphere "frozen," it was impossible to have social interests represented at that level, even if we assume that such a model remained a theoretically valid one in Latin America. As a result we find the politicization of social spaces, not as a result of postindustrial sensibilities to the crisis of modernity, but simply as a necessity of life under military or authoritarian rule. Nevertheless, this politicization of the social in Latin America also marks a break with earlier patterns of popular representation that tended to be dominated by political parties and clientelistic networks of patronage. The systematic dismantling of linkages of this type led popular groups to search for new, autonomous spaces for expressing their demands. Religious, cultural, and nonpartisan activities became the ideal spaces for rebuilding people's capacity to resist political, economic, and social exclusion. In the process, they also generated new ways of acting politically that developed into a parallel critique of the hierarchical nature of political parties.

Laclau concluded his essay in Slater's volume by asking whether the transitions from military rule in Latin America in the early 1980s would lead to the reproduction of traditional political spaces, which have tended to reduce all political practice to a relation of representation. Or, he continued, "will the radicalization of a variety of struggles based on a plurality of subject positions lead to a proliferation of spaces, reducing the distance between representatives and represented?" (Laclau 1985:41–42). That is, would the new social movements remain imprisoned by the political discourses of the past, such as the Leninist faith in the revolutionary vanguard or the national variants of populism, both with their cult of the leader and their invocation of a collective will? Or, would these movements break with the past and articulate a "radical democratic imaginary" from numerous rather than one central point of antagonism?

Laclau used the concept of antagonism to refer to social conflict. However, he went much further than this sociological definition by making it the central characteristic of any social order. Rather than assume that political structures contain their own principles of development, Laclau stressed the partial and incomplete nature of all structures, giving primacy to those elements that negate and undermine claims to any objective or necessary foundation. Following Derrida, he noted that all structures have a "constitutive outside," which both negates the structure's completion but also affirms its (contingent) existence. As a result, the only possible ground is one continually open to the actions of social agents. The constitutive role of antagonism replaces the unfolding of objective laws of history, providing room for hope in the transformation of oppressive conditions now and always (Laclau 1990:6–7, 16–17).

If we see society as constituted by antagonisms rather than by any predetermined principle of order, we are forced to recognize the *political* nature of antagonism because there is no necessary relation between a particular conflict and how that conflict is interpreted. Although some antagonisms do acquire a central position in a society's transformation, this is not an inevitable result of objective conditions. Instead, the dislocations within a structure (for exam-

ple, economic crises and restructuring) are open to their politicization by different forces. In this regard, new social movements can
be seen as acting upon a proliferation of antagonisms beyond those
that tended to dominate political imaginaries of the Left in Mexico
and Latin America. This is of crucial importance when addressing
the novelty and significance of the Zapatista rebellion.[3]

The argument that new social movements were indeed "new" did
not convince everyone. For some, it appeared to leave out the historical dimension of popular protest. Referring to the Mexican
case, Alan Knight (1990) described the continuities in popular
movements, noting that identity had always been problematical
and contingent. It was therefore no great revelation to find different
sectors of the working class simultaneously supporting the ruling
PRI, the Mexican Communist Party (PCM), or the far Right. Mexico's new popular movements of the 1980s could be understood by
reference to the effects of economic crisis on the poor, and the
supposedly "new practices" were simply an extension of traditional
strategies of appealing to those in positions of power. In short, the
popular movements in Mexico were not new in the way that new
social movements theorists believed. Although they may have involved new actors or new demands, their practices remained the
same and should not be misread as the sign of an emerging democratic political culture.

Knight's criticisms, however, were made at an empirical rather
than a theoretical level. Laclau's arguments could easily accommo-
date the presence of antagonism at any point in history. It was not a
matter of how far back we want to go, because the social, by definition, is always constituted by antagonism and never by the ideological closure of state discourses. The difference between Knight's
and Laclau's analyses concerns the novelty of contemporary movements, but here Laclau had not made any detailed reference to
Mexico or Latin America, beyond the fact that the transitions from
authoritarian rule potentially allowed for a proliferation of political
actors, rather than their reabsorption by the totalizing discourses of
Marxism and populism. That Knight did not see such a break-
through does not deny the validity of the theoretical distinctions
made by Laclau. Furthermore, that economic dislocations played
such a central role for Mexican popular movements in the 1980s in

no way implies that these movements automatically adopted a class character, still less a socialist consciousness. In fact, the two were not as far apart as it seemed, because they both gave primacy to agency and history rather than objective structures or interests. Knight's own interpretation of the Mexican Revolution is consistent with this less deterministic and more relational approach (Knight 1986).

Similar empirical problems were posed by a group of Latin American sociologists who, in the midst of economic crisis, saw not plurality and diversity but fragmentation, anomie, and a radical *disarticulation* of the social (Tironi 1988; Zermeño 1990). Postmodern politics in Latin America was not primarily about the discovery of new sensibilities and respect for difference. It was the crisis of development, the state, and the hope of social integration that marked the "lost decade" of the 1980s. Drugs, street crime, and gangs came to occupy the spaces vacated by the state and political parties. In these conditions, the political articulation of demands depended not on new practices of radical democracy, but on its antithesis: the caudillo, or charismatic leader who claimed to interpret the "collective will." The caudillo was certainly no stranger to Mexican politics (nor the Left) and, in the absence of strong civil associations and parties, the "return of the leader" appeared as the only possible means of integrating the masses. If hegemony was not to be used out of historical context, these writers demanded a sociological analysis of popular movements, their strengths and, in particular, their limitations (Zermeño 1985). However, this view of resistance as basically collective defensive behavior was unable to account for important differences in how popular movements engage the political system.

Significance of Popular Movements: Clientelism or Citizenship?

What, then, is the political significance of social movements in Latin America according to these authors? Slater and Laclau argued that they represent a "recasting of the political" as new social spaces are politicized within a broad critique of authoritarianism and tra-

ditional forms of representation. However, the return to democratic rule had ambiguous results for social movements. The old
political parties and practices tended to dominate once more as social movements found it difficult to carry over their radical critique
of authoritarianism into the more complex day-to-day negotiations
of democratic politics. Several authors noted how the decline in
social movement activity coincided with the reestablishment of
party systems and familiar patterns of clientelistic politics (Canel
1992; Cardoso 1992; Jaquette 1989; Schneider 1992).[4]

Referring specifically to Mexico, the contributors to Foweraker
and Craig (1990) attempted to deal with this issue by evaluating
the impact of particular movements on the political system. The
diverse nature of these movements made generalization hazardous.
At least two opposing conclusions were drawn from the case studies. On the one hand, it was argued that social movements had a
discernible effect on the opening of more political spaces for the
expression of popular demands. The impact was not measured in
terms of the radical transformation of the political system, but in
the gradual and piecemeal conquest of reforms that expand the
possibilities for democratic struggle. The effects were also felt in the
generation of new political discourses that upheld citizenship rights
in contrast to traditional appeals to populist leaders or benevolent
patrons. Another position argued for a more historical perspective
in judging the supposed novelty of contemporary movements.
Knight and Rubin questioned the whole idea that Mexico had a
strong corporatist state until the 1968 student movement unleashed
a new generation of organizers for new social movements. Taking a
regional and historical focus, Rubin (1990) showed how spaces for
voice and autonomy have been central to the lives of people in
Juchitán throughout the postrevolutionary period. The Worker-
Peasant-Student Coalition of the Isthmus (COCEI) has been significant because it represents the continuity of popular struggle, rather
than constituting a new challenge to a mythical corporatist state.
Even the guarded optimism of Foweraker and others was seen as
misplaced by another contributor, Sergio Zermeño, who described
increasing exclusion of the mass of the population from modern
spaces of political, cultural, and economic interaction. Instead, the
population's desire for integration, fomented by industrialization

and the oil-debt boom of the late 1970s, had been shattered by the unrelenting crisis of the 1980s (Zermeño 1990). In this view, social movements fight defensive actions to protect highly localized "restricted identities" in the face of political co-optation and repression. Put simply, social movements are a minute fragment of an increasingly impoverished and disorganized society, or, to use Zermeño's term, *México roto*. Zermeño's arguments also contrast with Carlos Monsiváis's more optimistic reading of a "society getting organized," in which the author chronicled the struggles of teachers, earthquake victims, peasants, urban activists, and students in the mid-1980s (Monsiváis 1987).

The debate over the significance of Mexico's popular movements continued to revolve around the challenge to traditional forms of representation. Some, like Zermeño, held out little hope that these movements could survive in the face of rapid social decay. Similarly, Judith Hellman (1994) saw only two, equally uninviting, alternatives for popular movements. Either they sacrificed their political autonomy for short-term material benefits, or they maintained their autonomy at the cost of repression or marginalization. Hellman observed that during the Salinas presidency most movements opted for the former. Citing Paul Haber's (1994) analysis of the urban-based Popular Defense Committee (CDP) in Durango, she concluded that clientelism remained strong as CDP leaders were prepared to negotiate agreements with the government in exchange for political quiescence on broader national economic and social policies. In fact, Hellman argued that we should not expect popular movements to formulate an agenda for democratic reform, because this was more properly the task of political parties. Grassroots organizations should concern themselves with meeting the day-to-day necessities of their members. If achieving this goal involves playing the clientelist game, then that is an inevitable consequence of living in a system that is adamantly resisting democratization. In sum, the connection between popular movements and democratization was overdrawn and perhaps influenced by arguments developed in the Southern Cone. So, prior to 1994, Mexico was not becoming more democratic, nor more repressive. It was simply "more Mexican than ever" (Hellman 1994:127).

Hellman raised important questions regarding the impact of popular mobilization. However, it is not entirely accurate to say that analysts assumed popular movements were part of an inevitable forward march toward democracy. Foweraker had been quite clear on this. For example, he had stated that one of the effects of popular movements in the 1980s was to make the challenge to clientelism and presidentialism more open than in the past. He then warned that this challenge would not necessarily be more successful, recognizing the longevity of clientelism and caciquismo. Foweraker concluded that although the dissolution of authoritarian control was occurring in some contexts, "there is no proof that the movements have arrived at a historical turning point" (1990:8). He restated this point by noting that the impact of popular movements within Mexican civil society may not translate into changes within the political system. "The government may be discredited," he argued, "but it seems that the state still has ample margin for reaction and recuperation" (1990:18). But at this point his analysis was more open to other alternatives than was the outlook Hellman portrayed. Arguing that popular movements have also limited the state's co-optive capacities, he suggested that "the future is no longer inevitably defined by an endless succession of PRI administrations." In sum, Mexico is not "more Mexican than ever" but is in fact undergoing a profound political transformation under the weight of economic crisis, neoliberal reform, and popular mobilization.

Unlike Hellman's analysis, Foweraker offered a third alternative outcome for popular movements. In fact, it is the ability of some movements to survive co-optation and repression that allowed Foweraker to conceptualize their political impact in terms of the struggle for effective citizenship. Without assuming the success of popular movements, Foweraker noted that the challenge to clientelism and caciquismo is now less restricted to individual patrons and caciques and more a matter of principle. This principle is expressed by the demand that rights be respected. The operation of the political system itself, not the aberrations of corrupt individuals, is being targeted. If this is the case, then the novelty of popular movements is not defined by their economic-corporate demands (which may be ancestral in the case of rural movements), but by their political practices. When movements no longer petition the government for favors but demand respect for rights, the practices inevitably change, even if the authorities attempt to reassert vertical lines of clientelistic control, as Salinas attempted with the National Solidarity Program (PRONASOL) (Cornelius, Fox, and Craig 1994). In Foweraker's words, "this is tantamount to challenging the prerogative of the PRI government to rule arbitrarily: [popular movements insist on] the application of the law, an *estado de derecho,* and accountable government; a return to the republic, and the constitution made real" (1990:8–9). The hallmark of Mexican popular movements is not their radical autonomy from the political system, but their institutionalism. For the most part, they have followed gradualist strategies and pressed the authorities to meet demands in line with legal and institutional norms (Cook 1990, 1996). This trend does not mean that movements only seek incorporation into the existing rules. Foweraker saw them, instead, as institutionalist *and* non-conformist. They negotiate in order to get demands met, but they also mobilize and challenge the way they are treated by state authorities. In his case study of the teachers' movement, Foweraker showed how the struggle for democratic control of local sectional committees took place on the legal and institutional terrain of the PRI government. This fact clearly conditioned the movement's possibilities, but it did not entirely determine the outcome. Rather, some advances were achieved and the struggle itself created new leaders, activists, and discourses. It is significant that much of this oppositional activity took place in Chiapas during the 1980s (Foweraker 1993).

From a methodological perspective, Foweraker's approach leaves more room for political strategy and contradictions within the state than Hellman's conclusion implies. It also allows us to affirm the political nature of popular movements in Mexico. The struggle for economic-corporate demands may, theoretically, be the appropriate horizon for grassroots organizations. In reality, the almost immediate need to confront or negotiate with the state politicizes social concerns and social policy and inevitably generates political discussion within and between popular organizations. That this is true is born out as much by movement alliances as by internal factionalism. Politicization may not occur democratically, but it does appear to be an inevitable consequence of engaging the Mexican political system.

Although the struggle for rights appears to distinguish recent popular movements from their predecessors, we cannot assume any universal meaning of rights to which these movements appeal. An analysis of the historical context of popular struggle is essential if we are to avoid imposing Eurocentric assumptions on culturally specific phenomena. If it is the case that Mexican popular movements are concerned with making "the constitution real," then they are not referring to some liberal democratic constitution of universal validity, but to the Mexican Constitution of 1917. The appeal of constitutional government is that it comprises a set of rights that were won through a bloody social and political revolution. These circumstances do not deny the importance of individual rights that constitutionalism enshrines. But it does add a specific Mexican element, or, more precisely, it forces us to ask how the meaning of democracy is constructed through different political discourses, rather than to assume only one possible definition. Moreover, if what defines popular movements are their political practices, then it makes more sense to talk of democratization as an unending process rather than democracy as a fixed set of rules to which all give their consent. We do not have to look far beyond the liberal democracies of Western Europe and North America to realize that the democratic revolution is far from over, despite ideological claims that we have reached the "end of history" (Mouffe 1992).

Cultural Constructions of Citizenship and Dignity

How, then, do Mexican popular movements understand democracy and citizenship? A regional and historical perspective provides an invaluable starting point for our analysis. One of the conclusions we can draw from the preceding discussion is that if popular movements are defined by their political practices, then we need to examine the cultural spaces in which new practices emerge. It has also become apparent that democratization in Mexico is driven as much by regional forces as national-level changes. The strength of the National Action Party (PAN) in several northern states and the increasing support for the Party of the Democratic Revolution (PRD) in southern and western Mexico can be seen as related to regional histories of opposition, negotiation, and accommodation with the federal government and the PRI. It is in these regional spaces that the meaning of democracy is defined through political struggle.

In his case study of politics in San Luis Potosí, Wil Pansters (1996) documented the evolution of a civic movement for democratic government. The struggle against the Gonzalo N. Santos regional power domain (*cacicazgo*) in the 1950s did not call the PRI or presidentialism into question. In fact, alliances with the center and the president were important in ousting those who abused what was considered to be a legitimate political system. By the 1980s, however, the same struggle for accountable government was directed against the system. At stake was not simply access to public goods, but how that access was to be determined. The struggle for rights was infused with an assertion of moral dignity, born of the moral outrage at consistent fraud, imposition, and corruption. Opposition struggle was therefore able to draw on historical claims to the moral high ground, but was also expressed within the democratic discourse of political parties and popular movements of the late 1980s and early 1990s. This marriage of dignity and democracy was clearly articulated in 1992 by Dr. Salvador Nava, leader of the Potosino Civic Front (FCP):

The installation of democracy cannot be delayed for long. The country demands it. This was demonstrated last year when we began the March for Dignity from the city of San Luis Potosí. The principle of dignity brought thousands of Mexicans without reservations about ideology or party. The dignity of the citizens has often been humiliated by power, violating the fundamental rights of Mexicans. It is because of this that today dignity demands the installation of democracy in Mexico. (cited in Pansters 1996:260, n.23)

Democracy in San Luis Potosí is not understood solely in liberal terms as the guarantees pertaining to individual citizens. The historical and cultural construction of democratic discourse includes a powerful collective identity to uphold the dignity of "the people" (not as isolated individuals) in the face of power.

Similarly, Jeffrey Rubin argued that radical popular mobilization in Juchitán should be understood in terms of the historical struggles of Zapotec Indians to construct spaces for voice and autonomy. He made the important observation that we should not assume the uniform presence of the postrevolutionary state in Mexico. Instead we need a regionally differentiated analysis of the struggles, negotiations, and accommodations that occurred between the federal government and local populations (Rubin 1994, 1996; Joseph and Nugent 1994). Rubin called his approach the "decentering of the regime" and argued that we should trace the roots of contemporary social movements in the regional histories of places such as San Luis Potosí, Juchitán, and highland Chiapas. The novelty of today's movements is that they have reconceptualized those struggles in broader terms of democracy and citizenship rather than restricting their scope to local struggles for autonomy in the face of outside pressures. Nevertheless, these movements are not guided by abstract universal principles of democratic citizenship. Instead, they are better understood from the vantage point of everyday life and the attempt to transform spaces where people experience power as illegitimate and an affront to their dignity (Rubin 1994:128). The importance of the post-1968 political leaders is that they helped build broader alliances through shared discourses of radical mobilization for change in Mexico. The localism of popular struggles was not necessarily subsumed into new political forces, and in many cases tensions exist between a local movement's autonomy and its engagement in regional or national alliances. Nevertheless, the novelty of popular movements consists in their ability to articulate local and culturally specific understandings of citizenship and democracy in broader struggles of regional and national scope.

That social movements are concerned about citizenship is hardly surprising. Especially in rural areas, the violation of basic civil and political rights is a constant reminder that associational autonomy is something to be won rather than assumed. Over 800 peasants were killed in land-related conflicts in Mexico between 1981 and 1987 (Paré 1990). Many others were imprisoned for their political activity in support of landless groups. Most of the violations of human rights in rural areas have been directed against peasant organizations not affiliated with the PRI (Amnesty International 1986). Similarly, David Lehmann argued that rural movements in Brazil have tended to turn more on questions of citizenship and fair treat-

ment than on the seizure of state power and the subsequent transformation of class relations. Land reform is valued not because it un-
dermines the capitalist mode of production (in fact it may bolster
agrarian capitalism), but because it embodies a political struggle
against the violation of rights and autonomy in land tenure relations
(Lehmann 1990:155–60). Given that the Catholic Church played
an important role in organizing landless rural workers through its
Pastoral Land Commission, it is not so surprising that the meaning
of citizenship was constructed through religious rather than secular,
liberal discourses. Democracy is valued less for its rules and procedures and more for the dignity it bestows to the poor. Citizenship
is understood as the collective enjoyment of social justice rather
than the embodiment of individual rights and obligations before a
liberal state. In this way, the religiosity of rural life overlaps with the
modernist and humanist concern for individual human rights. Tensions between these discourses exist, but the novelty of contemporary rural movements is that they express long-standing material
grievances within a discourse of citizenship that is at once local and
national, particular and universal. As a result, it becomes possible to
talk of democracy more as a process that, to be sure, is partial and
incomplete but which also occupies a meaningful place in people's
experience of political struggle. At the least, it moves us away from
the assumption that a total transformation of society is necessary
prior to the creation of democratic and egalitarian practices. This is
how Lehmann saw the influence of liberation theology and the
informal church in Latin America. The result may be effective pressure from below to democratize political institutions and spaces for
popular representation. He concluded by noting the irony that "an
almost millenarian zeal fired with religious invocations was needed
to 'get the people organized' in the manner of a modern *civitas*"
(Lehmann 1990:147).

The defense of dignity and personal or group autonomy are central to the everyday forms of resistance that, in James Scott's analysis, are characteristic of highly stratified societies (Scott 1985,
1990). Where open political dissent entails too many risks, the
oppressed may still resist domination by secretly subverting the
rulers' "public transcript" of natural hierarchies. Through their
"hidden transcripts," which Scott assembled from songs, jokes,

poems, and popular myths, the dominated create an infrapolitics of resistance. Scott did not argue that this level of resistance is the only expression of popular struggle in authoritarian contexts. However, he did suggest that it is more widespread than appearance of social peace would indicate, and that it is the original source for those rare occasions when dissent is expressed publicly. These important observations challenge the assumption that the absence of visible conflict implies the acceptance of dominant ideologies. In the Latin American context, however, open opposition has been present throughout its modern history, despite the lack of guarantees for free public expression. Perhaps this is due to the contradictory nature of constitutional government and mass politics — a very different context from the plantation societies, landlord-peasant relations, or caste systems that serve as the historical basis for Scott's analysis. The "public transcript" in postrevolutionary Mexico allowed for much more public contestation than that of the Porfirian regime. Whereas revolutionary nationalism actually encouraged mass participation in defining the public transcript, the positivism of "order and progress" was clearly exclusionary of nonelites. Nonetheless, although Scott's approach may be less useful for understanding state-peasant relations since the 1930s, it still has the merit of drawing attention to the infrapolitics of everyday forms of resistance. In this regard, his observation that resistance responds to daily affronts to dignity and autonomy is highly relevant to the study of popular movements in contemporary Mexico. In fact, unlike analyses that focus on struggles over material resources, Scott privileged the cultural meanings attached to domination and resistance where what are at stake are dignity and autonomy, not simply wages or benefits.[5]

If the impulse for mobilization comes from this defense of one's dignity, then the process is unlikely to be guided solely by the abstract principles of liberty and equality enshrined in the public transcript of constitutionalism. The existence of constitutional rights may provide groups with something to which they can legitimately appeal, but the process of mobilization will draw upon historical memory, cultural practices, and political symbols as much as on legal norms. The popular appropriation of institutional discourses and practices significantly changes their meaning by attaching them to alternative discourses on class, gender, ethnicity, or region. From the perspective of popular movements, what matters is whether dignity and autonomy, rather than the consistency of the law, are reaffirmed.

There is also a clear danger here for the consolidation of democratic institutions. If the logic of popular mobilization is driven by particularistic concerns and only tangentially by procedural issues, then the concept of rights can easily be replaced by interests, leading to fragmentation, sectarianism, and the dogmatic defense of small spaces. The struggle for democratic rights must therefore be kept analytically distinct from the demand for dignity and autonomy, which can just as quickly be fulfilled by benevolent patrons of a distinctly nondemocratic regime. A democratic assertion of dignity and autonomy implies a political decision that these aspirations can best be satisfied through specifically *democratic* means. This does not rule out ambiguity in democratic struggles where internal practices may reproduce hierarchical rules and discrimination, but it should alert us to the fact that popular movements are not inherently democratic. Indeed, it becomes a question for empirical analysis to explain the democratic nature of popular movements, their ambiguities and contradictions.

The critique of structuralist approaches has also been prevalent in the study of rural social movements. Earlier analyses assumed a necessary causality between the development of capitalism and peasant responses (Paige 1975; Wolf 1969). This supposition tended to present rural protest as simply reactive in the face of economic forces. In contrast, as Steven Stern noted (1987:6), we need to see peasants as "continuous initiators" who resist and adapt in the face of economic or political dislocation. Resistance plays a key part in peasant politics, but it does not necessarily find expression in revolutionary action or discourse. Similarly, Leon Zámosc (1986) argued that approaches that ascribe a "revolutionary" or "reactionary" consciousness to peasants are restricted by their essentialism to simplistic and inaccurate accounts of political agency. In his study of the Colombian peasant movement between 1967 and 1981, Zámosc showed how interests and consciousness evolved through the interaction of peasants with their changing political and economic environment. In Mexico, Warman found that peasant re-

sistance to collectivization programs in the 1970s did not represent
conservative parochialism, but a defense of economic options that
would be undermined by more centralized state control of production and marketing (Warman 1980:61–83). However, peasant resistance cannot be reduced to interests constituted independently
of structures. Samuel Popkin's attempt to show how the underlying
rationality of Vietnamese peasants explains their political behavior
suffers from the same essentialism as the more overt structuralists,
only in Popkin's study the final moment in the explanation is found
at the level of the rationally constituted individual (Popkin 1979).
A more accurate approach is to treat interests and identities as historically constructed through political struggle (Foweraker 1994;
Nash 1995; Tilly 1995).

The defeat of rural guerrilla insurgencies and the effects of agrarian restructuring in Latin America have also led to new ways of
understanding peasant movements. Rather than reify a unified
peasant class and its revolutionary potential, researchers have instead been challenged by the proliferation and differentiation of
rural producers and their political movements. Some maintain their
struggles for land reform, others resist displacement due to the
construction of hydroelectricity dams, and still others organize to
market their surpluses or obtain credit through autonomous producer organizations. Resistance to the loss of a land base is clearly
central to each of these struggles and in some cases may be expressed as a broader critique of the prevailing development ideology. This differentiation of rural agency does not prevent comparative research and generalizable statements. However, we need to be
aware of the distinctiveness of rural society according to time and
place.

What these diverse movements do appear to share is the political
problem of achieving voice, autonomy, and accountable government. Jonathan Fox, drawing on comparative research from five
Latin American countries and the Philippines, highlighted the specific challenges of democratization in rural areas. These include the
establishment of channels for effective representation in electoral
and sectoral arenas, accountability of state institutions, and protection of civil and political rights. Fox also interpreted the struggles
against local regional bosses, or caciques, and clientelism in terms

of the search for effective rural citizenship. However, he added that the political space for voice and autonomy is unlikely to be free of contradictions. Instead, we need to pay more attention to gray areas of state-peasant relations in which new channels for rural representation are indeed created but are still constrained by new state strategies of co-optation and control. Instead of assuming the achievement of a uniform level of citizenship, Fox called for better indicators of *degrees* of citizenship and *degrees* of democratization (Fox 1990:11–12).

These theoretical and political concerns have also been expressed in recent work on human rights and citizenship in Latin America. Elizabeth Jelin has argued that the challenge for analysis is to document the social processes through which citizenship is constructed, "that is, the ways in which the formally defined subjects of law actually become such — in social practices, institutional systems and cultural representations" (Jelin 1996:101). Jelin therefore questioned the teleological evolution of civil, political, and social rights that T. H. Marshall (1964) saw as the almost inevitable consequence of modernization in England. In its place we need to pay closer attention to the process whereby citizenship emerges as the contingent outcome of struggles for dignity, voice, and autonomy. In the case of indigenous peoples, we must also note that access to universal, individual rights cannot be guaranteed without positive steps to eliminate racism (Stavenhagen 1996:147).

Jelin's more historical and subjective approach to citizenship contrasts with the classical liberal interpretation offered by Fábio Wanderley Reis (1996). In the latter view, there are two dimensions to modern citizenship: a civil and civic citizenship. Civil citizenship entails the establishment of individual rights and personal autonomy. This was achieved in the West by the breakup of traditional, hierarchical social orders rooted in ascriptive categories of caste, race, or ethnicity. The liberal democratic revolutions were made possible, in this interpretation, by the birth of the capitalist market, where individuals were free to enter into transactions and pursue their rational self-interest independently of ascriptive categories. In short, people were freed from religious doctrines or monarchical absolutism and, literally, became free citizens with the capacity to control their own destinies. This liberal view recognizes that capitalism also generated new hierarchies and inequalities of status. When these inequalities became politically untenable and threatening to liberal hegemony, the purely *civil* dimension of citizenship evolved into a *civic* dimension. The latter dimension involves the self-organization of individuals in free associations that serve to hold the modern civitas together in the face of the disaggregating effects of unrestrained individualism. However, the process of individuation permits citizens to choose freely their form of political association. Unlike traditional, precapitalist societies, the market system provides the basis for civil equality and, consequently, for pluralism and tolerance of individual political choices. For Reis, the problem of democracy in Latin America can only be resolved through capitalist modernization. The region's economies are insufficiently market oriented, although the neoliberal reforms of the 1980s and 1990s have moved in this direction. The philosophical point is that democratic institutions will not be viable until a modern citizenry has been formed. In practice, this means the breakup of traditional ascriptive categories, the creation of a prosperous market system, and individual freedom to participate in civic life through a plurality of political associations. In the words of Reis (1996:131), "the problems of democracy, especially with respect to ensuring that various rights are upheld, will hardly have a stable solution if the problems of capitalism are not resolved and if capitalism itself is not made to flourish and mature."

There are obvious reasons why this perspective is appealing to neoliberal economists and politicians in Latin America. It promises what capitalism has never produced in the region, that is, a stable democratic system with respect for individual rights of all citizens. Its ideological appeal stems from the rejection of earlier modes of state regulation of the economy and the corruption of public administration through "rent-seeking" strategies of corporate interests. It offers to level the playing field among economic actors by removing preferential subsidies and tariff protections from uncompetitive sectors and individuals. It also promises to resume the positivists' faith in order and progress that led to the first wave of modern capitalism in the latter quarter of the nineteenth century. Ascriptive categories such as ethnicity become obstacles to modernization and the creation of a fully individuated citizenry. Expensive and obligatory rituals are deemed not only a waste of productive capital and human resources, but also a way to reproduce traditional forms of community-level control over individuals who could potentially improve their lot in the free market. Ascriptive categories are therefore seen as antithetical to modern citizenship. Indigenous or regional identities hold back democratization because they undermine the universal ethicopolitical values of individual liberty and equality before the law.

Jelin's approach is radically different and helps us problematize the meaning of citizenship in Latin America. According to Jelin, we should reject the notion of universal definitions of citizenship. Instead, we need to analyze the processes by which citizenship is constructed as a culturally meaningful concept. This pursuit requires more concern for ethnographic detail and sociopolitical processes and less reliance on the neoliberal assumption that free markets lead to free politics. A crucial distinction arises when we consider the relationship between ascriptive categories (such as ethnicity) and democratization. If, for Reis, the former had to give way if the latter were to succeed, Jelin presents a counterargument. For her, it is precisely the strength of community and social solidarity that enables people to see each other as members of an oppressed collectivity. People identify with each other as members of discriminated groups and express their demands not solely (or even primarily) in terms of individual rights, but as collective rights. Citizenship is understood more as a collective enterprise rather than an individual prerogative, and it is social solidarity, often rooted in ethnicity, gender, or class, that provides the basis for reconceptualizing political representation in this way. Jelin, citing the work of Herman van Gunsteren (1978), called for an analytical perspective in which the concept of citizenship refers to "a conflictive process related to power — that is, to a struggle about who is entitled to say what in the process of defining common problems and deciding how they will be faced" (Jelin 1996:104).

Rather than assume a legitimate and consensual definition of citizenship rights, we should instead accept the inescapable fact of competing claims and focus on the legitimacy of the debate itself. This means that there can be no final point of truth and universal acceptance. Citizenship and rights are continually in the process of construction and transformation. What matters is not so much a single definition of citizenship rights, but the expansion of new spaces for public debate. This is what Mouffe has referred to as the "return of the political" (Mouffe 1993). If we accept that all societies are characterized by innumerable points of antagonism, a democratic polity cannot aspire to resolve these antagonisms and create a completely harmonious community. In her critique of the communitarian strand of modern liberalism, Mouffe was concerned that individuality or group differences will be subsumed under the superficially consensual, but ultimately oppressive, ethical values of the community. Instead, the challenge for democracy is not simply who can vote, but where one can vote (Bobbio 1989). That is, the expansion of democratic control of more and more spheres of social life will not eliminate antagonisms, but it has the potential to redirect them against the diverse sources of class, gender, ethnic, or neocolonial oppression (Laclau 1990). The "political" can thus "return" to the center of analysis, rather than being a mere reflection of objective structural factors. Laclau and Mouffe called such a project "radical democracy" to both differentiate it from liberal, representative democracy and to give continuity to the socialist project after the fall of communism.

Although these authors have directed their concern toward the future of democracy in the postindustrial West, their approach can be made compatible with how democratization is conceptualized in Latin America. At first sight this may appear too Eurocentric. After all, if the right of all individuals to a free vote is not yet established, then is it not premature to talk of extending democracy to more areas of social life? But this argument could also restrict our analysis to electoral competition and miss the importance of struggles for democratic representation in rural unions, the creation of human rights associations, the search for different strategies of rural development, and the assertion of ethnic identities or women's rights. Each of these struggles can be seen as politicizing different social spaces through critiques of the prevailing models of rural development. Clearly a more liberal political environment would facilitate the expansion of democratic struggles in these and more areas, but there is no theoretical reason why democratization at one level automatically precedes struggles at other levels. In fact, in Mexico the sequence appears to be the reverse of the Western experience of citizenship. Free elections, if and when they occur, may be the outcome rather than the beginning of democratic struggles. So, although it is useful to talk of the proliferation of social spaces where democracy is contested, there is no necessary sequence in which these struggles occur. The sequence is instead contingent on the strategic and organizational capacities of popular movements and on the divisions and realignments within the state and the economy that may open or close spaces for political intervention.

In rural Mexico, the creation of new spaces for voice has been essential in establishing the most fundamental of human rights, which is quite simply the "right to have rights," that is, to be recognized as a legitimate member of the political community (Arendt 1949, cited in Jelin 1996:105). It might be argued, therefore, that the struggles of popular movements for dignity, voice, and autonomy are precisely attempts to constitute the "people" as a political actor; that is, as a people with the right to participate freely in public debate and uphold their right to have rights. Politically, securing this goal means contesting both the terms of representation and the performance of government institutions. It means asserting that it is the people who make history, that the struggles of indigenous peoples can be articulated in broader struggles for democratic elections, and that what is at stake is not who is in power but how power is exercised. Our task is to understand how people in Chiapas have come to make these claims and reflect on what they tell us about the politically contingent nature of democracy and citizenship.

Chapter 2

COLONIALISM, STATE FORMATION,

AND RESISTANCE

If the struggle for citizenship is born in local contexts, then we need to understand the historical patterns of power and resistance in particular regions. In the case of Chiapas, this involves an analysis of recurrent struggles against *ladino* elites.[1] This book focuses on three specific areas of recent popular mobilization: the Lacandon forest in the eastern portion of the state, the municipality of Simojovel in the northern highlands, and the municipality of Venustiano Carranza in the Grijalva river valley (map 2.1). The new peasant organizations that emerged in these locations are the forerunners of the EZLN. However, their different trajectories can also tell us something about the contingencies and paradoxes of popular struggle. As such, they should be understood in their own terms and not idealized or demonized for their achievements or failures.

If there is one thing that these diverse struggles have in common it is their opposition to rural bossism, or caciquismo. The roots of caciquismo are to be found in the concentration of political and economic power. Since the conquest of the province of Chiapas in 1524–27, regional elites have competed for control over Indian land and labor, provoking violent rebellions in 1712 and 1867–70. The sources of interethnic conflict were never addressed by the elites. Instead, we see the development of new techniques of power designed to govern indigenous communities more effectively. The emergence of intercommunity alliances or confederations was impeded not only by linguistic and cultural factors, but by a pattern of clientelistic control, which became institutionalized in the post-revolutionary period. Caciquismo today is the visible legacy of colonialism and nineteenth-century liberalism in Chiapas.

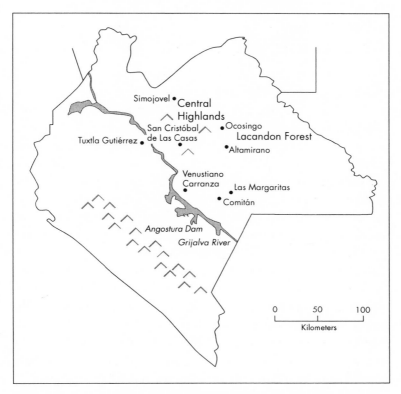

Map 2.1. Location of the Lacandon Forest, Simojovel, and Venustiano Carranza

The Zapatista rebellion can be seen as the latest in a long cycle of popular demands for dignity, voice, and autonomy. The novelty is to be found in the democratic discourse that articulates a broad range of demands, from access to land to peace, justice, and independence. However, the meaning of these demands is not given by purely abstract principles, but by their historical place in people's lived experience. In this chapter, I discuss the ongoing struggle to mark the boundaries between indigenous and ladino society in Chiapas. These boundaries are never fixed. Instead, we should understand them as constantly negotiated and disputed through political and cultural claims to citizenship and identity. The meaning of community is central to these struggles.

Patterns of Resistance in the Colonial Period

As several historians have noted, colonial Spanish America was marked by relative social peace for almost three centuries. The most common explanations for indigenous compliance are the demographic crisis caused by new diseases and the protection of community lands by colonial courts and the regular clergy (Coatsworth 1988; Katz 1988). In Chiapas, both factors were present. However, revolts did occur in response to increasing competition among elite factions for control of Indian labor and tribute. By 1570 the indigenous Mayan population had fallen by at least 50 percent and, in some areas of the province, by 80 or 90 percent. The population of the lowland central valley was affected most. In the highlands, the cooler climate and the geographical dispersion of communities meant that epidemics were less devastating (Benjamin 1989:4). Significantly, the decline began to bottom out by the mid seventeenth century, and the native population even recovered in the highlands and central valleys. This was due to the persistent economic depression of the province after the 1560s. Spanish settlers moved to more prosperous areas or engaged in activities that did not require large amounts of Indian labor. After the impact of conquest and the depredations of the first generation of Spaniards, indigenous communities survived in relative isolation, allowing for a quiet reconstruction of native society during the long depression of the seventeenth century.

In the aftermath of the conquest, Dominican monks led by Fray Bartolomé de Las Casas, protested against the harsh treatment of Indians and forced the Crown to enact reforms to abolish slavery and protect indigenous labor against Spanish colonists. The New Laws of 1542 also permitted indigenous authorities to control community affairs as long as they remained responsible to the Crown and their customs did not violate the church's teachings. Las Casas was also able to convince the king that only the Dominican order had the necessary, disinterested commitment to the native people to assure compliance with the new legislation. As a result, by the end of the sixteenth century the Dominicans, along with accumulating productive land throughout the province, had become the most important institution in the reorganization of native society. Villages were governed in accordance with colonial design, but the postconquest accommodation with the Dominicans meant that native leaders continued to enjoy a degree of local autonomy. This situation allowed for the persistence of indigenous religious practices, although they were expressed in a new Christian form. The clearest example of such syncretism was the colorful and enthusiastic celebration of saints' festivals, which frequently aroused the suspicion of those church authorities who favored more solemn rituals. The fiestas were organized in each village by religious associations, or *cofradías,* identified with particular saints. The Dominicans appear to have been highly pragmatic in allowing the cofradías some local autonomy in exchange for their devotion to Christianity. However, it was this ambiguity of ladino-Indian relations that permitted native leaders to establish a space of resistance to Spanish rule, culminating in outright rebellion in 1712.

By the end of the seventeenth century, the Dominican friars were under attack from both civil and religious authorities tied to the Crown. In particular, they were threatened by the growing importance of the secular clergy. This branch of the church was made up of diocesan priests who served under bishops but were not part of the missionary orders or of the regular clergy. The regular clergy, which included the Dominicans, Franciscans, and Augustinians, had been entrusted with the religious conversion of native society following the conquest. However, during the seventeenth century, the Crown promoted the establishment and expansion of new bishoprics throughout the colony. The secular clergy of parish priests and new bishops began to contest the control exercised by the regular clergy, leading to political confrontations that the Crown used to reduce the latter's power and influence.

The intensity of conflicts between the regular and secular clergy varied by region. In Chiapas, the long economic depression of the sixteenth and early seventeenth centuries meant that Spanish society remained weak and unable to challenge the position established by the Dominicans. This challenge came instead in the second half of the seventeenth century as a result of political crises in Spain that led the Crown to act more aggressively in exacting tribute from its colonies. A more centralized colonial administration was created, and the regional authorities (in particular, the king's provincial governors, or *alcaldes mayores*) sought to increase their own wealth and political control by monopolizing the trade of commercially valuable items. Similarly, the activities of new provincial bishops in this same period revealed that what was at stake was not simply who would attend to the religious needs of native society, but rather who would gain access to the material resources (labor and tribute) of Indian villages. For example, though the Dominicans were denounced for charging for the administration of the sacraments, the same practice was continued by the "reformist" bishops. The most notorious of these was the Franciscan Fray Bauptista Alvarez de Toledo, who went much further than the Dominicans, even imprisoning those parishioners who failed to provide tribute or pay for church services. The new bishops also denounced indigenous religiosity as a form of disguised paganism and led an aggressive campaign to combat native shamans and all practices of "idolatry and witchcraft." They also attempted to curtail the activities of cofradías, which had been central to the cultural accommodation achieved under Dominican pragmatism (Gosner 1992:58–66).

The combination of excessive tribute, crop failures, and lack of alternative employment led to increasing hunger in the Chiapas highlands. Indians responded to this crisis by invoking the religious practices and ethnic consciousness that had been evolving since the 1540s. Between 1708 and 1712 Indians claimed that the Virgin Mary had appeared to them in Zinacantán, Santa Marta, and Cancuc (see map 2.2). News of these appearances spread throughout the highlands. Thousands of Indians deserted the church and congregated at the new shrines to the cult of the Virgin Mary. Cult organizers elaborated a millenarian vision of the destruction of the ladinos, reinterpreting the scriptures by identifying Indians as the chosen people and the ladinos as the Jews to be run out of the Kingdom of God. The world would be turned upside down in a great cataclysmic moment of liberation.[2]

Although it posited a universal goal of liberation, the movement's immediate aim was to achieve autonomy from the church and the colonial government. A confederation formed of twenty-one communities extended throughout the central highlands. Over

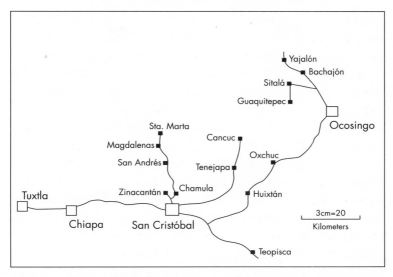

Map 2.2. Areas of Rebellion in 1712 and 1867. Source: Rus (1994: 226).

4,000 Indians joined the rebellion (Viqueira 1995). The leadership was based in the Tzeltal community of Cancuc, where the Virgin was said to have appeared for a fourth time in 1712. The rebels used the same terror tactics as their masters. They murdered landowners, took their wives and children, and destroyed crops and buildings. The royal government used its military supremacy and brought reinforcements from Guatemala, actions that proved decisive in suppressing the revolt three months after it began.

Although the rebels initially displayed a high degree of internal unity, they were nevertheless divided by factional rivalries and rapidly fragmented after their military defeat. Divisions were already apparent before the uprising, as the communities of Yajalón and Tila claimed to have their own cults. The leaders in Cancuc moved quickly to suppress any such rivalry. After the final rebel holdouts were "pacified" in 1713, the Indian confederation broke up and each community followed its own independent path.

There is some discussion among historians regarding the disunity of the Tzeltal rebels. For some scholars, it was the legacy of colonial "parcelization" that inhibited the consolidation of strong intercommunity ties. As a result, each pueblo was limited by a localized sense of identity, to the obvious advantage of the colonial authorities (García de León 1985, vol. 1:84). This theory appears to have been influenced by earlier conceptualizations of the closed, corporate nature of Indian villages, which assumed little if any migration or contact between communities (Wolf 1957). However, more detailed accounts of the Tzeltal revolt offer a different explanation. The celebration of saints' festivals, so central to the revitalization of native cultures after the conquest, provided for much greater contact between apparently isolated communities. In fact, the celebration of religious fiestas may even have allowed for a broader ethnic consciousness that went beyond local identities. In addition, during the seventeenth century there was a significant flow of migrants throughout the province as Indians sought to escape tribute obligations made even more onerous by the fact that, due to the effects of disease, most communities had relatively small numbers of people. This pattern of migration allowed communities to identify potential sources of aid, while enabling the formation of new social relations across a wider geographical area. The main source of disunity may not have been the legacy of parcelization, but rather the factional disputes between rival authorities within the rebel leadership (Gosner 1992:94–104, 135, 138–42).

The brutality with which the rebellion was suppressed demonstrated the extent of ladino fear of further uprisings. Interethnic relations were indelibly marked by this event because vengeful ladinos caught and physically mutilated rebel Indians by cutting off their ears. Other rebels were sent to work on lowland ranches and haciendas. The church was also able to reestablish credibility by capitalizing on the disunity of the rebel movement. The millenarian vision of destruction and conflict was contrasted with the Catholic vision of harmony, duty, and charity. Devotion to the church appears to have grown in the aftermath of the Tzeltal rebellion, although it is likely that the renewed display of compliance was also a strategy to avoid further punishment and physical mistreatment.

Consequently, resistance once again became invisible to the outsider and returned to the domain of infrapolitics. The material conditions of Indians did not improve after the revolt, and the crushing military defeat and persecution of suspected rebel communities negated ideas of social and political reform. In sum, the violent suppression of the 1712 rebellion left the sources of interethnic conflict unaddressed and likely to resurface in later years.

Indigenous Resistance in the Nineteenth Century

In the aftermath of 1712 many Indian communities were again decimated by epidemics and simply disappeared from the map. During the rest of the eighteenth century, the regional divisions in Chiapas became more evident. One that would have increasingly greater political relevance was between the central highlands and the lowland towns of the Grijalva valley, principally Chiapa, San Bartolomé de los Llanos, Tuxtla, and Comitán. By the start of the nineteenth century, the growth of an entrepreneurial class of land-owners and merchants in the lowlands was creating conflicts with the royal government and its representatives in Chiapas, who continued to be subordinated to the authorities in Guatemala. The lowland elites felt encouraged by the rise of liberal ideology in Spain during the 1810s and blamed the province's economic stagnation on the parasitic bureaucracy that supported the conservative elites of Ciudad Real.

Following a period of internal disputes between rival elite factions, in 1824 Chiapas decided to join Mexico rather than continue to be subordinated to Guatemala. The weakness of the newly independent Mexican state, combined with the geographical separation of Chiapas from the center, allowed the local elites a significant degree of autonomy. A strong regionalist sentiment continued to characterize these groups and would shape political conflict and patterns of Indian resistance in the nineteenth century (Benjamin 1989:6–12).

With the virtual absence of central authority, local military leaders who had supported the independence movement assumed control of their own areas of influence. None of these caudillos could maintain control of state government, and a period of political instability continued until the national liberal forces achieved supremacy over their conservative rivals at the end of the 1860s. Political rivalries were animated by the struggle for control over Indian land and labor. The Liberal forces viewed the highland elites, in particular the church, as the main obstacle in their efforts to gain access to the large supply of labor in the indigenous villages. They also sought to wrest control of lowland estates and plantations from the Dominicans.

Following the liberal revolt against Santa Anna in 1854, the struggle for national supremacy affected local politics by allowing for the lowland elites to win control of the state government and enact the liberal reform measures during the administration of Angel Albino Corzo in 1855–61. The most important of these were the privatization of lands held by both the church and indigenous communities and the nationalization of church properties. In response, priests encouraged Indians to defy the new laws and to support the conservative counterrevolution. By 1860, however, the liberals had defeated their rivals both nationally and locally, forcing the bishop of Chiapas into exile in Guatemala, along with members of the Dominican and Franciscan orders. The failure of the French intervention in 1861 to 1867 to consolidate conservative rule further weakened the power of the highland elites in Chiapas. After a brief period in 1863 to 1864, when a conservative government was established in San Cristóbal, the liberal faction regained political control with the support of the National Guard. By 1867 the interventionist war had ended. Conservatives were not completely defeated, however, and the new government was returned to San Cristóbal as part of the national accords that allowed for accommodation between the two factions. In Chiapas, the threat of Indian rebellion, occurring just as their own war was ending, united these two forces.

As elsewhere in Mexico, the liberal victory in Chiapas weakened the position of the Catholic Church. It also allowed for the private appropriation of lands held by Indian communities. The number of private estates and ranches grew from around 500 in 1855 to 949 in 1877 and 3,159 by 1889 (Benjamin 1989:27). Political power was subdivided between a handful of caciques, who had accumulated land and wealth as a result of the liberal reforms. The most important cacicazgos were those led by Sebastián Escobar in the Soconusco, José Pantaleón Domínguez in Comitán, Pomposo Castellanos in Tuxtla Gutiérrez, and Julián Grajales in Chiapa de Corzo. These family names would come to dominate the political and economic life of the state during the rule of Porfirio Díaz (known as the *porfiriato,* lasting from 1876 to 1911). For example, Grajales impeded the state government from collecting taxes in Chiapa de Corzo, while posts within the federal bureaucracy stationed in the Soconusco were appointed by Escobar. In a telling statement, Governor Manuel Carrasco complained to President Díaz in 1891 that "the sentiment of localism is very deeply rooted in the sons of each community in this state" (Benjamin 1989:2).

When it came to appropriating Indian land, political ideology was nothing more than a sideshow. In the first three decades after independence, lowland "liberals" took over fertile community lands located in the Grijalva valley. In the central highlands, "conservatives" also claimed lands that had previously provided some protection to native communities. The liberal and conservative governments that alternated in power between 1826 and the 1850s enacted legislation with one and the same goal: to remove restrictions on the private appropriation of land, including so-called vacant lands, or *terrenos baldíos.* These lands had been held in trust by the Spanish Crown as a buffer around indigenous communities. Although Indians were restricted by colonial law to the use of lands close to their village church, or *ejidos,* in practice, many had settled on the "vacant lands" as a result of population growth. Between 1826 and the early 1850s, it is estimated that over a quarter of Chiapas's Indians were therefore converted from "free" villagers into peons, or *baldíos,* who were obliged to work for new private landowners (Rus 1983:132–33; Wasserstrom 1983:119).

A second effect of the factional struggle between liberals and conservatives was the increasing burden placed on indigenous communities by higher rates of taxation and new demands for labor. Following the civil war of 1856 to 1861, when economic disruption momentarily relieved Indians of the depredations of either ladino faction, even greater demands were made by conservatives as they fought to regain control of San Cristóbal and the highlands. After the defeat of the conservatives and the restoration of liberal rule, the new civil authorities in the Indian villages, or *secretarios,* ordered parishioners to refuse to pay taxes to their priests. The uncertainties of the moment led many Indians to feign compliance with both factions. However, the potential liberation from exploitative conditions (which were particularly evident during the conservative of-

fensive of 1862 to 1863), gradually led many Indians to assert
greater autonomy from their traditional overlords. Using the space
opened by the liberal victory, highland Indians withdrew from their
churches and villages and established their own marketing and religious centers. In Chamula, however, the church fought to retain
its control, obliging Indians to honor their tax duties in spite of
liberal proclamations. With a zeal that matched that of the provincial bishops of the early eighteenth century, a new vicar attempted
in 1865 to restore the profitability of Indian parishes in Chamula,
provoking a new rebellion.

For Indians in mid-nineteenth-century Chiapas, neither of these
factions offered more than continuing exploitation. Beginning in
1848, a series of conflicts occurred in the Tzeltal and Tzotzil regions,
culminating in the rebellion of 1867 to 1870. As in 1712, it was
native religious practice that united diverse communities in a defensive struggle against the encroachments of ladino society. For
Indians, at stake were the economic options represented by community markets and freedom from taxation, combined with the
defense of religious autonomy. An early indication of resistance was
the decline in those rituals controlled by the clergy (specifically
Holy Mass and the Sacraments) and the enthusiastic celebration of
those events controlled by Indian authorities, such as saints' festivals and carnivals. Indeed, it was the Carnival of 1848 that provided the space for Tzeltal Indians in Chilón to organize their own
rituals. The church claimed that Indians were plotting to extermi-
nate all ladinos and began to increase its attacks on what were
deemed to be paganism and indigenous superstition. The effects
were counterproductive.

In 1867, Augustina Gómez Checheb, a Chamula Indian, declared
that three stones had fallen from the sky. A community leader
claimed that the stones were sacred and could communicate with
Augustina. It was then reported that Augustina had given birth to a
clay idol; the idol was then placed at a special shrine in the Chamula
hamlet of Tzajalhemel. News spread quickly, and thousands of Indians flocked to honor the new shrine, which the church naturally
refused to bless. Throughout the highlands, independent markets
and shrines allowed Indians to exercise the kind of freedom from
ladino society that had been blatantly violated by the intraelite

struggles of the previous decade. As in 1712, this assertion of indigenous autonomy was a response to the exploitative treatment suffered at the hands of both factions of the ladino elite. Significantly, resistance was made possible by the affirmation of religious-cultural identities that were clearly not reducible to the political ideologies of either conservatism or liberalism. It was this space for resistance that allowed Indians to contest ladino rule and affirm a distinctive ethnic consciousness. For conservatives, the threat of losing a vital source of income "obligated" a violent response and, by 1870, their militia had succeeded in suppressing the rebellious villages. It is important to note that the rebels' goals were limited to defending a measure of community autonomy, rather than taking over highland society. This did not stop ladino politicians using the imagery of a caste war (complete with an imagined threat to San Cristóbal itself) to unleash a brutal offensive whose violence bore no relation to the armed threat of the Chamulans. The rebellion was not therefore a caste war, but an attempt (more peaceful than violent) to defend access to land, markets, and religious practices of cultural importance (Rus 1983). The final "pacification" of the highlands gave the lowland elites the opportunity to at last reduce conservative control over Indian labor. This would benefit the plantation owners and ranchers of the Grijalva valley, who had consistently complained about the obstacles the church presented in their efforts to hire workers for use in commercial agriculture. Highland elites accepted accommodation with the new times, retaining control over the recruitment of labor in the Indian villages, but never recovering their traditional monopoly over the product of that labor.

The traditional suspicion of church authorities toward the Indian population was complemented by the racist assumptions of nineteenth-century liberalism. Particularly after the rebellion, the state government, imbued with the positivist ideology of the day, espoused the need to civilize the Indians by incorporating them into the modern agrarian economy. In Chiapas, as in Guatemala and El Salvador, vagrancy laws were introduced in 1880 that obliged Indians to be employed at certain times of the year. A new head tax and reforms to municipal government were added in the 1890s, further reducing the autonomy of indigenous authorities. Racist commentaries of indigenous culture abounded. For example, the liberal state governor in 1869, José Pantaleón Domínguez, declared that only colonization of Indian lands could restore social peace and contain the "savage objectives of the rebels." As would occur throughout the twentieth century, the opening up of new lands was seen as the solution to indigenous rebelliousness, leaving the sources of conflict alive. For the liberals in 1869 it was unoccupied scrublands in the central valleys that would provide the Indians with the means to progress as citizens of the new republic (Marion Singer 1988:54).

By the 1870s it was clear that indigenous communities in Chiapas had lost much of their land and autonomy. Although several highland communities continued to limit the church's intervention, the impact of commercial agriculture was felt in virtually every corner of the state. Chiapas divided itself into economic regions, each controlled by political bosses through various combinations of coercion and paternalism. The pattern of resistance in the early twentieth century would reflect this new reality. Ethnic differences persisted but political conflicts became increasingly characterized by regional and class divisions.

Porfiriato and Revolution

When General Agustín Castro arrived in Chiapas in 1914, sent by Venustiano Carranza to take control of the state's affairs in the name of the constitutionalist forces, he was immediately confronted by the resistance of the landowning oligarchy of the central valleys. Ardent supporters of the dictator Porfirio Díaz, these ranchers and *finqueros,* or plantation owners, had benefited greatly from the administration of Díaz's proconsul Emilio Rabasa. Rabasa became state governor in 1891 and was succeeded by four other loyal *porfiristas* during the next two decades.

This period marked the birth of an export economy in Chiapas and its rapid integration into the world market. Following the final settlement of borders with Guatemala, which included an agreement on the final surveys delimiting the Soconusco region in 1892, the Díaz government began to attract foreign investment (map 2.3). Between 1892 and 1894 Governor Rabasa implemented a

Map 2.3. Departments of Chiapas in 1911. Source: Benjamin (1996: 36).

series of new laws designed to break up what remained of indigenous communal lands. These measures had two important effects.

First, as Indians lost access to land, they began to seek work on the newly established coffee and cacao plantations of the Soconusco. Others were forcibly taken to mahogany lumber camps, or *monterías,* on the eastern edges of the Lacandon forest, where they were held in virtual slavery. The "voluntary" labor force that arrived in the Soconusco was subjected to traditional forms of indebted servitude. Given that dispossessed Indians had little or no resources to cover transportation costs and living expenses, they became dependent on taking obligatory loans that could only be paid off with labor. However, their work was remunerated in tokens that could be exchanged at company stores, or *tiendas de raya,* for food and other basic items. In this way, workers rarely accumulated enough to pay back initial loans, were obliged to accept new loans, and, as a result, accumulated more debt. Bosses could also increase their workers' dependency by financing religious ceremonies and selling cheap alcohol at the company store. Furthermore, because permanent workers were not permitted to leave plantations until they had paid off all debt, their servitude was assured. Similarly, migrant wageworkers *(jornaleros)* were indebted by their dependence on cash advances made by labor contractors at the beginning of each season. The export boom of the late nineteenth century was underpinned by these types of relationships. When wages were paid they remained at the subsistence level of thirty-seven centavos for the entire twenty-year period from 1890 to 1910 (Benjamin 1989: 88). By 1910 as much as 50 percent of the rural workforce was made up of indebted servants. It was this extensive and intimate control of Indian workers that regional landowners were to defend in their counterrevolution against Carranza and the constitutionalists.

The coffee economy in the Soconusco proved so lucrative that plantation owners began to extend their holdings to the northern highland department of Simojovel. Foreign entrepreneurs who had worked for the colonization companies were rewarded by the Díaz government with the concession of lands in Simojovel, Huitiupán, Tila, Yajalón, and Tumbalá. By 1900 coffee had replaced tobacco as the area's major crop, and by 1911 there were 167 plantations operating in Simojovel and Huitiupán alone (Pontigo Sánchez 1985:28). In addition to the German and British families who bought land, other plantations were purchased by prominent ladinos from San Cristóbal, Comitán, and Tuxtla Gutiérrez. The large labor force required for coffee picking was provided by Tzotzil and Tzeltal migrants who had lost their lands in the central highlands during the porfiriato. In Simojovel, migrants from Chamula, San Andrés Larráinzar, and Yajalón accumulated so much debt that they were prevented from leaving the plantations. They became permanent indebted workers, or *peones acasillados,* and were obliged to work for the *patrón* in exchange for the use of a small plot of land within the plantation boundaries.

Besides the indebted workers, there were two types of sharecroppers. Some, known as baldíos, were the long-term occupants of previously designated vacant lands that were appropriated by ladino elites during the nineteenth century. They exchanged their labor for the right to continue to use a small plot of land within the new private estates. A second category was made up of season-to-season sharecroppers, known as *mozos* or *laboríos,* who were given land for a year in exchange for their labor. The number of days per week a sharecropper was expected to work varied according to local conditions. With both sharecropping systems the landowners benefited from cheap labor and produce without having to finance crop failure or workers' debts. Tenants, or *arrendatarios,* were also allowed a plot of land on the estate but paid in cash or, more commonly, with part of their production.

The second major effect of the policies of Díaz and Rabasa concerned expansion of private landholdings by Mexican and foreign capitalists at the expense of Indian communities. Overall, the number of private estates in Chiapas increased from around 1,000 in 1880, to 4,500 in 1896, and 6,800 by 1909 (Benjamin 1989:86–87).[3] In the central valleys ranchers employed mozos from highland villages to clear scrubland for their own use on the condition that it be left as pasture after one or two years. The mozos were then obliged to move on to clear more areas, facilitating the expansion of ranching and further land concentration. For example, in San Bartolomé de los Llanos, the liberal reform laws accelerated the private appropriation of lands that had been recognized as the property of the Indian community since 1769. In that year the Spanish Crown had granted the community title to an area of 70,142 hectares. Most of this was nonarable land, but it did include some fertile areas located close to rivers and the municipal center, features that attracted the interest of ranchers (Molina 1976:61–3, 78–80). The Indians were left with the poorest areas and forced to clear scrubland at ever greater distances from their homes. Many became sharecroppers and depended for employment and land on the region's caciques.

Despite the variety of these labor relations, all arrangements were enforced by patronage and coercion. Peasants and workers depended on their bosses for loans, work, access to land, and payment for their production. At the same time the rural state police, or *rurales,* guaranteed compliance and subservience. In this way, different factions of the landed oligarchy competed to extend their control over land and labor, so by 1911 several landowning families had consolidated regional networks of power relations, or cacicazgos.

At this point it is useful to note that the caciques who would be challenged by peasant movements in the municipalities of Venustiano Carranza and Simojovel in the 1970s were descendants of the dominant families in those same regions in 1911: Orantes, Castellanos, and Coutiño in Carranza (known as San Bartolomé de los Llanos until 1934) and Peñagos, Zenteno, and Coello in Simojovel. Power relations were based on the local elites' particularistic interpretations of the law. Prior to the 1930s the formal institutions of the state remained weak and easily co-opted by the caciques.[4]

Carranza's troops were thus viewed as outside enemies when, in October 1914, General Castro promulgated a Labor Law that abolished debt servitude and granted workers the right to a minimum wage and other benefits. This moment marked the beginning of a counterrevolution, and several influential landowners in the central valleys met to sign the Act of Canguí, calling on all the population to fight against what they considered to be an army of occupation.[5] Through loyalty or coercion, ladinized peasants joined the armies of these counterrevolutionaries, known as the *mapaches*.[6] Support came from landowners in the departments of Tuxtla, Chiapa, La Libertad, Comitán, Mariscal, Tonalá, and Soconusco.

The revolution in Chiapas was essentially about who would control access to Indian land, labor, and production. In 1911 the highland elite based in San Cristóbal sought to take advantage of the fall of Porfirio Díaz by declaring themselves *maderistas* and mobilizing a mainly Indian army, the Brigada de Las Casas, to fight against the lowland porfiristas. Indians from Chamula and other highland communities had their own reasons for joining the Brigada Las Casas. Their main goal was to rid themselves of the municipal authorities that had collaborated with the porfirista regime in enforcing new taxes and coerced labor. However, they were roundly defeated within less than three months, with over 300 Indian troops being killed. By the end of 1911, antiporfirista sentiment among highland Indians was turned against those community officials identified with the old regime. The conservative elite, seeing that it no longer controlled the course of this struggle, began to warn once more of the Indians' propensity for violence, eventually allying with their traditional rivals, the lowland porfiristas, in the counterrevolution against Carranza, Castro, and, most important, the 1914 Labor Law (Rus n.d.). In 1915 a prominent highland landowner, Alberto Pineda, reorganized the Brigada Las Casas on the basis of ladino ranch hands and *cristobalenses* and led them against *carrancista* troops in the departments of San Cristóbal, Chilón, Simojovel, and Palenque (Castillo Burguete 1985:82). Indians did not support Pineda and spent most of this period trying to survive a war that was largely made on their lands and over who would eventually control their labor.

The Indian population was manipulated by all sides during the civil war. Many communities sought to protect themselves by turning inward and surviving as best as they could. This retrenchment would continue until the 1930s (Rus 1994:270). In some cases, such as Simojovel, the turbulence of the 1910s allowed for isolated acts of vengeance by plantation workers against their bosses and overseers. Rather than demonstrating coherent support for the carrancistas, these workers took the opportunity presented by the constitutionalist army to throw off the impositions of the local porfirista authorities. When Carranza sent reinforcements to Chiapas in 1917, Indians in Simojovel offered themselves as volunteers. They forced plantation owners to flee and retook communal lands. However, Pineda's Brigada Las Casas eventually defeated the carrancistas, killed the Indian leader who had organized the volunteers, and reestablished the control of the finqueros allied to this conservative faction. Throughout the highlands, Pineda's forces terrorized villages, destroying crops and homes, and in the Tzeltal village of Bachajón suspected carrancista Indians were hung from a ceiba tree.

Similarly, Indians in San Bartolomé de los Llanos saw their land overrun for six years by warring armies of mapaches and carrancistas. In 1920 the constitutionalists finally left and in the following year a mapache leader, Fernando Borraz, was installed as municipal president. There was no *zapatista* movement in San Bartolomé; instead, Indians were enlisted into one of the two contending armies. With the end of the armed conflict, Indians continued to clear scrubland for their bosses and the traditional forms of clientelistic control persisted.

Despite reinforcements from Tabasco and Yucatán, the carrancistas were unable to prevail, and by 1920 it was clear that a military victory was impossible. As a result, when General Alvaro Obregón became president of the republic in 1920, the mapaches declared themselves loyal *obregonistas* in exchange for de facto autonomy to continue governing Chiapas without federal intervention. They therefore ensured that agrarian reform would not affect their own class interests and that the latifundio system would persist.[7]

It was only in the more developed region of the Soconusco, where clientelistic ties were less established, that workers attempted to build an independent union movement. Here, due to greater contact with outside ideologies and activists (including political exiles from Central America) an agricultural workers' union organized several strikes on coffee and banana plantations between 1914 and 1920. In 1921 the Socialist Party of the Soconusco was founded, and three years later it affiliated itself with the Socialist Party of Chiapas (Spenser 1988). The support of the socialists was important in the victory of Carlos Vidal over Tiburcio Fernández Ruiz in the gubernatorial election in 1925. However, Vidal was assassinated in 1927, and the state government returned to the hands of the mapaches. As a result, it was not until the Cárdenas period that peasants and workers would be provided with a more favorable conjuncture for the presentation of their demands.

The Institutionalization of Community in the Central Highlands

The second major clash between regional caciques and the revolutionary government occurred during the presidency of General Lázaro Cárdenas. Nationally, this period saw the political incorporation of the mass of the peasantry into agrarian committees tied to the ruling party through the CNC. Philippe Schmitter (1974) defined the nonvoluntary, compulsory, and hierarchical nature of this type of interest representation as "state corporatist" in order to differentiate it from the pluralistic aggregation of interests in non-compulsory, autonomous associations of "societal corporatism" characteristic of Western liberal democracies. In the case of Mexico, the term *corporatism* came to signify the statist variant in the work of many political scientists (Córdova 1979; Hellman 1988; Reyna and Weinert 1977).[8] However, the capacity of peasant movements to achieve agrarian reform varied according to the regional balance of forces and the government's priorities for agricultural development. In Chiapas, the strength of regional landowners became increasingly apparent as the new forms of state-directed labor organization and land distribution engendered new, institutional forms of caciquismo.

Several studies of rural Mexico have demonstrated how the formal but highly fragmented institutions of the state operate through informal networks of local and regional power (R. Bartra 1976; de la Peña 1986; Friedrich 1986; Schryer 1990). These networks, which de la Peña called *redes sociales* (1986), functioned as the privileged access points to strategic resources that were gradually monopolized by the federal government. Power was both centralized and dispersed. Regional brokers were subordinated to central government and the party, but, in their own domains, they were empowered by this same relationship. De la Peña thus described the Mexican political system as a "hierarchical patronage network" in which "different levels of articulation" are vertically interconnected through a vast array of political intermediaries (1986). Institutional power operated through distinctly noninstitutional mechanisms such as clientelism and violent coercion but also sought to make these mechanisms functional for the centralized control of resources. Brokers were not free to pursue any interest. If they wanted to stay in the game, then they inevitably had to accept their dependence on state patronage. This combination was reflected in the symbiosis of clientelism and corporatism in many areas of rural Mexico. Independent organizations were usually denied access to resources because they did not belong to the informal red social and were unwilling to subordinate their members' demands to conditions imposed by the state.

Peasant organizations such as the CNC functioned within a power structure that made state-provided goods indispensable for community development and, in turn, made communities dependent on the state for their provision. The strength of the CNC rested not on its capacity to organize and represent the demands of its members, but rather on its position in the centralized allocation of resources. Clarissa Hardy (1984) maintained that this "institutional legitimacy" helps explain the support the CNC continued to command in spite of its evident failure to influence agrarian policy after 1938.[9] The right of associational autonomy was consequently denied in practice by the institutionalization of clientelism. In this way, clientelistic practices formed the basis for an authoritarian state that assured the continued concentration of land and capital by private owners.

During the 1930s a new group of local leaders was promoted by the federal government in indigenous areas. Between 1936 and 1940 Cárdenas employed a native of San Cristóbal, Erasto Urbina, to mobilize political support among highland Indians for his reformist policies and for his candidate for state governor, Efraín Gutiérrez. After organizing a successful campaign that installed Gutiérrez as governor in 1936, Urbina proceeded to take control of Indian affairs as head of the newly created Department of Social Action, Culture, and Protection of Indigenous Peoples (DPI) and the Union of Indian Workers (STI). These agencies established control over the supply of labor to the coastal plantations. Urbina also directed the creation of local agrarian committees, which, by 1941, were incorporated into the state-level League of Agrarian Communities of the CNC (García de León 1985, vol. 2:201–30; Rus 1994:274–80).

Leaders of these committees were appointed by Urbina, thereby consolidating a new group of political brokers for the ruling party.[10] Furthermore, the postrevolutionary state not only co-opted native leaders but also the community structures that had allowed indigenous communities to insulate themselves as much as possible from the pressures of ladino society. The civic-religious cargo systems were not dismantled, but they were taken over by Urbina's appointees. The *muchachos de Erasto* were bilingual and (where possible) literate young men who replaced the older municipal secretaries as village scribes. The new brokers did not go against tradition, but instead sought to bolster their new positions internally as well as externally. They therefore accepted the responsibilities that went with occupying costly and time-consuming civil and religious offices *(cargos)*. The new brokers could uphold "community tradition" while at the same time expanding their influence as labor contractors, leaders of agrarian committees, and representatives of the CNC and the PRI. They could also take advantage of federal policies that the National Indian Institute (INI) chose to first implement in highland Chiapas in the early 1950s. The goal of the INI was to bring modern services to indigenous communities under the auspices of the state. Its programs for agrarian commercialization required much more intimate relations with communities than had existed in the past. The new brokers were therefore essential to the success of the state in establishing its presence in highland Chiapas. They clearly knew this and used it to their personal advantage whenever possible.[11] Local ladino elites similarly came to accept that it was preferable to make alliances with local indigenous elites rather than continually engage in ethnic battle. The outcome was the consolidation of a group of bilingual, politically connected indigenous caciques whose alliances with the PRI and with ladinos enabled them to accumulate wealth and land within their communities. The private use of publicly funded resources (trucks, machinery, credit, etc.), combined with the sale of cane liquor *(posh)*, created the conditions for internal social stratification and the exercise of political control through the PRI. The outcome was not an autonomous defense of community against outside agents, but the penetration of community life by the state and the party, or, in Jan Rus's words, the creation of the *comunidad revolucionaria institucional* (Rus 1994). By the 1970s those who dissented from the ruling cliques were being forcibly expelled on the pretext that they were "enemies of tradition."

Community and Land Struggles in Simojovel and Venustiano Carranza

As we might expect, not all communities were penetrated and transformed to this degree. Rus based most of his analysis on the case of Chamula and surrounding villages, but he also drew a useful distinction with those communities on the northern and eastern edges of the central highlands, where state presence was much weaker and more ambiguous in its effects. For example, reforms to federal agrarian law in 1934 allowed tied peons to petition for land for the first time. In Simojovel rural schoolteachers and agronomists began to inform Indian workers of their new rights, organize agrarian committees, and help the Indians file their land petitions. Despite threats from their former bosses, many Indians stopped working on plantations and joined the new agrarian committees. Although some ejidos were formed in this period, the political effect was to tie the new committees to the CNC and the ruling party.[12] This meant that the gradual abandonment of agrarian reform after 1940 went largely uncontested. As a result, the number of unresolved land petitions accumulated while the population pressure on the available ejido land increased. Further distribution would require the expropriation of powerful finqueros, and the CNC, without the kind of backing it had enjoyed during the Cárdenas administration, was clearly unable to make an impact. Sixteen more ejidos were created from 1940 to 1960, but most were formed on uncleared "national lands" rather than affecting the plantations (Pontigo Sánchez 1985:38). After 1960 land reform in Simojovel practically halted. Only six more ejidos were created in the subsequent two decades. By 1980 the ejido sector represented less than 20 percent of the land in Simojovel. Private owners could file an injunction *(amparo)* to prevent land redistribution. Many were also able to protect themselves with new certificates of nonaffectability *(certificados de inafectabilidad)*. In response, some land claimants engaged in isolated direct actions throughout the 1950s and 1960s, but it was not until the 1970s that a coordinated movement for land reform emerged.

The experience of land reform in San Bartolomé de los Llanos (renamed Venustiano Carranza in 1934) shared some similarities with the Chamulan case. However, the outcome more closely resembled the situation in Simojovel. The first attempts to recover community lands from ladino ranchers came out of the reshaping of internal structures. Prior to the 1930s the Tzotzil community had been represented by its indigenous council *(ayuntamiento indígena)*. The council was governed by a hierarchy of civil and religious cargos, and the maximum authority were the community elders, or *principales*. Earlier efforts to regain land had failed for the same reasons as in Chamula. The Spanish-speaking scribes who acted as the community's representatives in its dealings with the ladino authorities were appointed and manipulated by those same authorities. Furthermore, the traditional system of providing free labor for the community *(tequio)* began to be abused as the council allowed tequio labor for the benefit of private landowners. The harsh punishment of those who questioned the principales (which included imprisonment) helped fuel internal dissent against the structure of the ayuntamiento indígena.

The catalyst for the reorganization of the community was a rural schoolteacher, Donaciano Zamudio, who arrived in San Bartolomé in the 1920s. As a result of his teachings, younger Indians began to refuse tequio work for the ladinos, and the council elders found it increasingly difficult to imprison dissenters. This younger generation saw the principales as conservative and easily manipulated by the local ranchers. At the same time, Zamudio's prestige and authority grew when Lázaro Cárdenas met with him during his presidential campaign in early 1934 (Renard 1985).

The implementation of land reform in Venustiano Carranza led to a radical reordering of internal community structures. The ayuntamiento indígena was abolished and replaced by a new body, the Administration of Communal Property (Comisariado de Bienes Comunales). The Indians with rights to communal land became known as *comuneros*. With the support of Cárdenas, Zamudio was instrumental in linking comuneros to the state. In 1935 the Comisariado de Bienes Comunales was incorporated into the peasant wing of the ruling party. The authority of the principales was gradually displaced by a new group of comuneros, whose legitimacy was tied to their relations with the federal government and the agrarian bureaucracy. Unlike Chamula, however, Venustiano Carranza did not develop into a comunidad revolucionaria institucional. The state had indeed penetrated community life, reordered internal structures, and even tied them to the PRI, but here relations with the ladino elites were more closely bound up with land disputes than in Chamula. This meant that the new, younger leaders could only establish their legitimacy by successfully recuperating communal lands. In Carranza, this dilemma was further complicated by the alliances that local caciques did establish with leaders of new ejido settlements in the region. In fact the most important cacicazgos in Carranza (the Orantes and Castellanos families) were created through the subversion of agrarian reform. Carmen Orantes was one of the principal ranchers in the area. In the early 1930s, at the same time as the indigenous community was being restructured, Orantes formed a clientele of supporters among migrant workers and organized them into an agrarian committee to petition for ejido land known as Vega del Chachí. This ejido was established on land belonging to the indigenous community. It also became the center for his cacicazgo. Personal and family ties underpinned his growing influence. Virginia Molina cited one *ejidatario* as recalling how "every family in Vega del Chachí has something for which to thank Uncle Carmen, whether it be for financial help to overcome some difficult situation or for purchasing land and cattle, negotiating with the authorities, or mediating in family quarrels" (Molina 1976:95). His popularity among ejidatarios grew as he financed the construction of the local church, the basketball court, a bandstand, and an unpaved road linking the ejido to the main highway to Tuxtla Gutiérrez.

Numerous clashes occurred in the 1950s and early 1960s as comuneros tried to protect their lands from encroachment by the clientele of ejidatarios loyal to Orantes. In 1959 Orantes became municipal president and used his ties to the state governor to finance his cacicazgo. Ranching was also encouraged by government policy. In 1961 a state-level ranching law was passed, reducing taxes on livestock production, allowing the rental of unused ejido land for cattle raising, and even permitting the use of armed groups *(guardias blancas)* to protect private ranches. The economic consolidation of prominent ranchers was clearly assisted by their connections to the state government (Benjamin 1989:224; Fernández Ortiz and Tarrío García 1983). In 1959 a local ranchers' association was formed with twenty-nine member families, including the Orantes and Castellanos families. By 1969 this number had risen to fifty-nine. At the state level, various local associations united in 1939 in the Regional Union of Cattlemen of Chiapas. By 1944 there were twenty-three associations, the regional union, and three other local unions. Ranching was further encouraged by the construction of new roads and the development of internal markets for meat. The completion of the Pan-American Highway in the state in 1947 meant that live-stock could be transported more easily to Mexico City. In Carranza, ranchers benefited greatly from the opening of new markets in Tuxtla Gutiérrez, Tapachula, and the capital. By 1970 some ranchers in Carranza had up to 2,000 heads of cattle, and nineteen families controlled 40 percent of private property in the municipality (Molina 1976:116).

Finally, in 1965, the land petitioning of the comuneros paid off. A presidential resolution was published in the *Diario Oficial*, recognizing the community's legal right to 50,152 hectares. Although some 41,000 hectares of this land were of poor quality, there were another 8,000 hectares of good quality land, part of which had been taken over by ranchers. The struggle to recuperate this land would transform Venustiano Carranza into one of the main centers of popular mobilization in the next ten years.

The Remaking of Community in the Lacandon Forest

Without generalizing too much we can say that the central core of the Tzotzil region corresponded more closely to the comunidad revolucionaria institucional, whereas in the Tzeltal and Chol regions young men were able to escape the control of the village scribes by settling in the Lacandon forest. In fact, federal agencies, particularly the INI and the Department of Agrarian Affairs and Colonization (DAAC), encouraged Tzeltal and Chol Indians to migrate rather than confront Indian or ladino elites in the highlands. The first colonists were therefore made up of former peons on the private estates and plantations near to Ocosingo, Yajalón, Chilón, and Bachajón. The flow of Tzotzil Indians would only really begin in the 1970s as communities such as Chamula began to expel thousands of its members who had begun to resist indigenous caciquismo (Rus 1994:296).

Between the 1930s and 1970s the Lacandon forest became the

safety valve for land pressures elsewhere in the state.[13] The availability of unoccupied land allowed the government to avoid affecting private owners, particularly in the areas of dense indigenous
population. By 1970 an estimated 100,000 colonists had settled in
the forest. Most were Tzeltal and Chol Indians from the eastern and
northern highlands. Smaller numbers of Tojolobal Indians from the
border area east of Comitán also settled in the southern valleys of
the Lacandon forest. The colonists were former plantation workers
or peasants who had lost land to the encroachments of private
owners (Ramos Hernández 1978:26). The population of Ocosingo, the region's largest municipality, more than doubled from
13,940 in 1950 to 34,356 in 1970 and doubled again to reach 69,757
by 1980. In the following decade, the annual rate of population
growth for the municipality was 5.66 percent (higher than the 4.41
percent registered for Chiapas as a whole), reaching 121,012 inhabitants by 1990 (Ascencio Franco 1995:368, table 23).

One of the results of this out-migration was the transformation of
community structures in the new lowland settlements. Until the
1980s, state presence was certainly much weaker in the Cañadas
of the Lacandon forest than in the densely populated highlands
around San Cristóbal. This factor is important in understanding
how the origins of the EZLN were rooted in social rather than
institutional forms of community organization. The first people to
actively organize in the forest were Protestant missionaries associated with the U.S.-based Summer Institute of Linguistics. Beginning
in the early 1940s groups of missionaries were invited by the Mexican government to assist in the acculturation of the indigenous
population (Dichtl 1987:45). Traditional cultural practices were
discouraged, while individual effort and conversion to new crops
were promoted. These goals resembled those of the INI in the
central highlands. However, in the 1960s Catholic missionaries also
began to work in the Lacandon forest. Their approach differed in
that they sought to revive indigenous communal practices through
the creation of village cooperatives. This approach reflected the
Catholic Church's "preferential option for the poor," which the
diocese of San Cristóbal had begun to promote at the time of
the Medellín Council of Latin American Bishops in 1968. Samuel
Ruiz García, who had been named bishop of the diocese in 1960,

participated in the Medellín conference and became an important proponent of an autochthonous, popular church.

Prior to Medellín the diocese had already begun to adapt its own structures, creating special teams of priests assigned to regions inhabited by the four largest indigenous groups (Tzeltal, Tzotzil, Chol, and Tojolobal) and two predominantly mestizo areas in the central and border regions of Chiapas. In contrast to the situation in the highland villages, the colonists were able to reconstitute communities independently of state agencies, that is, the CNC and the PRI. However, it would be a mistake to assume that the remaking of ethnic identities grew naturally from the experience of colonization. For here too we find the creation of a new set of community leaders supported by the institutional resources of the church.

In fact, colonization was interpreted quite effectively through biblical reference to the Exodus. According to Xochitl Leyva Solano (1995), the idea of Exodus came from Marist missionaries who began the first training courses for indigenous catechists in San Cristóbal. These courses began in 1961 and were designed to overcome two problems. The first was the critical lack of priests in the diocese. The second was the need to incorporate the indigenous population into the structures of the diocese. At first, the methodology reproduced the ethnocentric bias of the institutional church. Gradually, this gave way to a new strategy that consciously sought to break with paternalism. This shift coincided with the discussions leading up to the Second Vatican Council of 1962 to 1964 and the Medellín conference in 1968. Bishops throughout Latin America were seeking innovative ways to make the teachings of the Bible more closely relevant to the lives of the poor majority. In Chiapas, Bishop Ruiz approached this challenge by calling for the "incarnation of the evangelis" within the region's indigenous cultures. His goal was not to displace native customs and traditions but to bring out the evangelical message of Christian love and salvation from within these same traditions. For this, the church would need to prepare young, bilingual, and literate catechists from the indigenous communities themselves. The new catechists would be responsible not only for religious instruction but also for community activism, as organizers of the colonists in their daily struggles for survival in their new promised land. The church termed this a *cate-*

quesis de integración, one that would promote broad-based community participation in problem solving and in the analysis of economic and political oppression.

The lowland ejidos therefore differed from the highland communities in that the hierarchical system of civil and religious posts was replaced by more horizontal forms of internal organization. The demographic composition of the colonists lent itself to this restructuring of community life. By 1990 only 4 percent of colonists were over 50 years of age. Forty-six percent were aged between 15 and 49, and about half of the population was under 14 years of age (Leyva Solano 1995:401, n.43). In addition, the courses imparted by the catechists encouraged all to speak and reflect on their current situation. The democratizing effects of this approach to community organization contradicted earlier beliefs that only the principales, who had worked all the way up the cargo system, possessed sufficient wisdom to speak on community affairs. This is not to say that the elders and religious festivals lost all significance. In some places this may have been true, but it is also the case that elders continued to command respect (especially as healers in an inhospitable environment, far from the nearest clinic). Similarly, religious festivals continued, and the founding of the new settlements was always accompanied by the worship of patron saints. The names given to the new ejidos were often drawn from the Old Testament (Betania, Nuevo Jerusalén, Monte Líbano, etc.).

Rather than reject native traditions, lowland colonists reworked them in a new discourse of liberation and struggle. In this they were clearly oriented by the church and the anti-imperialism that united a generation of Mexican youth in the 1960s. The meaning of community differed radically from that of the comunidad revolucionaria institucional described earlier. People were participating for the first time as citizens. In some cases as much as 40 percent of villagers occupied some office or other, while community assemblies became the center of decision making. The catechists revived indigenous forms of consultation and consensual decision making, known in Tzeltal as *tijwanej,* allowing all to speak and express their views (or, more poetically, "to bring out what's in another's heart"). This broader level of participation was also significant in how elected leaders carried out their tasks. In contrast to the highland villages such as Chamula, colonists and catechists insisted that officeholders should govern by obeying *(mandar obedeciendo)*. The maximum authority remained with the community assembly. Internal pressures for accountability came before external alliances with powerful ladinos (Leyva Solano 1995:383). These factors clearly distinguished lowland communities from the highlands. They also provided the organizational and ideological basis for the reinvention of ethnic identity. Because the Cañadas received migrants from each of the different indigenous groups, this pluriethnic mix obliged communities to either maintain or transcend linguistic and cultural differences. The catechists played a fundamental role in helping communities adopt the latter position. As a result, community cohesion in the lowlands was given not by strict adherence to native traditions, but by a shared organizational militancy and a common set of religious beliefs. Ethnic identity was in this way re-created as the basis of political unity (Leyva Solano 1995:399).

This pattern of resistance was indeed only one of several. Nor was it free of internal contradictions, which, as we shall see, often fragmented political unity. While reminding us that there can be no essential Indian community ethos, this newest form of resistance also gave continuity to the struggle against racism, poverty, and caciquismo in Chiapas. Its trajectory, however, would inevitably be shaped by how communities engaged the political system, the strategies they would adopt, and the actions of outside leaders and governmental agencies during the early 1970s.

Community and the Postrevolutionary State in Chiapas

In this chapter we have seen how different patterns of indigenous resistance have been constructed in local contexts. Rather than assume the existence of pristine native traditions, we must instead acknowledge the historical fact that communities in Chiapas have been restructured in the process of resistance and increasing involvement with ladino society. This restructuring has taken several forms. Whereas Rus has spoken of the institutionalization of community structures in Chamula and other central highland villages, the experiences of Simojovel and Venustiano Carranza can be thought of in terms of the creation or renewal of community in the context of agrarian reform. The migration of colonists to the Lacandon forest and their organization in community-level cooperatives through the Catholic Church can be interpreted as the remaking of community and ethnic identity. In each case the meaning of community is contingent on the increasing interaction with the post-revolutionary state. The "everyday forms of state formation" varied according to local factors and resulted in a markedly uneven presence of state authority across the different subregions of Chiapas (Joseph and Nugent 1994).

State presence tended to be more concentrated in the densely populated central highlands and became less so the farther one moved out. On the northern and southern edges of the highlands (Simojovel and Carranza, respectively), the institutions of the state were less visible, and they were completely absent in the Cañadas of the Lacandon forest. The unevenness of state presence had contradictory effects. Whereas in the highlands it helped bolster the position of both ladino and Indian caciques, in the periphery it allowed ladino elites to either avoid or subvert agrarian reform, thereby perpetuating ethnic divisions while simultaneously upholding revolutionary promises of land and justice. In this sense the role of federal agencies was much more ambiguous in the periphery than in the core area of the central highlands. Given the state's inability to completely co-opt the internal structures of indigenous communities, the new leaders could operate more independently in pursuing their communities' land claims. However, they did so in the face of staunch opposition from the local landowners and their friends in the state government. The most obvious example of this contradictory state presence was the publication of the presidential resolution in Venustiano Carranza. This decision opened up the opportunity for community leaders to pursue the agrarian cause that had constituted the basis of their legitimacy since the 1930s. By contrast, in the lowland forest, the absence of party and state allowed the church to play a predominant role in building a new social order. These different levels of centralized, contradictory, or weak institutionalization affected the meaning of community identity in relationship to the state. Whereas community leaders in Chamula accepted the expansion of state agencies and alliances with prominent ladinos, in Simojovel and Carranza the state was seen more ambivalently, first as an ally in the struggle with local landowners, then as indifferent, and eventually as a hostile enemy. In the Cañadas, the state was seen as either irrelevant or as an obstacle to the goal of popular liberation. These different political views could only emerge in the local contexts of state formation and the negotiation of political rule in Chiapas. As a result, they helped define distinctive political identities, forms of internal organization, and strategic choices in the Lacandon forest, Simojovel, and Venustiano Carranza.

Chapter 3

LEADERS AND BASE IN THE

LACANDON FOREST

In Chiapas, one of the principal sources of ambiguity within peasant movements has been the relationship between leaders and base. This phenomenon is not of course unique to Mexico. Ever since Roberto Michels ([1911] 1959) wrote of the "iron law of oligarchy," social scientists have had to contend with the recurrent pattern of bureaucratization of popular movements, unions, and political parties. Referring specifically to a regional peasant movement in Mexico, Jonathan Fox and Luis Hernández (1989) provided a useful counterargument to Michels. Departing from the assumption that the divorce of leaders from the base is only a tendency, rather than a law, they investigated the shifting pattern of internal relations over a twenty-year period. Their findings help shed light on the general problems facing rural social movements that simultaneously strive for independence and representation in an authoritarian political system. Their main conclusion was that leadership accountability requires the existence of effective intermediate instances of participation. These instances may include "formal or informal opportunities for members to make, carry out and oversee important group decisions" (1989:9). If leaders are to be held accountable, grassroots organizations need to encompass local-level free spaces for membership participation, effective channels for exchanging information among members and between members and leaders, active participation of members in decision making, and implementation of agreements and decentralization of responsibilities through training in political, technical, and administrative skills. These authors found that leaders could be held accountable, and the organization be more successful, when these conditions were present. However, they noted that it is unlikely that they all exist simultaneously. The authors described the result of this situation as the "ebb and flow" of leadership accountability in regional organizations. This model appears to be more realistic than assuming the "iron law of oligarchy" and forces us to identify those elements that strengthen or undermine popular organizations.

In rural Mexico, the concern with leadership accountability has conflicted with traditional practices of *caudillismo*.[1] In Mexico during the turbulent first decades of national independence, regional caudillos competed in violent struggles for political supremacy. The weak implantation of impersonal juridical norms allowed for the continuation of the caudillo tradition, incorporating it into the political practices of modern mass organizations such as parties, unions, and peasant confederations. For those who aim to democratize their communities and their organizations, the practice of caudillismo has been a constant source of tension. On the one hand, they need leaders who are experienced political negotiators. On the other, they resist manipulation and demand participation in more and more areas of decision making. This tension is intrinsic to popular struggles in authoritarian political systems such as Mexico's. However, this tension does not imply a cultural determinism condemning new movements to repeat the caudillismo of the past. The nature of the EZLN draws from this history, but it also reflects multiple efforts to promote more decentralized forms of organization in Chiapas. Our task is not to show how one dominant form of political practice has been expressed in contemporary struggles, but to document resistance to caudillismo in the construction of popular notions of democratic community and citizenship. During the 1970s pastoral workers, students, and national peasant organizations played a significant role in this struggle.

Catechists and the Word of God

Priests and preachers can be seen as potential caudillos. They possess the training and vocation of natural leaders. They are also backed up by a formidable set of institutional and theological apparatuses that encourage compliance and trust on the behalf of members. Until the early 1970s, the Catholic Church seemed to be continuing with this role even as it underwent a complex process of

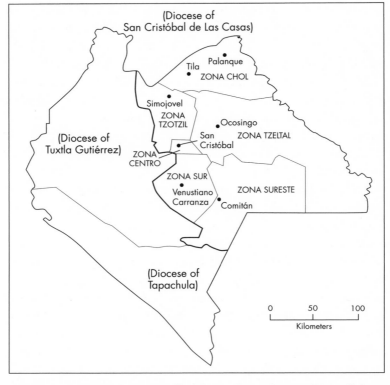

Map 3.1.   Diocese of San Cristóbal de Las Casas. Source: Leyva Solano (1995:389).

internal renewal. Prior to 1960 the diocese covered the entire state of Chiapas. In that year a separate diocese was created for Tuxtla Gutiérrez, and the following year saw the establishment of the diocese of Tapachula. This left the highlands and eastern lowlands under the supervision of San Cristóbal's newly appointed thirty-five-year old bishop, Samuel Ruiz García (map 3.1).

After Oaxaca, Chiapas has the highest proportion of indigenous population of any state in Mexico. According to official census data for 1990, over one-quarter of the state's 3 million inhabitants belong to one of seven major indigenous groups (table 3.1). Over 80 percent of the indigenous population of Chiapas is located within the diocese of San Cristóbal (table 3.2). The areas with the highest percentage of indigenous population are located in the northern

Table 3.1. Indigenous Population in Chiapas, 1990

Indigenous languages in Chiapas	Number of speakers of indigenous language over 5 years of age	Percentage of total population over 5 years of age in Chiapas
Tzeltal	258,153	9.52
Tzotzil	226,681	8.36
Chol	114,460	4.22
Tojolobal	35,567	1.31
Zoque	34,810	1.28
Kanjobal	10,349	0.38
Mame	8,726	0.32
Total	688,746	25.39

Source: INEGI (1992, "Chiapas" section).

and central highlands and Lacandon forest, corresponding mainly to the *Zonas* Chol, Tzeltal, and Tzotzil. The percentage is lower in the southern and southeastern zonas, which include the Comitán region and the Grijalva valley.

Samuel Ruiz brought with him the contradictions of the times. A new church was in the making, a church that had to respond to the twin threats of materialist individualism of the West and the communistic atheism of the East. The church needed to renew its appeal to the masses and modernize its own structures and message. Ruiz was as anticommunist as his mentors in the Catholic hierarchy. Fidel Castro was roundly denounced for his espousal of socialist values, and the diocese began to organize communities in the spirit of President Kennedy's Alliance for Progress (MacEoin 1995:24). The problems of poverty and landlessness could be resolved without social revolution. The task was to dismantle the many barriers to modernization in Latin America. Land reform, agricultural cooperatives, education, and health programs were seen as necessary elements of a nonrevolutionary path of social change. These ideas were taken up by the young renovators of the Catholic Church in Latin America. Just as occurred in northeastern Brazil, Bishop Ruiz promoted the transformation of indigenous communities through the direct intervention of a new generation of lay preachers.[2] Two

Table 3.2. Indigenous Population in Diocese of San Cristóbal de Las Casas, 1990

Diocese zonas in map 3.1	Number of indigenous speakers over 5 years of age	% of total population in zona over 5 years of age	% of indigenous population in diocese	% of indigenous population in Chiapas
Zona Chol	118,221	57.4	19.6	16.5
Zona Sur	19,439	26.8	3.2	2.7
Zona Sureste	51,399	11.9	8.5	7.1
Zona Centro	25,093	33.1	4.2	3.5
Zona Tzotzil	159,435	86.8	26.4	22.3
Zona Tzeltal	230,112	89.7	38.1	32.1
Total for Diocese	603,699	51.0	100.0	84.2

Source: INEGI (1992, "Chiapas" section).

schools for indigenous men and women were created in 1961. By 1970 over 1,000 catechists had been trained and now transmitted the Word of God (*La Palabra de Dios*) throughout the lowland ejidos. However, there were two negative consequences of this evangelization. First, native cultural practices were suppressed by the emphasis on Western models of social change. Second, the methodology of consciousness-raising promoted passivity rather than active engagement among community members. The new catechists often reproduced vertical relations of power based on their knowledge and outside contacts (Diócesis de San Cristóbal de Las Casas 1978). In other words, they became new caudillos.

The diocese began to change its top-down practices in response to internal criticism and external developments. Internally, many community members began to complain that the church appeared to be only interested in spiritual liberation and religious matters, while ignoring the need for economic and political change (Floyd 1996:155). At the same time, Samuel Ruiz had participated in the Medellín Council of Latin American Bishops in 1968. The adoption of the preferential option for the poor occurred in the context of an emerging radical consensus that the causes of poverty in Latin America were structural in nature and were rooted in the expansion of U.S. imperialism. Marxist class analysis and dependency theory overlapped with the bishops' own concern for their largest and newest constituency — the rural and urban poor. If the church were truly concerned with renewal, then it had to confront the economic and political obstacles to liberation.

The diocese of San Cristóbal began to address these issues in 1968. The catechists were no longer trained to simply take the Word of God and deliver it to their communities. Instead, they were to incarnate it within their cultural traditions and practical daily lives. That is, the Word of God did not exist externally but was already present within the communities. The task was to bring its message out, respecting and promoting the cultural practices of the people. The emphasis shifted from instruction to reflection. The teacher-centered method of *nopteswanej* (to make another understand) was replaced with the dialogical practices of tijwanej, which means "to bring out what's in another's heart" (Leyva Solano 1995:403). The role of the catechist was to open up reflection and collect all the different opinions. This reorientation toward community over leader also helped address the problem of passivity noted earlier. Catechists were no longer restricted to religious matters and instead promoted discussion of economic and political issues in people's daily lives. Communities began to reflect in a more systematic fashion on the low wages paid on plantations, the lack of security in their land titles, the corruption of government agencies, and the abuses of merchants and landowners. This method also helped revive indigenous practices of decision making. Reflection and discussion continued until an agreement was made that would be binding to the whole community. These *acuerdos* were therefore the result of dialogue rather than preestablished doctrines and were interpreted by the diocese as theological statements, not simply as a list of complaints or demands. They were the theological expression of how the Word of God lived within people rather than occupying a position of exteriority. This theological expression provided not only the analytical framework for reflection, but also the practical tools for collective action. The indigenous poor were not simply the passive victims of structural oppression; they used their religious faith and interpretation of the Bible to create concrete solutions to immediate problems. Even prior to the Indigenous Congress of

1974, the lowland communities of the diocese had begun to establish new transport and food cooperatives, community health projects, and literacy programs. These initial efforts to remake community would be essential when the struggle for land and political rights began in the mid-1970s.

The work of the catechists was complemented by the decision to train a large number of community deacons whose main responsibility would be to help the priests administer the sacraments. It was the communities themselves that expressed the need for their own deacons so they would not have to rely on the already limited supply of pastoral workers in the diocese. Each community would choose their deacon, or *tu'hunel,* through consensus and generally they elected those who had served well in other capacities. The diocese agreed to ordain deacons after a three-year trial period (Tangeman 1995:9). The importance of the deaconhood was that it was made a permanent feature of community organization, whereas prior to the 1970s it represented more of a temporary solution to the lack of priests.

In 1975 and 1976 some 600 communities reflected on the need for deacons who not only spoke indigenous languages but also understood their cultures and traditions. As a result, the election of deacons was taken very seriously. Finally, in the summer of 1976, all community members debated their preferences over a period of three months. The election was not limited to deciding who would occupy the new positions, but also defined their precise functions and responsibilities, which tended to vary among communities. For the diocese, this was the clearest manifestation of an autochthonous Christianity, an expression of the incarnation of the Word of God within indigenous cultures. The effect was to create a network of community leaders who went beyond religious activity to inspire new forms of political and economic organization that would eventually be absorbed by the EZLN. This was, in the words of the popular movement literature, the "people" constituting itself as a political actor.

The conception of power within these communities was not based on competition between rival groups or individuals. Instead, it referred to the ability to serve the community. When the Tzeltal talk of political positions in a community they use the noun *a'tel,* meaning communal work or service. Those who have been elected must govern by obeying (mandar obedeciendo), a principle that retained its appeal to such an extent that it now forms the central idea of the Zapatistas' political philosophy.[3] The final decision remains with the entire community, not the catechists nor the deacons, who are simply expected to carry out the agreements (acuerdos) made in assemblies. Those elected to positions of authority are not paid, and they should work in unison with other officeholders rather than making individual decisions for the community (Latapí 1994). Community cohesion is central to this form of governance. As an example, one community received the sacrament of the holy Eucharist only after three days of discussions to resolve internal conflicts between its members.[4]

In contrast to the practices of caudillismo, leaders depended on maintaining the confidence of the base through their constant involvement. The role of the church changed as a result. Its pastoral work was reinterpreted as one of accompaniment, rather than leadership, of the people. In the words of Bishop Ruiz, "becoming acquainted with the painful reality of our brothers, the poorest of the poor, we chose to accompany them, like the good Samaritan, in their search for a new society, structured on justice and fraternity" (cited by Floyd 1996:161). In practice, this has meant accompanying indigenous peasants in their struggles for land, respect for human rights, and democracy (Floyd 1996; Gómez Cruz and Kovic 1994). This type of community structure was certainly more open to debate, but it also allowed for new tensions to surface. The displacement of traditional elders by a new generation of young, bilingual catechists and deacons was never fully accepted. Charges of caudillismo were then leveled against these new community leaders, who owed their position to the political and organizational space created by the diocese. Other outside activists promoted similar organizational strategies but were also denounced for their caudillismo. The fact that caudillismo was seen as a problem was itself indicative of a change in how people viewed political participation. The discourse of liberation theology had provoked this change by building an authoritative structure around its core political teachings: "all have the word in their heart," "to govern by obeying," and "accompaniment in liberation." Each of these messages contrasted with and negated the practices of caudillismo. Their precise effects can only be understood in the context of a series of new institutional linkages that evolved during the 1970s.

Indigenous Congress of 1974

The early 1970s saw a rebirth of agrarian populism in Mexico. President Luis Echeverría came into office promising to restore the government's revolutionary commitment to workers and peasants. His administration attempted to regain popular support in the aftermath of the brutal repression of the 1968 student movement. A political opening to the opposition was announced and some left-wing activists were co-opted into new agencies and programs of an expanding federal bureaucracy. In the rural sector, Echeverría outraged private landowners by permitting land invasions and renewing the land reform program. The biggest confrontation occurred at the end of his *sexenio,* when over 100,000 hectares of prime irrigated land in Sonora were expropriated from private farmers for the purpose of redistribution among peasants (Sanderson 1981). However, most of Echeverría's actions fell short of seriously affecting the landed elites, although they did create a new legal and institutional terrain for state-peasant relations in subsequent years. The most important changes in this respect were the Federal Agrarian Reform Law of 1971 and the failed program of collectivization in the ejido sector. The new law stipulated that those ejidos that joined together in new, productive units, known as *uniones de ejidos* (UE), could receive increased government support through subsidized inputs and preferential rates of credit. Public investment in agriculture grew, and the government believed that its program to collectivize 11,000 ejidos (half the total number in existence) would overcome declining productivity of basic food staples. The government promoted new courses in agrarian law, marketing, and agricultural techniques with the intent of displacing intermediaries and fomenting a self-sufficient peasant economy.

In practice, these measures mostly benefited the irrigated ejidos of the northwest states, and by the end of Echeverría's term only

633 collective ejidos were operating (A. Bartra 1980; Moguel and López Sierra 1990; Montes de Oca 1977). Nevertheless, the greater presence of federal agencies created frictions with local caciques. The organization of UES and the courses in agrarian law were often directed by activists who had participated in the student movement. This was the case in lowland Chiapas, where church catechists were now joined by activists from the urban Left who brought different skills and views on how to modernize the region's social relations.

It was in this context that the state's governor Manuel Velasco Suárez imitated Echeverría's populist style by calling for the celebration of an Indigenous Congress in Chiapas. The official motive was to mark the 500th anniversary of the birth of Fray Bartolomé de Las Casas. It would take place in San Cristóbal in October 1974, but, recognizing the government's limited presence in the areas of greatest indigenous population, Velasco Suárez asked Bishop Ruiz to assist in the preparation of the congress. The diocese was indeed well placed to begin organizing the delegations from the different indigenous regions. Its catechists now numbered over 1,000, and the new method of reflecting on social conditions provided a solid base upon which concrete proposals could be formulated. The diocese also asked for assistance from teachers, students, and lawyers in directing new courses in agrarian law, history, and economics in preparation for the congress.

It was through such courses that community leaders gained a political education. In fact, some of the delegations to the congress were made up of indigenous men and women who had participated in a School for Regional Development, a program supported and led by teachers and researchers at the INI. In Simojovel, for example, community assemblies elected fifty young people from the municipality to attend the school's courses on agrarian law and political economy. The project was designed to form groups of community representatives from the Tzotzil, Tzeltal, Chol, and Tojolobal areas. These groups would then present their problems and demands at the Indigenous Congress.[5]

The congress was held in San Cristóbal de Las Casas in October 1974. 587 Tzeltal delegates, 330 Tzotziles, 152 Tojolobales, and

161 Choles were present, representing 327 communities (Mestries 1990:473). On agrarian matters, delegates demanded the titling of ejido and communal land and denounced encroachment by ranchers. They attacked the corruption of officials of the Department of Agrarian Affairs and Colonization (DAAC), specifically for their acceptance of bribes from landowners seeking protection. They also alleged that DAAC officials unduly demanded payment for each step in the processing of land petitions and often threatened to drop those cases where the peasants were unable or unwilling to pay (Congreso Indígena 1974). Plantation workers, newly aware of their labor rights, demanded respect for the provisions of the Federal Labor Code such as the minimum wage. Members of the Chol delegation illustrated how conditions on plantations in the northeastern municipalities had not changed significantly since the porfiriato.[6] Others called for greater access to markets, complaining how local intermediaries manipulated prices and controlled transportation and access to credit. Delegates also demanded education in their own languages and the defense of indigenous cultures. Finally, poor sanitation and the lack of medical services and clinics outside of the main towns were denounced as responsible for high indexes of disease and infant mortality, which was estimated at forty-two deaths per thousand births in 1970 (Mestries 1990; Morales Bermúdez 1992).

If the government had hoped that the congress would allow it to co-opt the new indigenous leaders in a populist alliance, then it was disappointed. The delegates directed their demands against the arbitrariness and corruption of government agencies and called for land reform and respect for indigenous cultures. The congress was also determined to remain independent of the government and the PRI. In the words of Samuel Ruiz, "the Congress should be of and for the Indians." Governor Velasco Suárez recognized the delegates' autonomy, proclaiming that "in no way should you feel your freedom threatened, so that you may express your reality as you live it" (Congreso Indígena 1974:1–2). The delegates took up this offer, thanking the governor for his open-mindedness. However, relations soon deteriorated when, shortly after the Congress, the army was used to violently evict peasants in six villages of the Lacandon forest.

Maoism in the Lacandon Forest

The Indigenous Congress proved to be a catalyst for grassroots organizing in the central highlands, but its impact was felt most in the Lacandon forest. This difference was probably due to the weaker presence of governmental institutions outside of the highlands, whereas within the highlands the INI, CNC, and PRI had subverted earlier forms of indigenous organization through the imposition of vertical and clientelistic lines of control. In the more peripheral and dispersed settlements of Ocosingo, on the other hand, the Catholic priests and catechists were able to build support for more autonomous forms of representation. This development is important in understanding the process of popular organization in the Lacandon forest. The origins are more social than institutional. Organization followed an intense period of political learning, achieved through a shared social and religious identification. Consequently, when the government began to promote the formation of uniones de ejidos (UE) in Chiapas, the new organizations that emerged were not controlled by interests loyal to the PRI but by the delegates who had participated in the Indigenous Congress. In this respect, the three most important cases were the UE Quiptic Ta Lecubtesel (in Tzeltal, "Applying our strength for a better future"), in Ocosingo, and UE Tierra y Libertad and UE Lucha Campesina, in Las Margaritas, each of which was recognized by the Ministry of Agrarian Reform (SRA) in 1976 (Ovalle Múñoz 1984).[7]

The largest of these was the UE Quiptic, which represented eighteen communities located in the Valley of San Quintín, sixty kilometers to the southeast of Ocosingo. Among the advisers the church had invited to help prepare for the Indigenous Congress were members of the Maoist group, Union of the People (UP). The most prominent of these were René Gómez, an agronomist trained at the Universidad Autónoma de Chapingo, and his wife, Marta Orantes. They were instrumental in bringing to the attention of Quiptic members the possible threat of eviction facing twenty-six communities in the region. The eviction threat was due to a presidential resolution issued in March 1972 that gave sole land rights for over 660,000 hectares to just sixty-six Lacandon families. However, the designated *comunidad lacandona* included at least 3,000 Tzeltal and Chol families who had settled in the area with government approval in the previous decades. Behind the decree was an agreement between the representatives of the Lacandon Indians and the state-owned forestry company (COFOLASA), which allowed for the latter to exploit 35,000 cubic meters of mahogany and cedar for a period of ten years. The UP advisers began to warn of possible evictions in 1973, and this issue contributed to the decision to form the UE Quiptic.

The network of community deacons and catechists proved to be essential in organizing opposition to a new perimeter road, or *brecha,* that was to demarcate the comunidad lacandona. The struggle to stop the brecha revealed the organizational capacity of these communities. This is how one of the leaders of the UE Quiptic described the initial response:

In 1973 we began to go from ejido to ejido in commissions to inform everyone that they would be affected. We went by foot. It took many weeks and months. We only heard about the brecha from René Gómez. The government had told us nothing.

In 1978 we were told that the brecha was getting nearer, that it was between fifteen and twenty meters wide, so we felt it even closer. We saw that the authorities would not agree to our demands, so we decided to stop further construction. In March 1978, eight hundred people went to the place in the forest which the soldiers were clearing for the road to pass through. Now, eight hundred people walking through the forest make a lot of noise! We surrounded them and began to speak with them, explaining that we had settled there long before the *decreto* [decree] and that it would be very difficult for us to give up what we had, and that they should not continue with the brecha. We were committed to this. They understood, saying that they were only following orders. But the brecha did stop there, and we saw that we could win our demands. As a result, our organization grew rapidly. From 1978 onward, we negotiated with the authorities and presented our proposal that we would respect the brecha if the authorities respected us. The brecha was not completed, although they did carry out the topographical studies and the survey by satellite. Day and night we moved, from ejido to ejido. (Interview with administrative secretary of Unión de Uniones, Ocosingo, October 12, 1987)

Twenty-six ejidos formed the backbone of this movement. Other ejidos did accept relocation and promises of government support, credit, and subsidies in new settlements of Frontera Echeverría, Nueva Palestina, and Marqués de Comillas. Those that remained received advice and leadership from the church, René Gómez, and another Maoist current, People's Politics (PP). Activists from this latter current arrived in Chiapas in late 1977. They came from Torreón in the northern state of Coahuila, where Samuel Ruiz had met them during a visit in the previous year (*Proceso* 1994:28–31). Bishop Ruiz believed the diocese needed the support and organizational skills of activists who were prepared "to go to the people," that is, to integrate themselves on a permanent basis in the struggle against land evictions. The first group arrived after hearing of an armed clash at Nueva Providencia, one of the threatened ejidos, in July 1977. The conflict had arisen when the local cacique kidnapped the son of an ejidatario who had begun to participate in the UE Quiptic. When the authorities failed to reply to appeals for his release a group of several hundred ejidatarios armed with machetes and rifles attacked the house where the boy was being kept. In the shoot-out seven police officers were killed, the cacique was taken prisoner, and the boy freed. Groups of peasants closed down nearby landing strips to avoid repression (Interview, adviser to UE Quiptic, October 1987).

People's Politics (PP) has its roots in the 1968 student movement and its principal leader was Adolfo Orive Berlinguer, an economics professor at the Universidad Nacional Autónoma de México (UNAM). In November 1968 Orive wrote a pamphlet entitled "Hacia una política popular" ("Toward a politics of the people"), which criticized the traditional Left in Mexico for its lack of insertion among the masses. Seeking to apply the Maoist "mass line" to Mexico in a nonviolent struggle for socialism, brigades of students went out to poor urban neighborhoods and ejidos to build bases of popular power at the grass roots. The most significant advances were made in the northern cities of Monterrey, Torreón, and Chihuahua and among ejidatarios in La Laguna and Nayarit.

In 1976 the PP joined with nonviolent factions of other groups, including Union of the People (UP) and became known as Proletarian Line (LP), which also developed an important presence in the national unions of teachers, telephone workers, and steelworkers. The arrival of LP activists in Chiapas was therefore part of a broad movement to build new forms of popular organization in Mexico. It should be stressed that they did not promote armed struggle. In fact, one of their central strategic decisions, "fighting with two faces" *(la política de dos caras),* was to avoid confrontations with the state, earning the criticism of many on the Left who concluded that LP was progovernment, or *gobiernista.*

The northerners *(norteños)* from LP were not immediately accepted by those indigenous leaders who had the support of the church. The northern advisers complained that the church gave too much power to the same leaders who had been delegates at the 1974 congress, creating a new clique rather than fostering grassroots participation. Some of the methods the advisers tried to introduce undermined the centralization of decision making. One was to revive a traditional element of indigenous democracy, the division of community assemblies into "small assemblies," or *asambleas chicas.* These were each made up of six or seven people who discussed problems or proposals that were then forwarded to the community assembly. A second strategy was to create horizontal links between the members of each community, rather than simply between the leaders or delegates. Drawing on their Maoist training, they promoted contacts and exchanges between different communities at a grassroots level. Through a method known as "from the masses, to the masses" *(de las masas a las masas),* commissions were sent to inform other communities of the threat of eviction from their land. This was painstaking work, involving treks of several days to reach distant settlements. Drawing from Fox and Hernández's (1989) analysis, we can note that the "iron law of oligarchy" was offset by the simultaneous promotion of autonomous spaces for grassroots participation and the horizontal flow of information between communities rather than through the vertical structures that had emerged from the Indigenous Congress.

Sensing that the advisers were attempting to displace them as leaders, the delegates *(delegados)* refused to cooperate and forced the

norteños to leave the region in late 1978. The church replaced the
LP activists with its own pastoral workers. However, new problems
emerged. The communities still lacked sufficient organizational
skills, and the delegados were often accused of neglecting their
responsibilities. Some allegedly took advantage of their position to
avoid work in the fields and to spend their time drinking. On the
other hand, the norteños had overextended the communities' interest in consciousness-raising. Political meetings and intellectual discussions lost their appeal as the day-to-day problems were left unresolved. At the national level, LP also suffered an internal division as
many of its members criticized the drift of their central body, the
Ideological Leadership Organization (OID) away from its grassroots orientation and toward a centralized, partylike structure.

It was in this context that René Gómez and five other LP activists
were able to resume organizational work in the Lacandon forest in
1979. The communities saw the continued need for organizers and
advisers. They were dissatisfied with the church's delegados and
anxious to move beyond ideological issues to deal with practical
problems. The local LP activists were freed from the overly ideological strictures of the OID, and René was not so "burned" as
others due to his longer association with the local catechists and
community deacons. In early 1979 these advisers began to reincor-
porate themselves in the UE Quiptic. Their political strategy shifted
from one based on ideological training to one that stressed economic issues. Throughout 1979 and 1980 they promoted a statewide movement to improve the terms of coffee marketing for peasant producers, known as the Comisión Coordinadora del Café. Two
main problems were identified: the high cost of transporting coffee
was absorbed by the producer, and the Mexican Coffee Institute
(INMECAFE) delayed paying producers for their crop. During
1979 several coffee growers' organizations, including the UE Quiptic, pressed INMECAFE to respond. A partial solution was achieved
in November 1979 when an accord was signed in which INMECAFE
agreed to pay 50 and 100 percent of ground and air transport costs,
respectively. At this point, the significance of intermediate instances
of participation was more closely linked to the need to address
pressing economic issues than to pure concern for democratic governance. In other words, economic survival was seen to depend on

greater levels of participation, rather than relying on the capacities of individual leaders. Participation was highest when the organization was directly addressing the most important needs of the base and when it rotated positions of responsibility among community members.

The convergence around coffee marketing culminated in the formation in September 1980 of the Union of Ejidal Unions and United Peasant Groups of Chiapas (UU). The UU brought together the three uniones de ejidos that had been formed in 1976 and other smaller producer groups from the highlands, Lacandon forest, and the border region. This was the first and largest independent peasant organization in Chiapas, representing 12,000 mainly indigenous families from 180 communities in eleven municipalities (Harvey 1992b): Ocosingo, Las Margaritas, Tila, Sabanilla, Huitiupán, El Bosque, Larráinzar, Yajalón, Comitán, Frontera Comalapa, and Motozintla (see map 3.2).

The unification of these diverse communities was achieved through a method known as pretexts and objectives (*pretextos y objetivos*). The advisers took a particular demand as the pretext for the broader objective, that of building an independent peasant organization. In this case, the problems surrounding coffee marketing were chosen as the pretext because they affected nearly all the communities of the Cañadas as well as many areas of the highlands and the border region. All had to deal with the impositions of middlemen *(coyotes)* and the corruption of INMECAFE. Coffee marketing, rather than land tenure, was chosen as an issue that could more feasibly be resolved in the short term. In order to build support around this objective, the advisers promoted from the masses to the masses strategy. The more politicized communities sent commissions to areas where political awareness was much lower. Their task was to explain how the coffee issue could be resolved through organization. This activity also served to give the UE Quiptic a central role in directing the struggle. It had the effect of renewing the organization's leadership through the formation of new commissions of peasant leaders dedicated to the specific problems of coffee marketing.

From the beginning, the rivalry between advisers was a source of

Map 3.2. Area of Presence of Unión de Uniones in 1980

potential conflict for the UU, or Unión de Uniones. Whereas René Gómez had established his popularity with the UE Quiptic, the ideological father of LP, Adolfo Orive, was supported by communities in the highlands and Motozintla region. Orive arrived from Torreón with the first group of People's Politics activists in September 1977. They immediately went to live in the communities on the northern edge of the highlands (between Huitiupán and Tila) that had participated in the Indigenous Congress. Orive spent the next two years integrated into the life of these Chol and Tzotzil communities. Unlike the LP advisers in the Cañadas, Orive's group was able to maintain support from the base. During 1978 Orive accompanied Tzotzil and Chol leaders on a trip to Monterrey to meet labor and peasant activists from northern Mexico. These connections partly offset the silent but increasing opposition from some sectors of the diocese. By 1980, as René Gómez worked to unite coffee growers, Orive was formulating his plans to attack the problem of insufficient credit and prohibitive interest rates. In 1979 he had helped establish a credit union for the Coalition of Collective Ejidos of the Yaqui and Mayo Valleys (CECVYM) of Sonora. This contact enabled indigenous peasants from Chiapas to visit CECVYM in the spring of 1980 and learn how their credit union worked.

During 1981 the two factions led by René Gómez and Adolfo Orive appeared to complement each other. Both leaders agreed on the strategy of pretexts and objectives as the best way to avoid overpoliticization of struggles and the hostility of the state governor, Juan Sabines. This discourse was able to exploit the federal government's new support programs for subsistence producers, thereby creating an effective counterweight to politically motivated opposition in Chiapas. Its emphasis on matters of production and marketing was a strategic choice that allowed the UU to take advantage of a margin of maneuver for uniones de ejidos at a time when the federal government was declaring an end to land reform. The UU leaders were aware of divisions between Sabines and the federal government and successfully isolated the former by proposing an alternative solution to the land tenure problem that gained acceptance within the SRA in Mexico City. This proposal involved the suspension, pending investigation, of the eviction orders against twenty-six ejidos located within the comunidad lacandona. Rather than confront the local caciques head on as in Carranza, the UU adopted a strategy of fighting with two faces (política de dos caras), appearing externally to support official policies while internally building the critical perspective of an independent mass movement.[8] For example, the UU did not openly denounce the agrarian policies of President José López Portillo (1976–82). Whereas other organizations condemned the 1980 Law of Agricultural Development for potentially opening the way for privatization of the ejido sector, the UU welcomed new programs designed to boost productivity, declaring:

We are organized to increase and improve our production and market it in a freer way at better prices, contributing in this manner to the

Mexican Food System (SAM). Proof of this are the two Agreements on Production and Marketing that we have established with INMECAFE and the support that we have given to the president's assistance programs for marginalized areas: National Company of Popular Subsistence–Federal Coordinator of the National Plan for Deprived Zones and Marginalized Groups [CONASUPO-COPLAMAR] and Mexican Social Security Institute–COPLAMAR [IMSS-COPLAMAR]. We are willing to collaborate with the different institutions, with the state government and with the federal government, in solving our problems of production and marketing.[9]

From this perspective, the capacity for independent political action depended less on denunciations and confrontation and more on the economic viability of peasant organizations. Economics became the key to political emancipation. The retention of surplus value through autonomous control of production, credit, and marketing became the goal for a new type of peasant movement that sought to go beyond the struggle for land. The Unión de Uniones, together with CECVYM, was therefore a pioneer of what became known throughout Mexico as the peasant struggle for the appropriation of the productive process (see chapter 5).

The state government of Juan Sabines unsuccessfully attempted to co-opt the leaders of the new organization. Instead, the group's strategy of fighting with two faces worked to isolate his opposition to an "unofficial" popular organization. The UU held a march and demonstration in Tuxtla Gutiérrez on October 12, 1981, to back up its demands for the suspension of the eviction orders. Over 2,000 peasants participated in a three-day sit-in at the palace of government. In a show of solidarity, LP activists organized a support demonstration outside the offices of the SRA in Mexico City. An agreement was reached. Evictions were suspended, and the UU was able to negotiate directly with the federal authorities. Another outcome was the signing of a new accord with INMECAFE that improved the terms of coffee marketing and, in February 1982, an agreement was made with the Autonomous University of Chapingo to provide technical assistance. The UU was quickly able to occupy a space for new producer organizations, which coincided with reformist initiatives from within the federal bureaucracy. As such, it represented one of the earliest examples of the type of new political linkages that could feasibly be established between independent peasant movements and reformist functionaries (Fox 1992).

This does not mean that members of the UU escaped local-level repression. Sabines also attempted to use the CNC to divide communities that lacked definitive land titles. The most serious attack occurred in the municipality of Ocosingo in August 1982, when a group of over 100 CNC peasants from the ejido Velasco Suárez violently evicted UU supporters from their homes in the neighboring ejidos of Flor de Cacao, Cintalapa, and Nuevo Progreso. In this action, which was motivated by the dispute over the demarcation of the comunidad lacandona, two people were killed, twenty-three UU members were kidnapped, 149 homes were burned down, and crops and equipment were stolen. The kidnapped persons were released in the same month, and the state delegate of the SRA promised a full investigation. Nevertheless, members of the UU feared the attacks would continue as long as its members' legal title to land went unrecognized.[10]

For Orive, the UU's main task was to secure approval of a credit union that would allow its members to directly control the financing of their productive projects. The National Banking Commission finally granted the extension of 25 million pesos to help establish the credit union in May 1982.[11] However, the way this happened led to a serious split within the UU. The leaders of the UE Quiptic accused Orive of attempting to rush through approval of the creation of a credit union for the UU and of bypassing internal democratic procedures. Orive drew on the support of smaller organizations in the highlands, not all of whom had contributed to the start-up capital. Orive was anxious to win official approval of the credit union prior to the end of the sexenio, fearing that his contacts within the López Portillo administration would no longer have the same leverage in the new government. Tensions grew throughout 1982 as the UE Quiptic once more raised the problem of caudillismo. In the opinion of one of its members, "Orive became obsessed with the credit union. He came to run the show. In 1980 and 1981 the Unión was very strong, but we let Orive in and that was a big mistake" (Interview, member of administration committee of the Unión de Uníones, Ocosingo, Chiapas, October 12, 1987). A related criticism was that Orive neglected other issues, particularly the problems of land tenure, in his effort to secure the credit union. This was revealed by his failure to respond more vigorously to the evictions of August 1982. Whereas the UE Quiptic and UE Tierra y Libertad reacted by sending commissions of community represen-tatives to Mexico City, the Chol and Tzotzil regions participated with only one representative each (Rubio López 1985:64–65).

Tensions came to a head at a general assembly held in Rizo de Oro (Las Margaritas) on January 22 to 23, 1983, when the two factions accused each other of trying to undermine their UU. René Gómez alleged that Orive tried to provoke him with insults but failed and, in his frustration, declared that each should go their own way. "Orive personally divided the Unión de Uniones," Gó-mez concluded. Orive's supporters naturally had their own version of events. According to one, Orive had tried to promote more community-level participation and this did not please "those who wanted to be at the top and control everything." They could also point to the obstructive tactics of the church in Ocosingo and Las Margaritas, where the two largest uniones de ejidos (Quiptic and Tierra y Libertad) were located. Ever since the UE Quiptic had driven the norteños out in 1978, Orive and his followers had been critical of the pastoral workers in the Cañadas.

Both sides accused the other of being caudillista, invoking the "community" to back up their own position. The meaning of com-munity was inevitably reified in this factional struggle for leadership of the Unión de Uniones. According to Marín Rubio López, the division was due more to factionalism than to any grand ideological dispute, although each group tried to theorize its position as the correct one (1985:77). True to their Maoist origins, both factions conceptualized this struggle in terms of the "mass line." This strat-egy was directed against Leninism and social democracy as models of revolutionary change because they relied on the vanguard role of trained professionals, intellectuals, and political leaders. In con-trast, Maoists (in a manner not unlike the *basistas* of liberation theology) sought to let the masses decide *(que las masas decidan),* minimizing the role of leaders and intellectuals. In reality, the mass line never took an effective hold, and it was not difficult for each side to accuse the other of caudillismo or, just as pejoratively, social democracy. Instances of corruption in the administration of the credit union helped fuel charges that the new practices were really not much different from those of the PRI. However, the most damning criticism, and the one that went beyond mere intellectual rationalization, was that the Orive faction was unwilling to confront the government when it was most necessary. The failure to respond to the evictions in August 1982 was the final straw for the UE Quiptic. Its members had just seen their homes destroyed and their lands taken over by the CNC. Mass mobilization was called for, but this might have endangered final approval of the credit union. The strategy of "fighting with two faces" was immediately perceived as "fighting with one face" and that face was labeled gobiernista, or progovernment. The ideological formation of the masses in their struggle for socialism was, without a blink of the eye, transformed into accommodation and quiescence. The UE Quiptic accused the credit union of fulfilling the role of any social democratic institution — that of co-opting and controlling the workers and peasants. Unfortunately for the basistas, the situation in the Cañadas was not much better. The split in the Unión de Uniones led to a period of retrenchment and weaker participation for the rest of the decade. One of the advisers, commenting in 1991, recalled that "the division was really a big blow to the Unión. It had the effect of *vaccinating the people* against any type of organization. Their trust has still not been recovered" (emphasis in original statement; interview, Mexico City, August 1991). Regaining this trust would be the first political task for the EZLN.

Chapter 4

MOBILIZATION AND REPRESSION

IN SIMOJOVEL AND VENUSTIANO

CARRANZA

Along the Grijalva river basin lie three hydroelectricity dams: Las Peñitas, Chicoasén, and La Angostura. The largest of these, La Angostura, is located in the municipality of Venustiano Carranza, some sixty miles south of Tuxtla Gutiérrez. The economic crisis of the 1980s stopped the Federal Electricity Commission (CFE) from building another, the Itzantún dam, in the northern municipality of Simojovel. In each case peasants have faced the loss of cropland and have had to fight for compensation. A detachment of federal army soldiers guards the road leading to the Angostura dam. Although most of the area is designated property of the CFE, some parcels of community land remained within its boundaries. Peasants from Venustiano Carranza must pass through a military checkpoint in order to farm some of their land. Each time they remind the soldiers that they are going to their land and that one day they will recuperate the rest, which has been stolen from them.

Most analysts have traced the origins of independent peasant organizing in Chiapas to the Indigenous Congress of 1974 (Barry 1995:161; García de León 1995; González Esponda 1989; González Esponda and Pólito Barrios 1995; Hernández 1994a). As we saw in chapter 3, the congress was called by the state government and organized by the Catholic diocese of San Cristóbal, a relationship that seems almost inconceivable now. The governor's objective was to co-opt indigenous leaders into a new alliance with an expanding state apparatus that promised, in true populist style, to attend the demands of the poor. The congress escaped these parameters and instead helped new organizations establish a measure of political autonomy from the PRI and the government. We have seen how this was the case in the Lacandon forest. However, although the congress was indeed an important event in the emergence of new peasant movements, it was not the only one. Two other areas of agrarian struggle in the 1970s were Simojovel and Venustiano Carranza. Representatives of the Chol and Tzotzil Indians attended the congress from Simojovel but were more independent of the diocese than were the colonists of the Lacandon forest. For its part, the Tzotzil community in Carranza had a more indirect relationship to the congress and the diocese. Unlike the Unión de Uniones, the organizations that emerged in each of these municipalities had to confront the violent resistance of local caciques and found much less margin for maneuver in their relations with federal and state government. However, in both cases, the practices of caudillismo would also be a constant source of tension.

Struggle for Land in Simojovel

The resurgence of land conflicts in Simojovel began in 1971, when Tzotzil and Chol Indians engaged in a series of land invasions on private coffee plantations.[1] According to participants, the decision to invade was taken because of the lack of response to petitions filed with the DAAC, some of which dated from the 1950s (Interviews, Simojovel, August 2–3, 1987). By 1970 some 10,000 hectares of the best land in the municipality were controlled by just nine families. These same families also exercised political control through the rotation of key positions in the local ranchers' association, Chamber of Commerce, Confederation of Private Property Owners, and municipal government. At the same time, of the landless population in Simojovel (which constituted 50 percent of the municipality's total population in 1970), only a small proportion was employed on a permanent basis. The majority was employed in seasonal work, obliging many to migrate to the Lacandon forest or urban centers (CIOAC 1983:132). Most of the workers on the plantations were peones acasillados, who exchanged their labor for a piece of land for their family's subsistence. As in Carranza, further land redistribution was blocked by a well-organized and intransigent fraction of the landowning class, descendants of the same families who had defeated the *carrancistas* during the Mexican Revolution.

In 1971 peons and landless peasants began to invade areas they had been petitioning for several years. Repression quickly followed, and one of the leaders was killed. Significantly, the failure of the CNC to provide adequate leadership or achieve solutions led these petitioners to form an independent organization that would combine mobilization with negotiations. Moreover, the failure of the DAAC to prevent encroachment by private owners onto ejido land and the impunity of acts of violence against land claimants deepened the latter's hostility toward the state government.

The early leaders in Simojovel emerged from the courses that prepared the regional delegations for the 1974 Indigenous Congress. It was through these courses that community leaders began to make contact with each other and exchange experiences of their respective struggles for land. Following the congress, a group of leaders began to work together as a coordinating committee. They also helped set up local committees in over thirty communities. This expansion facilitated broader participation and reduced the nascent organization's vulnerability to repression of its leaders (Pérez Castro 1981:232). Although these communities had split from the CNC, at this point they did not adopt a new name. As in Carranza, the organization's first actions were demonstrations to win the release of peasants who had been arrested following the eviction of the Vista Hermosa plantation in 1974.

The struggle to democratize ejido authorities also served to unify the new organization. Ejido assemblies and elections for new ejido presidents *(comisariados)* provided the arena for this struggle. Most of the ejidos were controlled by authorities who had been imposed by the PRI. However, during 1974 and 1975, the new militancy inspired by the Indigenous Congress led to their defeat and to the growing influence of independent leaders. In April 1976 a new round of land invasions began and by the end of the year, the organization claimed to have the support of thirty-seven communities in Simojovel and the neighboring municipalities of Huitiupán, Sabanilla, and El Bosque (Pontigo Sánchez 1985:90). Under pressure from the region's landowners, the new state governor, Jorge de la Vega Domínguez, called a meeting on April 29, 1977, with representatives of the CNC, INI, SRA, and the peasant organization itself. In Simojovel, landowners took advantage of the presidential succession in December 1976 to form what they themselves called "counterinsurgency militia" and called on the government to carry out evictions.[2]

The SRA agreed to examine each claim on a case-by-case basis on the condition that the land invasions were lifted. This was barely an acceptable offer, and the organization's leaders looked for assistance from outside activists associated with the Independent Confederation of Agricultural Workers and Peasants (CIOAC). The CIOAC was a national confederation with close ties to the Mexican Communist Party (PCM). It had its roots in the Independent Peasant Confederation (CCI), which was formed as an alternative to the CNC in 1963. The CCI split into an official and an independent wing following the repression of its leadership. It was the independent wing that took the name of CIOAC in 1975. The CIOAC differed from other peasant movements in that besides working to achieve land reform, it also fought for the right to organize independent unions of agricultural workers. It began to operate in Chiapas in 1976 in the municipality of Huitiupán, organizing tied peons who had taken over land within private coffee plantations. It was following the meeting with de la Vega that the leaders of the independent organization in Simojovel requested the assistance of the CIOAC activists. However, this first contact had negative results. Part of the agreements reached in April 1977 required the abandoning of invaded land in exchange for new land in other areas of the state, principally in Socoltenango, near Venustiano Carranza, and in the Lacandon forest. The CIOAC saw that the balance of forces was decidedly against the struggle for land and recommended relocation in exchange for some concessions in Simojovel. This went against the decision of land invaders, who refused to give up the fight. The most militant were those who had taken a plantation named Chanival, and they began to accuse CIOAC of simply helping the government to carry out its relocation plan. Tensions between the two sides even led to violent clashes and the death of one peasant at Chanival. Finally, on June 10, 1977, federal troops were used to evict Chanival and other disputed lands. Various incidents of beatings and killings were reported, including the dropping of bodies from army helicopters. The troops were also supported by the landowners' militia. (Marion Singer 1984:28).[3] The CIOAC activists fled Simojovel, while the national leadership appealed to the minister of the interior, Jesús Reyes Heroles, to withdraw the troops and stop the repression. The peasant movement in Simojovel went into decline until the arrival of new CIOAC activists in 1979. In the meantime, the army continued to patrol Simojovel, Huitiupán, and Sabanilla and during 1979 was reported to have harassed communities and made arbitrary arrests (see "Chiapas" 1979:22–27).

This new group of activists adopted a different strategy to the land struggle. They began to promote an independent union of plantation workers and the defense of labor rights. The new strategy led to the formation, on October 26, 1980, of the "Miguel de la Cruz" Agricultural Workers' Union (SOA), encompassing workers on twenty-two plantations.[4] The new leaders were also careful not to repeat the same mistakes as their predecessors and sought ways to promote broader participation. The most important of these was the promotion of assemblies in each community where land and labor rights were being claimed. Through these assemblies, special committees were elected to carry out specific tasks, while the organization as a whole became more open, encouraging the formation of local leaders (Interview, member of regional committee of CIOAC, Simojovel, June 28, 1987).

Nevertheless, differences between base and leaders over strategy continued to cause internal dissent, although not on the scale seen in 1977. The main difference of opinion concerned how to respond to a new initiative from the state government concerning land reform. Juan Sabines, who replaced interim governor Salomón González Blanco in 1979, offered to purchase disputed lands and resell them to peasant communities as private smallholdings, or *copropiedades*. The CIOAC leaders were accused by some communities of having agreed to the plan without consulting with the base. Three communities left and joined the Coordinadora Provisional de Chiapas, arguing that they should not be obliged to pay for land on which they had a legal claim (Colectivo 1983).

This problem did not halt the consolidation of CIOAC in Simojovel. The new union (SOA) provided a rallying point for an increasing number of communities in Simojovel, Huitiupán, Bochil, and Jitotol. The original twenty-two plantations were represented by over 300 delegates at the union's founding in October 1980. By the end of 1981 strikes had been organized at forty-seven plantations. The main demand at this point was for the recognition of the independent union. This was seen as a necessary step in the promotion of such basic demands as the right to a minimum wage, collective contracts, the right to organize, an eight-hour workday, and provisions concerning health and safety. The request for official recognition was first rejected in April 1981 by the Ministry of Labor's Local Arbitration and Conciliation Board (JLCA) in Tuxtla on the grounds that "the name lent itself to confusion" because it included "Miguel de la Cruz" (Pontigo Sánchez 1985:125–30). In response, strikes broke out on every plantation in the area, obliging the landowners to withdraw to the municipal center where they demanded the intervention of the state government. A second application for the *registro* was rejected in June. The JLCA now argued that it could not rule on the matter due to absence of formal wage relations on the plantations. The workers were classified as tenant farmers who received access to land in exchange for their labor and, as such, had no legal right to organize as workers (Pontigo Sánchez 1985:97). This principle, however, did not stop the same board from granting registro to a group of strikebreakers organized by the CNC (which went by the name of Solidaridad). Then the local landowners' association successfully filed an injunction against a third attempt at registro in the same month. The decision of the JLCA allowed the landowners to break off wage negotiations with the union and begin a campaign of attacks against its members. Despite the failure to win the registro, and in the face of increasing repression, the strikes in 1981 paralyzed sixty-eight plantations, bringing the coffee harvest to a standstill (Marion Singer 1984:34).[5] By the end of the year CIOAC began to see the strikes more as a means to press for the break up of the plantations and the redistribution of the affected land as ejidos. As a result, labor demands ceased to have relevance and the struggle for land reform regained prominence.

In February 1982 the registro was again denied, and four CIOAC leaders were arrested while attending talks with Governor Sabines. In response, some 2,000 CIOAC supporters marched from Simojovel to Tuxtla Gutiérrez to demand the leaders' release. They won the release of three of the detained and an agreement from Sabines to begin talks with the union's representatives. However, the registro was never granted. In October 1982 two other CIOAC members in Simojovel were killed following a demonstration in support of the union's demands (*Uno Más Uno,* October 30, 1982).

Despite these obstacles and repression, the state government could not ignore the support for CIOAC in Simojovel. At the same time as the strikes were taking place, another issue allowed CIOAC to redirect the struggle from labor rights to land redistribution. This concerned the impact of the proposed construction of the Itzantún hydroelectricity dam by the Federal Electricity Company (CFE). Although the site for the dam was located in neighboring Huitiupán, the flooding of lands required for its operation would directly affect Simojovel. Some 14,000 peasant families in the area faced resettlement, exacerbating the already critical demand for access to land. These families included 11,000 who were to lose ejido or communal lands and 2,000 tied peons who lived and worked on coffee plantations. The CIOAC demanded that the affected families should be compensated with an average of ten hectares each. Faced with the prospect of their plantations being taken over by peons and land claimants, the landowners offered to sell parts of their properties to the CFE while the state government offered generous compensation for lands that would be used to resettle displaced peasants. However, according to Marion Singer (1984:34), many purchases were overvalued by state functionaries who sought to keep part of the compensation money for themselves.

In response to this corruption and the lack of guarantees for displaced communities, CIOAC demanded that work on the dam be suspended until the houses and infrastructure of the new communities were completed. It also insisted that no compensation be paid to landowners until a wage agreement was reached with CIOAC's local union. These demands were presented at meetings with the CFE and state government in March and December 1981. The position of CIOAC at the second meeting was strengthened by a march of over 3,000 supporters to the CFE offices in Huitiupán. The march also called for recognition of CIOAC as a legitimate representative of the affected communities because the government only negotiated with the CNC.[6] A subsequent demonstration blocked the entrance to the construction site and forced the CFE to suspend operations until the state government reached agreements with CIOAC.

The CFE's decision to halt construction allowed CIOAC some space from which it could adopt a more offensive strategy in proposing alternative solutions for the region's problems. First, the CIOAC demanded that the government issue a formal decree of expropriation that would clearly state the areas of land to be compensated, the affected individuals, and the amount of compensation to be paid. Second, it called for the expropriation of a further 11,000 hectares from private owners for the purpose of resettlement. It argued that such a measure would help transform power relations in Simojovel by displacing the most traditional landowners and helping to modernize the local economy. In calling for the breakup of the coffee plantations, CIOAC proposed an alternative it believed would win support from modernizing sectors within state and federal government:

From the point of view of the state, [land redistribution] would help to break up old fiefdoms, the rule of caciques represented by backward-thinking landowners who prefer to subject their workers to superexploitative conditions and take over ejido and community lands to extend their holdings with little or no capital investment, rather than invest in the modernization of their farming techniques. Our proposal is that the creation of a group of new ejidos with sufficient urban infrastructure, roads, credit, etc. will allow for the sort of social and economic development which has not been possible in the past seventy years, which is the cause of the social injustices and unrest in the region today. (CIOAC 1983:139)

Related proposals included the formation of credit unions to allow the new ejidos to raise productivity and overcome obstacles to efficient marketing posed by intermediaries. The CIOAC also insisted on speeding up the construction of the new ejidos so that production would not suffer.

Although these proposals coincided with the productivist discourse of the López Portillo and Sabines administrations, they implied political changes the state government was unwilling to contemplate. On the one hand, they required the breakup of large landholdings. On the other, they would have strengthened the CIOAC, not the CNC, as the legitimate representative of the area's peasant communities. The fear that radical alternatives to the CNC could gain ground in Chiapas was also influenced by a similar pattern of mobilization and repression in Venustiano Carranza.

The Casa del Pueblo and Agrarian Struggle, 1965–76

In 1965 a presidential resolution finally granted the indigenous community of Venustiano Carranza the rights to over 50,000 hectares of land. Shortly after the news arrived, a group of comuneros began to meet at a private house in the San Pedro barrio of the municipal center.[7] The first meetings were kept secret in order to avoid detection by the caciques. They set up special committees (comisiones), which were responsible for pressing for the implementation of the resolution at the DAAC offices. Each member of the community cooperated with twenty-five centavos. Prior to 1965, when the DAAC sent surveyors to carry out land measurements they were bribed or threatened by the caciques and so their work always remained unfinished. It was the new comisariado, José Córdoba Ayar, and a retired teacher, Gaspar Díaz Reyes, who reopened the negotiations with the DAAC in 1965. Córdoba Ayar was killed almost immediately. He was succeeded by Manuel Gómez Ortega, who was able to bring a new surveyor from the DAAC to Carranza. Then, in 1971, the secretary of the comisariado was assassinated. In the same year the new comisariado, Gaspar Díaz Reyes, was murdered inside his home. One of the comuneros vividly recalled these events:

Gaspar and Manuel had great vision, great clarity of thought. They had been key figures. Everything was done clandestinely in 1971–72. In mid-1973 some students arrived and began to promote organizational work. We distributed pamphlets by night, all clandestinely, pamphlets of three or four pages, with denunciations against the caciques. The caciques patrolled the town and stood on street corners with rifles and guns." (Interview, member of the Casa del Pueblo, Venustiano Carranza, June 24, 1987)

The most active figure in the struggle for land was Bartolomé Martínez Villatoro. His grandfather had participated with the teacher Zamudio in the land struggles of the 1930s. Following the death of Gaspar Díaz Reyes, Bartolomé was chosen as the new comisariado in May 1972. During his administration the community built a new meeting place and office in the municipal center, which was named the Casa del Pueblo, or "People's House." This building would soon become the most visible target for the caciques.

Many of the comuneros recalled how Martínez Villatoro suffered various attempts on his life. "When we went to get a permit from the Forestry Commission offices, he was shot at and injured by a *pistolero*" (this and quotes throughout remainder of chapter are from interviews with members of the Casa del Pueblo, Venustiano Carranza, Chiapas, June 12, 1987). At a meeting in the municipal presidency another attempt on his life failed. In San Francisco barrio he was attacked with a machete and lost an eye. In November 1973, based on the accusations of Carmen Orantes and the municipal president, Jesús Domínguez Herrera, he was imprisoned for the murders of three comuneros. On his release in July 1974 Orantes allegedly told him "look here Indian, if you don't get out of here, you'll pay with your life." Orantes recognized that Bartolomé was his biggest enemy because he was the most active in pressing for land distribution. Despite his desire to do everything himself and his faith in the legal channels, the other comuneros admired and respected him. "Bartolomé was the only one who mobilized. He believed a lot in laws and lawyers, but if we went with him on comisiones he would leave us silent at the door."

In the spring of 1974 four students arrived to promote an independent organization in Carranza. They included one of the sons of Gaspar Díaz Reyes, Ismael, who had been imprisoned in Lecumberri prison in Mexico City after the 1968 student movement. He argued that it was necessary to use force to get Martínez Villatoro out of jail. They tried to organize a guerrilla movement in Carranza, and some comuneros went to the camp for training but returned after only a month. "We had to look after the milpa and the family," recalled one.

The level of political consciousness and base organization was still weak, so strategies brought from the outside were unsuccessful. The camp was at a place called Jeshtontic, 20 km from Carranza. The students attempted to get people to join, but there was a low level of awareness. But there was a lot of discontent with the municipal president because of the detention of Martínez Villatoro. People were willing to act, but it never developed into a full-time movement. The combatants went to the camp for a week or so, then returned to look after the milpa and the family; there was no total integration, more of a *guerrilla de semaneo* [weekly guerrilla].

The army easily discovered the location of the camp and the identity of the guerrilla leaders. A peasant hired by Carmen Orantes successfully infiltrated the group and passed on information to the government. The repression followed immediately in May and June of 1974. Many did not realize what was going on at Jeshtontic, Martínez Villatoro included. Over seventy were arrested, including the students. They were held at a farm called El Brasil and tortured with electric shocks from car leads. Nine were imprisoned: five students (including Ismael) and four peasants. Gradually they were released, but three people were disappeared: Javier Coutiño Gordillo, Bartolo Pérez Hernández, and Sebastián Vásquez Mendoza. All in all the guerrilla movement lasted no more than three months.

Shortly after the repression, Martínez Villatoro was released. He resumed the struggle for the community's land, establishing contacts with students of the Mactumatzá rural teachers' college in Tuxtla who were involved in their own struggles for financial aid and administrative reforms. The main goal was to win the state government's authorization of the demarcation *(deslinde)* of communal lands. In November 1974 the Casa del Pueblo participated in joint demonstrations with the Mactumatzá students and bus drivers of the Cuxtepeques transport cooperative. The drivers blocked roads in the center of Tuxtla for four hours in support of the negotiating team that was meeting with Governor Manuel Velasco Suárez. The demonstration was timed for maximum effect: President Echeverría was scheduled to arrive for an official visit the next morning. Following a long night of negotiations, an agreement was signed at 4 a.m.

The negotiations were a partial success for the Casa del Pueblo. Besides winning the recognition of some communal lands, it also won compensation from the Federal Electricity Commission (CFE) for land that had been flooded by the construction of the Angostura hydroelectricity dam. Altogether, the community's land had been reduced by 8,229 hectares. The Angostura dam accounted for 5,045 hectares of this, but there were another 3,184 hectares left out of the deslinde. This land corresponded to the most fertile and productive areas, which the caciques refused to give up. As a result, the area that was finally approved in 1975 was not the 50,152 hectares promised in 1965, but 41,924 hectares. Because only 1,000 hectares of this were arable (averaging 1 hectare per comunero), the Casa del Pueblo demanded the restitution of the "missing" 3,184 hectares. It also demanded full compensation from the CFE, which had paid for only 2,545 hectares of the 5,045 hectares that were flooded.

Martínez Villatoro insisted that the compensation money be used collectively, not divided individually. As a result, the Casa del Pueblo bought 830 head of cattle, two tractors, a ten-ton truck, and several nixtamal mills. They also bought 150 hectares of good farmland close to the Río Blanco. The lawyer who had helped win the deslinde used his fee to buy twelve new sewing machines to help establish a women's sewing cooperative in Carranza. He also donated 100,000 pesos as start-up capital.

The deslinde began in 1975. The team of surveyors stayed with the comuneros for three months. "We did not let them out of our sight. We went out with the surveyor, Licenciado Elías Múñoz, and helped lay the blocks of cement for the fences. The people were very enthusiastic since they now saw that they were going to get their land back."

Martínez Villatoro was reelected as comisariado in May 1975. An official from the DAAC came and officially handed over part of the land, but the caciques did not want to give it up. The documentation for the deslinde was then sent for final approval to Mexico City. The papers were in Oaxaca when Martínez Villatoro was killed on

August 1, 1975. He had received a call requesting his presence at a meeting with DAAC officials in San Cristóbal regarding a possible solution to the land problem. On the way his vehicle was ambushed by four assassins near Laguna Aguacatenango, and he was killed alongside his driver. News of his death "ran like wildfire." "He was much loved and respected. He lived to see the carrying out of the deslinde and the formal act of possession."

The community reacted violently to the killing. It was now led by two comuneros: Bartolo Gómez Espinoza and Santiago Espinoza Hernández. The willingness of these leaders to engage in direct actions earned them the following of the Casa del Pueblo, though they would eventually create a new faction. They argued that Martínez Villatoro had been too respectful of the legal channels. It was time to run out the caciques and occupy the land. Among their main targets were Carmen Orantes and Augusto Castellanos, whom they saw as responsible for the murder of Martínez Villatoro. A house belonging to Castellanos was burnt down, fences were destroyed, and lands were taken back by force. The caciques began to retreat, Orantes leaving Carranza in early 1976, Castellanos trying to calm the situation by giving back some ranches (Renard 1985:209–10). Castellanos was killed on May 8, 1976, and the Casa del Pueblo was made responsible, although its role in the murder was never proven. Nevertheless, the murder provided the government with a pretext to intervene against the Casa del Pueblo.

On May 11, 1976 federal army troops were deployed in an attempt to take the Casa del Pueblo building and arrest its leaders. There was a shoot-out between soldiers of the Thirty-first Military Regiment and comuneros in which seven soldiers and two comuneros died. About 100 people were arrested, including the entire leadership, while soldiers searched houses for other supporters of the Casa del Pueblo. Gradually the detained were set free until thirteen remained in detention, among whom were Gómez Espinoza and Espinoza Hernández.

By 1976 the Casa del Pueblo had learned two important lessons that would leave an imprint on its strategic choices in subsequent years. First, the state was no longer perceived as a neutral arbiter in the struggle for land but as the direct enemy of the comuneros and an ally of the caciques. The strategy of mass arrests and intimidation

led a new generation of comuneros to adopt a more radical oppositional stance toward the state. This position was encouraged
through the personal networks that linked the struggle in Carranza
to other peasant movements in Chiapas in these years. Second,
attempts to repress the movement had relied mainly on the murder
or imprisonment of its leaders. From 1976 onward the Casa del
Pueblo would be characterized by the absence of a single leader, a
decision that although initially was a purely pragmatic measure,
soon became part of the organizational structure in that it opened
the way for broader participation.

Outside Linkages and Internal Divisions, 1976–82

Following the repression of May 1976 the Casa del Pueblo functioned without a recognized leader but through two comisiones,
one dedicated to achieving the release of prisoners, another that
continued to press for the restitution of communal lands. For the
next twelve months the community worked through its barrio representatives until a new comisariado could be elected in May 1977.
During this period one of the main achievements was the release of
most of those detained in the shoot-out with the army. The most
significant action, however, was the mobilization in 1978 to gain
the release of thirteen leaders. During this period the role of outside
activists became crucial.

Those who escaped arrest sought the support of peasants in
nearby communities, particularly in Villa Las Rosas. Contacts had
been established during the mobilization in 1974, and the comisariado was able to introduce them to Arturo Albores Velasco, an
architecture student at the National Autonomous University of
Mexico (UNAM). He and his wife, Marisela González, had carried
out studies in highland Chiapas since 1974 as part of an extension
program to support self-managed and affordable housing projects
in indigenous communities.[8] Albores also participated in the Indigenous Congress and became active in promoting courses in Mexican history, law, and economics. At first he worked in the highland
communities of Zinacantán, Huixtán, and Chenalhó. Through this
work he got to know other community leaders from throughout

the highlands and Lacandon forest. The congress provided the basis for new personal networks that linked community leaders and activists from across the state. Toward the end of 1975 Albores moved to Villa Las Rosas to promote literacy classes. However, he soon became active in supporting the struggle of local peasants to name their own candidate for municipal president in 1976. He also took a job as a teacher at the agricultural school and worked to unite students behind the peasants' struggle. This cost him his job, and he was forced to abandon Villa Las Rosas in the face of threats from caciques. The strength of the peasant movement was revealed when it occupied the town hall for almost two months, obliging the authorities to accept peasant representation within the new municipal government.

When invited to participate in Carranza, Albores accepted and began to teach the comuneros new forms of struggle. Although the Casa del Pueblo had been active in retaking land, it did not have experience of marches, demonstrations, political-cultural acts, propaganda, and alliances. The successful occupation of the town hall in Villa Las Rosas was now copied in Carranza. During 1977 Albores won the confidence of the Casa del Pueblo and, in February 1978, organized the first occupation of the municipal presidency in Carranza's history. Although the building was evicted by the army, the action did win the subsequent release of the remaining prisoners. The Casa del Pueblo could view this as a victory and a vindication of the new tactics and strategy introduced by the Albores, who continued their work by promoting agricultural and craft cooperatives. Their willingness to integrate themselves so deeply into the community won much respect. Moreover, it appeared to give the Casa del Pueblo a reason to believe in a nonviolent political strategy. This is how one member of the Casa del Pueblo recalled his initial feelings:

I wanted to follow Arturo because he was something else! I thought he was a guerrilla. I used to tell myself (I never said this to Arturo), "if I'm not mistaken, they are with Lucio Cabañas." You see, we really loved the guerrillas, because our people have been screwed over so many times and we had enough of the caciques. When the people decided, the people hit back too. It was a violent place and so we looked for violent leaders and we thought Arturo was one of those "good guys" [*de los buenos.*] Lucio Cabañas was very popular in those days and we thought they were with him, but no, they weren't. Then I thought they were with the Liga 23 de Septiembre, that they were also really tough, but they weren't with them either. In fact, they didn't like any of that and Arturo was really a very calm man. He was like us, trying to find a solution, only that he came from a higher position, with more experience, from a place where science is more developed. We learned a great deal from him. (Interview, Mexico City, April 16, 1992)

Albores did not promote the armed struggle. He believed that political conditions in Mexico were not conducive to popular insurgency. Instead, he insisted on the more painstaking work of gradually building independent organizations in the cities and the countryside. He believed that leaders should give direction but not become caudillos. The main task was to promote broad-based participation of peasants and workers in the construction and development of their own organizations. He was respected for his honesty and his ability to pass on organizational skills. According to three members of the OCEZ interviewed in December 1991:

Arturo really worked hard to train us so that our organization could achieve its goals, whether it was land, water, credit, roads, bridges or electricity in our communities. In fact, that was what he was about. He was never concerned with his own benefit, nor did he want a job in the government. No, he wanted us to be independent. He was not playing some game. The goal was to raise our awareness so that we would have a clear vision of what we were up against.

I admired the fact that Arturo was very honest and very committed to political work. I saw how he gave his time to the struggle. He also had a lot of patience and knew how to treat the *compañeros*. He was not aggressive. On the contrary, he was polite and we came to understand the struggle better and respect each other.

He helped the women in their efforts to organize. Before we only worked in the home and felt that we did not have the strength to participate, but he came and told us that "no, look, your participation is valuable also, organize yourselves in the struggle too." Thanks to Arturo we began to wake up.

The potential rebirth of the Casa del Pueblo was thwarted by a new division in 1979. One of the main leaders who had been released in February 1978, Bartolo Gómez Espinoza, formed a group in opposition to the Casa del Pueblo. During his time in jail it appears that he was bought off by the government. On his release he began to argue against the continued struggle for land. Instead, he proposed that the community accept the government's offer of credit, machinery, and subsidized inputs. With the backing of a hundred comuneros, he began a struggle for the leadership of the Casa del Pueblo.

At weekly assemblies Gómez Espinoza accused others of being "communists and terrorists" and, according to one comunero, sent a list of the most active members of the Casa del Pueblo to a local rancher. Unable to win control of the Casa del Pueblo, his group left and formed a parallel organization that affiliated to the National Peasant Confederation (CNC), the peasant wing of the PRI. In fact, Gómez Espinoza's group benefited from the simultaneous strengthening of the CNC in Chiapas and Carranza.

In 1979 Gómez Espinoza was named regional secretary of the CNC and immediately began to take control of the distribution of new agricultural inputs in the area. This event coincided with the implementation of a federal plan to boost output of basic grains, the Mexican Food System (SAM). The new subsidies provided under SAM helped to renew alliances between the state and peasant communities in the aftermath of widespread land conflicts throughout the 1970s. Gómez Espinoza also made an alliance with a group of comuneros who lived in El Paraíso, a settlement of small ranchers who had split from the Casa del Pueblo with the backing of Carmen Orantes in the early 1970s.

In 1979 the new governor of Chiapas, Juan Sabines Gutiérrez, added state subsidies through the Pact for Agrarian Support (CO-DECOA). Gómez Espinoza traveled throughout the state promoting CODECOA and SAM, gaining support in communities that had been complaining of the lack of credit for many years. This new money further isolated the Casa del Pueblo at the local level. Whereas in the rest of Mexico the CNC was in decline, in Chiapas it had never been so important, and its newfound strength was intimately tied to the government's strategy of displacing land struggles with programs to raise productivity. For example, in other regions the SAM subsidies were mostly handled and distributed by the Ministry of Agriculture and Water Resources (SARH). Yet in Chiapas this responsibility was given to the CNC. In Carranza, this economic function had the clearly political goal of isolating and deactivating the Casa del Pueblo (Moncada 1983:73).

Albores gave a new name to Gómez Espinoza and the CNC group: the *coras*. This was the name of indigenous people in Nayarit state who collaborated with the Spanish conquerors. The coras presented new problems for the Casa del Pueblo. The Ministry of Agrarian Reform (SRA) did not recognize the comisariado following the coras' decision to form their own parallel organization in 1979. The division also impeded the restitution of communal lands and full payment of compensation for the areas flooded by the Angostura dam. The SRA argued that the deslinde document of 1975 could only be approved if the two groups in Carranza united behind the leadership of the CNC group. In addition, there were several violent attacks by coras against members of the Casa del Pueblo. In February 1979 a group of coras attempted to take over the offices of the Casa del Pueblo but were immediately surrounded by a larger group of comuneros and were forced out. The division also provided ranchers with a new line of defense in their attempts to hold on to over 3,000 hectares of communal lands. In the words of one of the leaders of the Casa del Pueblo, "it was better when the struggle was directly with the rich. Now the rich stay out of it and put the coras in the front line" (Interview, Venustiano Carranza, Chiapas, June 13, 1987). By the end of 1979 the coras numbered about 300 of the 1,000 comuneros.

The nature of this division was clearly political because it sought to deny the Casa del Pueblo the right to defend communal lands through its own authorities. The struggle to overcome this limitation required mobilizations and alliances with other popular movements. The Albores provided the contact with other regional organizations of land claimants. In August and October 1979 a delegation from the Casa del Pueblo attended the founding meetings of the National Coordinating Committee "Plan de Ayala" (CNPA), an umbrella grouping of more than twenty peasant organizations that declared itself independent of the government and political parties. The group from Carranza came away from those meetings with the goal of constructing an independent land reform movement in Chiapas. In early 1980 it met with groups of land petitioners from Simojovel, Chicomuselo, and La Independencia and in July it formed the Provisional Coordinator of Chiapas, which was later renamed the Emiliano Zapata Peasant Organization (OCEZ) in July 1982. Paradoxically (although not unusual for Chiapas), the network of activists who would provide the leadership for the OCEZ was formed in the state prison, Cerro Hueco.

In September 1979 the Casa del Pueblo held a protest march and occupied the municipal palace for five days to demand recognition of its elected leaders and to denounce violent attacks by coras against its members (CNPA 1981:6). The governor's position left little room for doubt. In May 1980 the state and municipal governments called for an assembly in Carranza with the objective of forcing the election of the cora Gómez Espinoza as comisariado. The only officials required to attend such assemblies were usually the delegates of the SRA. This meeting, however, was attended by the state governor, the state delegate of the SRA, the commander of the Thirty-first Military Regiment, local PRI deputies, judicial police, members of the coras group, and people from outside Carranza. In response, the Casa del Pueblo filed an injunction against the legality of the election and succeeded in frustrating the efforts of the coras to impose their candidate. At the same time, it issued an ultimatum to the coras that they had two months to comply with communal work obligations as comuneros, invoking Article 87 of the Federal Agrarian Reform Law of 1971. Because the lands occupied by the coras belonged to the community, this legal argument was used to pressure them to rejoin the Casa del Pueblo.

Violent clashes between the two groups became more frequent. In April 1980 three comuneros were shot at by coras, one of whom died of the injuries sustained. Two months later another member of the Casa del Pueblo was allegedly killed by coras (Renard 1985: 174–78). Governor Sabines responded by ordering a curfew in Carranza in July. The comisariado, Manuel Vásquez Vásquez, was then held by coras for ten hours and forced to sign an agreement handing over authority of the Casa del Pueblo and the communal lands. Once again, an injunction was filed and the document overturned. Nevertheless, the constant threat of repression hung over the Casa del Pueblo in the period preceding the new elections for comisariado, which were scheduled for May 1981.

The Albores played a vital role during this period. They organized the march and occupation of the municipal palace and provided the contacts to lawyers who were able to file injunctions against the coras. They were clearly identified as enemies by the local caciques and their allies in the CNC and the state government. Then, in March 1981, a cora was killed in another attack on members of the Casa del Pueblo. This provided the pretext for the arrest on April 6 of Albores and two comuneros, Victórico Martínez Hernández and Ciro Coello Ruiz. Against their constitutional rights they were held incommunicado for two days during which time they were beaten and tortured (Amnesty International 1986: 74–76). In the same month, one of the defense witnesses was also detained and sent to the women's penitentiary in Tuxtla. Although their detention negatively affected the struggle in Carranza, it provided the beginnings of a broader network of peasant activists in Chiapas. This is how Albores and Martínez Hernández recounted their arrest:

We were detained on April 6 at five o'clock in the morning when three of us were traveling from Carranza in a private truck. As we were leaving the town we saw a white minibus at the turnoff and we thought it was a passenger bus. A few seconds later it drove up beside us. They were shouting at us "Stop, son of a bitch!" and they forced us off the road. We thought they were going to rob us and we ran but they fired at us and caught Victórico and beat him around the face with a gun. It turned out they were judicial police [judiciales]. They stopped us without explaining the charges. They forced open the door of the vehicle in which we were traveling. They beat us and threw us into the minibus where we were handcuffed and taken to Tuxtla Gutiérrez. On the way we found out that they had been waiting for us for three days. There was no arrest order, no explanation, just beatings.

We were kept handcuffed, face down on the floor of the minibus while they kept kicking us and standing on our backs. What were we accused of? They did not even tell us when we got to the police station. Bartolo Gómez Espinoza, the cora, was in the minibus. He had a gun and was wearing a helmet. He got out before we reached the police station and we didn't see him again. In the minibus, the police officers were relieved when they found out our names. "Thank God!" they said. "At last we've got them." "You're the sons of bitches who don't respect our governor." "You're the ones who want to change the government." "You're the agitators." Punches and insults, no explanation, but lots of threats.

When we arrived at the police station, they pushed us and dragged us by the hair to the office. There they took our names and took away everything we had on us. We then found out the name of the officer who had ordered our kidnapping. They kept some of our things, including Arturo's diary. In taking us from the office to the cells, just ten meters away, we were again beaten and kicked by the police. Their blows broke one of Arturo's eardrums.

We were kept for an hour in the cells and then told to sit facing the wall with our hands between our legs. If we moved, they would hit us. Then we heard the police commander order, "Don't hit these people!"

Then they took us upstairs to some other offices, handcuffed again. They took our photos, measurements, personal information, fingerprints. But still no explanation. Then, sitting again facing the wall with our hands between our legs. We were like that for another two hours. Two judiciales came up behind us, beat us on the back and insulted us. "These are the agitators." "They should have killed them straight away." "Hey, where are you from?" "Are you from El Salvador?" "This one is the foreigner." Arturo was asked his place of birth and the name of his wife.

At ten-thirty in the morning they took us to Cerro Hueco prison. On the way they kept asking if we were from El Salvador. When we arrived at the prison, we found out what we were being accused of: kidnapping and, in the case of Victórico, homicide. They didn't let us ask any questions or try to defend ourselves. The next day they called us again to the prison's main office. Once more the photos, fingerprints, lots of photos this time, left side, right side, full body and a number plate. When we told them that they had taken all this information the day before, they said that it had been lost and that they were just following orders.

On the Friday, April 10, without any notification, they took us before a judge to present our preparatory declaration. There we found out that we were both accused of kidnapping, injuries and homicide. A few days later they tried to make us sign our formal criminal indictment [*auto formal de prisión*] based on a list of false and contradictory accusations which had been drawn up by a group of coras.

Forty days passed and we were again called to the office to have our photos and fingerprints taken. We want to know how is it possible that so many lies can be fabricated in order to detain us? How is it possible that, on the basis of such accusations, without any grounding and without prior investigation, so many police officers were mobilized to arrest us? Why is there so much support for the Cora? What goal do the government and all its repressive apparatus have against the community, its leaders and those who work with it? Why has this witch-hunt been stepped up one month before the election of the new comisariado in the community?

These questions can only be answered politically, not through legal arguments. The state government in Chiapas is only interested in crushing discontent and in controlling the community of Venustiano Carranza. We demand that the state recognize its responsibility for all the aggressions which the community has suffered for so long." (CNPA and FNCR 1981)

On May 17 the elections for comisariado went ahead. The candidate of the Casa del Pueblo defeated his rival from the coras. However, the authorities refused to recognize the election because the delegate of the SRA was not present. This lack of recognition remained until 1987. Repression continued throughout 1981 with over forty arrest orders issued against comuneros whom the coras had denounced as "communists and terrorists."

Negotiations were granted with the Casa del Pueblo in October 1981. Governor Sabines attempted to condition the release of the detained to acceptance of the permanent division of communal lands, CNC leadership, and expulsion of Albores and Martínez Hernández from Chiapas. These provisions were clearly unacceptable, and the struggle for the leaders' unconditional release continued. A further wave of arrests in February 1982 led to another march and demonstration to Tuxtla, which was halted by the army. Another prominent member of the Casa del Pueblo, Agustín de la Torre, was arrested and also detained in Cerro Hueco. Although the Casa del

Pueblo had successfully resisted the imposition of the cora as leader, it was permanently under attack. This meant that the agrarian and economic demands were forced down the agenda and replaced by the more immediate concerns of gaining official recognition for the comisariado, obtaining the release of political prisoners, and calling for an end to repression.

The repression did have the result of bringing the Casa del Pueblo into contact with other popular movements. After her husband's arrest, Marisela González, fearing for her own safety and expecting their first child, left for Mexico City, where she organized a support group to campaign for the release of Albores and all political prisoners. The problems in Carranza thus began to gain a wider audience among CNPA and the National Front against Repression (FNCR), a network of human rights advocates and popular movements. Links were also made with the democratic currents in the teachers' union, which had come together as the National Coordinator of Education Workers (CNTE) in 1979. The CNPA and CNTE jointly organized a march on May 12, 1981, in downtown Mexico City. A delegation from the Casa del Pueblo participated in this act and a sit-in protest outside the National Palace. It was able to denounce repression in the national press and win commitments of support from other peasant organizations and the teachers' movement (*Uno Más Uno,* May 15, 1981, p. 7).

In Cerro Hueco, Albores and Martínez Hernández came to know other peasant leaders from different parts of Chiapas. Together they discussed the problems in each community and began to coordinate actions from their prison cells. One such leader from the community of Lindavista in the northern, oil-producing region of Chiapas recalled that "it was when we were imprisoned in Cerro Hueco that we first met the compañeros from Carranza, Las Rosas and other places. It was there that we all came to see that the problems were the same in each region" (Interview, Linda Vista, September 13, 1987).

In the space of just three months Albores organized the first hunger strike in Cerro Hueco's history. Through the work of his wife, the protest gained recognition beyond Chiapas. There was simultaneous participation by peasants in prisons in Michoacán, San Luis Potosí, and Veracruz. The hunger strike lasted twelve

days, from July 20 to August 1, 1981. It won the release of eleven
prisoners in Chiapas, but not that of Martínez Hernández and
Albores.

The hunger strike was organized with a great deal of care. Albores
wrote to his wife about the preparations:

We have been talking about how to organize the hunger strike and we
have agreed that we are going to be six *compas* [companions — short for
compañeros] here, and the two compas in the women's prison and in
Carranza. We need to make sure that we can keep communications
going between us, because it could get difficult especially if they get
repressive. We are trying to work out the details.

We think we should send a communiqué signed first by four of us
here in Cerro Hueco, and then by all eight from Chiapas.

We will inform all the other cells here a day before the action to see if
they support us or at least do not go against us.

In the event that the prison officers try to separate us we will resist as
far as we can and see what support and protection we get from the
other prisoners.

We think they may stop visitors coming in, so we have to work out
how we are going to communicate with the outside. In the event that
they try and break up the hunger strike we will have someone who will
be responsible for getting the word out to you.

We are also organizing for our own safety with the support of
some compas who will watch out for provocateurs sent by the prison
authorities.

We have to be prepared so we each know what to say if we are
separated and interrogated. We have to keep working. Right now we
are really enthusiastic about it. (Letter to Marisela, June 27, 1981)

Six other peasants joined the hunger strike in Chiapas to make a
total of fourteen. The action began according to plan on July 20.
Within a few hours the guards began to beat the *huelguistas* (strikers) and ordered that they be confined to a special cell. Albores had
previously made friends with one of the guards of this cell, who in
turn told the other guards to protect the prisoners. Martínez Hernández recalled how, when police agents tried to get into the cell
to beat the prisoners, the guards stood in their way and fought
them back with sticks, bottles, and broken lightbulbs (Interview,

April 16, 1992). Outside, Cerro Hueco supporters gathered to demand the release of the prisoners. Demonstrations were held at the governor's office in Tuxtla. Ten days into the hunger strike, the governor offered to release eleven of the fourteen prisoners in Chiapas. This was accepted with the belief that the other three cases could be resolved with further actions.

The weeks and months went by. Marisela gave birth to a son, Arturito, on October 18. Albores received the news in prison. He clearly understood the political nature of his continued detention:

It seems like the damned governor wants to keep us as hostages to force the community to sell out. Shamelessly he has proposed "your freedom in exchange for the division of the communal lands." How can we negotiate with someone who is so intransigent? It is the height of shamelessness! He says, "I want to talk with Arturo," but what do I have to say to him? I will never lend myself to such deceit!

I hope that the denunciations and pressure will work and that soon I can be with you, supporting you in looking after our son. In the meantime we must be patient and not despair so that we can still be useful. Despair would mean defeat for us and we must keep moving ahead. We know that victory will be ours and we must act with resolve and not lose our concentration. Let's hope we soon get signs of our release! (Letter to Marisela, November 1, 1981)

Their cases were held up another four months. In March 1982 new witnesses were called and testified against the declarations of the cora, demonstrating a number of contradictions in his accusations. However, the arraignment hearings *(careos)* were not held until June 2; it was then that Albores and Martínez Hernández finally had the chance to defend themselves in the presence of their accusers and prosecutors. Albores wrote to Marisela about the hearings:

Victórico and I presented the reasons for which we think we are accused, declaring ourselves to be political prisoners and explaining the land disputes in Carranza. The coras repeated their accusations against us. If their declarations were already full of contradictions, then now they really messed up. They even got some very obvious things wrong. Nonetheless, as we know, they are going to try to sentence us and we will have to present an appeal which could take up another few months if we just depend on the legal process. But the political pressure could speed things up. We think that the different actions which are being organized are very important. Hopefully they will bring results. I felt very good about the hearings because we clearly had better arguments than the coras and this can provide legal protection for you and the other compas who are being persecuted. (Letter to Marisela, June 3, 1982)

The political pressure for their release increased during the second half of 1982. In July the Casa del Pueblo hosted the national meeting of CNPA, which helped publicize the struggle and consolidate support in Chiapas. The Coordinadora Provisional was renamed Organización Campesina Emiliano Zapata (OCEZ), one of the most important members of CNPA. Its first task was to mobilize for the release of the prisoners. Several demonstrations were held, culminating in a second hunger strike in November 1982. This time the wives of the detained led the protest at the University campus in Tuxtla Gutiérrez. They succeeded in winning a meeting with representatives of the state government and promises that Albores and Martínez Hernández would be released, together with Agustín de la Torre, who had been detained in February 1982. Albores felt his release was near:

Today is the first day of the hunger strike. I am very concerned about what is going to happen. It is likely that one of us will be released, but I am worried that someone will remain and we will not win all that we are demanding. The authorities have not given us a firm response. However, we have heard from others that I will go free but Victórico will be denied his release because he is accused of homicide although he still has not been sentenced. I think that this is the right moment to apply pressure because Sabines is trying to clean up his image before he leaves office in December and the president [López Portillo] will be attending his *informe* [address to the local congress] next weekend. (Letter to Marisela, November 22, 1982)

The government had also promised to suspend all the arrest warrants, review the cases of other peasants imprisoned because of land disputes, and set up a meeting with the agrarian reform authorities. Political pressure appeared to be paying off. Alongside the protests in Chiapas, demonstrations were organized by CNPA and FNCR in Mexico City. Amnesty International had also adopted Albores and Martínez Hernández as political prisoners, and letter campaigns were organized in England where one of Albores's sisters was doing graduate studies. Several days later Albores wrote:

Well, now it is Friday the 26th and we are all unsure whether the government is going to fulfill its promises. What should we do? We have publicized things well in the last few days. The demonstration and hunger strike were very important in prizing commitments from the government. I think that the protests in Mexico City yesterday had a big impact. The INI representative in San Cristóbal came to see me with a message from the governor that I am to be released on the 30th on the condition that I stay away from anyone until the new governor [Absalón Castellanos Domínguez] takes over, because he does not want the coras and *paraiseños* [those from the ejido El Paráiso] to go crazy between November 30 and December 8. Apparently Absalón is not in agreement, but Sabines is going to risk it anyway. But now they are talking only about my release. We told the INI representative to remind the governor that there was a commitment to release three prisoners and to suspend the arrest warrants. What happened? We want him to find out and let us know tomorrow. We accepted not to appear in public before December 8.

We must not despair and this precisely is what the struggle is about. Sometimes we have to make concessions while trying to win as much as is possible and, if they do not follow through on their promises, we must work even harder to force them to act. Be patient, you will see that everything will work out well. I have my things packed, so does Victórico and we are planning our next steps already. I'll see you on the 5th or 6th of December, if not before and if they fulfill their promises. Take care. We'll soon be together." (Letter to Marisela, November 26, 1982)

Albores won his release on December 6, 1982, two days before Sabines left office. Martínez Hernández would have to wait until May 1987, and de la Torre until October of that year. The Casa del Pueblo had resisted attempts to divide communal lands and maintained its political struggle for autonomy and representation. However, another division awaited it.

Chapter 5

NATIONAL MOVEMENTS,

LOCAL FACTIONALISM

The emergence of new movements in Chiapas in the 1970s was not an isolated phenomenon. Throughout Mexico new organizations of landless peasants, agricultural workers, and ejidatarios began to displace the CNC as the sole representative of rural demands. The new movements shared a long history of rural protest in Mexico and again revealed the central role of peasant struggles in the formation and exercise of state power. In particular, they showed the incomplete nature of the state and the continuing appeal of the agrarian promises of the Mexican Revolution. At the same time, the new movements sought a type of national convergence that differed from earlier experiences. New networks of regional organizations decided to promote a less centralized structure than had been the case with previous confederations, while they adopted a more critical stance toward alliances with political parties. These decisions facilitated convergence between many new organizations, but the associations were not without ambiguity and conflict. Leadership struggles over tactics, alliances, and strategy threatened to frustrate the search for unity. In Chiapas, divisions within the OCEZ reflected these dilemmas in a dramatic way.

At the same time, in the aftermath of Echeverría's confrontations with the agrarian bourgeoisie in 1976, the new government of José López Portillo attempted to shift the emphasis of rural policy away from land redistribution and firmly toward modernization of production and marketing (Moguel and Robles 1990). As federal agencies expanded their presence in the remotest areas of the countryside, possibilities emerged for a new type of peasant movement that could use a productivist discourse to assert greater autonomy from the PRI. This trend was most clearly manifested in the second half of the López Portillo administration, 1979 to 1982. These years proved to be significant for the reconfiguration of state-peasant relations in Mexico and for the evolution of regional movements such as those in Chiapas.

Peasant Movements and the Incompleteness of State Formation

The role of peasant movements in Mexican history has generated much interest and discussion. Within the Latin American context, rural rebellions in Mexico have displayed at least two distinctive features. First, they have made significant contributions to national political upheavals (the wars of independence, the defeat of the French intervention, and the Mexican Revolution). Second, peasants did achieve greater short-term gains than is often assumed (Katz 1988). Their participation in these national struggles enabled peasants to resist depeasantization for another generation. However, over the long term, the greatest impact was on state formation rather than on rural livelihoods (Coatsworth 1988).

Historians are divided over the significance of peasant movements in the Mexican Revolution. Early studies by North American scholars such as Frank Tannenbaum (1929) upheld the idea that the revolution was predominantly agrarian based. Later writers, particularly John Womack (1969), tended to support this interpretation. However, in the 1970s, revisionists began to question the real extent of peasant participation, noting that in many regions peasants were acquiescent, necessitating a "revolution from without." For example, David Brading (1980) argued that rural movements were created and led by regional caudillos for political gain. He added that land concentration was probably not as great as was presumed and that the large estates, criticized as backward feudal legacies of colonialism by revolutionary intellectuals such as Andrés Molina Enríquez, were often in fact productive commercial enterprises. For Brading the real impact of the peasant movement was to strengthen Carranza and the Constitutionalists in their struggle against Victoriano Huerta and the Porfirian oligarchy. That Carranza succeeded did not guarantee significant gains for the peasantry, but simply their incorporation into populist rhetoric of the postrevolutionary state.

A critique of this revisionist position has been developed in various works by Alan Knight (1980, 1985, 1986). For him, the Mexican Revolution was different from other crises of the oligarchy in Latin America because of its mass base. The popular movement had to be taken into account in the design of the new Constitution. The landed oligarchy had lost political power, at least nationally, and a new form of state could only be constructed out of the regional bases of the revolutionary armies. Knight argued that peasants were not simply used by local caudillos or by the political machinations of Carranza. They fought instead for specific goals of land and local autonomy from a centralized state. Their relations with nonpeasant leaders therefore differed according to regional conditions, rather than following the single pattern of caudillismo suggested by Brading. The outcome of the revolution was therefore more of a contingent articulation of popular demands within a nationalist and statist discourse than the bourgeois revolution "from above" favored by the revisionists.

Knight's approach appears to be the more realistic in that he recognized the historically contingent nature of the postrevolutionary state. He gave due emphasis to the political relations between caudillos and peasants, rather than affirming the inevitable subordination of the masses to the new Leviathan. It is not that centralization of the state did not occur, but this centralization should be understood in terms of the multiple conflicts generated by the negotiation of rule, rather than the unfolding of a predetermined history. These conflicts are rarely resolved in any definitive manner and, as the reemergence of *zapatismo* in Chiapas tells us, the structures of the state are only as permanent as the security of their political underpinnings. In the words of Jeffrey Rubin, the Mexican state, for all its appearance of omnipotence over a malleable civil society, has been something of a "Swiss Cheese," shot full of holes and weak spots (Knight 1990:95; Rubin 1990). The incompleteness of the state is a useful starting point for considering the persistence of peasant movements since the 1920s before we consider the novelty of movements that emerged in the 1970s.

One factor that presents itself as central to the mobilizing capacity of peasant movements is their degree of autonomy from the state. The revolutionary army led by Emiliano Zapata in 1910 to 1919 grew out of the indigenous villages of Morelos. The villages provided the political and physical space with which to organize and plan the recuperation of communal land from encroaching sugar planters. Moreover, they were centers of self-government, where decision making was organized independently of the state and the ruling classes. The struggle of the zapatistas was therefore not simply for land but also for municipal autonomy (Gilly 1980; Warman 1988). Their military and political defeat, combined with the assassination of Zapata in 1919 by supporters of President Venustiano Carranza, undermined the autonomy of peasant communities. Agrarian reform became institutionalized by the postrevolutionary governments and the zapatistas had to petition for recognition of lands they had recuperated during the armed struggle.

Land reform proceeded slowly as national politicians feared alienating the more productive landowners. During the 1920s, redistribution was dependent on the linkages between the federal government and regional strongmen, or caudillos. The administration of President Plutarco Elías Calles (1924–28) and those of his loyal successors tried to subdue reformist state governors whom they considered a threat to the centralization of power. Repression became commonplace, forcing many peasant leagues into a defensive position.

Consequently, when Lázaro Cárdenas ran for the presidency in 1934, he received massive support in rural areas. As governor of Michoacán he had implemented a broad program of land redistribution. In his struggle to free himself of the influences of Calles, Cárdenas found important allies in the labor and peasant movements. The reorganization of peasant leagues affiliated to the official party was completed with the foundation of the CNC in 1938. The repression of the Calles years, combined with Cárdenas reforms, led most of the organized peasantry into forming an alliance with a government committed to expanding support for the social sector (Hamilton 1982:141–83).

However, the subordination of the CNC to the ruling party and the state was made clear after 1940, when official policy shifted in favor of private agribusiness interests. The shift had begun toward the end of Cárdenas's presidency due to fears of lost investment and landowner support for fascism in Mexico. The policy was unam-

biguously adopted by the administrations of Manuel Avila Camacho (1940–46) and Miguel Alemán (1946–52). Reforms to the
Agrarian Code in 1942 and 1946 made protection from expropriation easier to obtain, while public investment in irrigation works
and rural infrastructure and preferential credit were targeted toward large-scale agro-export enterprises in the Northwest. The political weakness of the CNC was revealed by its failure to mobilize effectively against the counterreform measures (Huizer 1982;
Hardy 1984). At the same time, attempts to organize along independent lines were frustrated by the governments of Miguel Alemán, Adolfo Ruiz Cortines (1952–58), and Adolfo López Mateos
(1958–64).

From the mid-1940s on, regional independent movements
emerged as grassroots leaders became frustrated with the slow pace
of agrarian reform. The most significant of these occurred in the
state of Morelos. Between 1945 and 1962 Rubén Jaramillo led a
mass movement in protest against the corruption of local sugar mill
owners and in favor of land reform and democratization of municipal and state government. The movement not only fought over
agrarian issues, but also on the electoral front as the Agrarian and
Workers' Party of Morelos (PAOM). The two fronts of struggle, as
had been the case for Zapata, remained inextricably linked due to
the economic power wielded by those in political office. It was
precisely the political threat of the PAOM that provoked the in-
transigence of the authorities. Perhaps a less "political" and more
"agrarian" movement would have been accommodated more readily, but in Mexico the "agrarian" is always "political." The problem
for peasant movements has traditionally been how best to operate
politically: in the narrow sense of electoral struggle, in the broader
sense of mass mobilization, or, as in the case of the PAOM, through
a combination of both. As it was, the *jaramillistas* were forced into
clandestinity by government repression, and they set up armed self-
defense units to protect peasant lands against local caciques. Although Jaramillo won the solidarity of other popular movements in
nearby Mexico City, that support was not enough to resist the
attacks coordinated by local elites. Following a brief period of legal-
ized political activity, in May 1962 Jaramillo and his family were
kidnapped and executed by troops and judicial police. No culprit

was ever found (A. Bartra 1985:90; Carton de Grammont 1988a; Manjarrez 1967; Ravelo 1978).

The reversal of Cárdenas's reforms provoked widespread discontent and, in 1949, dissident labor unions and peasant movements formed the General Union of Mexican Workers and Peasants (UGOCM), which was affiliated to the new People's Party (PP). In the northwestern states of Sonora and Sinaloa, the UGOCM and PP were met with similar responses to those seen in Morelos. When the UGOCM led land invasions in 1958, its principal leader, Jacinto López, was imprisoned along with other important members. Moreover, when the disputed lands were redistributed, it was the CNC and not the UGOCM that benefited most, despite the fact that the latter had been at the forefront of the struggle (A. Bartra 1985:81–83; Carton de Grammont 1988b). Whereas in Morelos, the party-movement link provoked repression, in the case of the PP and UGOCM the response was more complex. The PAOM was a regionally defined party, and its candidates did not aspire to seats in national government. The PP, on the other hand, was a national opposition party led by the former *cardenista* Vicente Lombardo Toledano. The PRI offered some concessions to the PP leadership in exchange for its "loyal opposition" in the Chamber of Deputies. This agreement coincided with Lombardo's preferred strategy of avoiding confrontations with the government and with his goal of gradually winning seats in the Congress. This strategy was seen by Jacinto López as doomed to failure, given the size of the PRI majority. In fact, Lombardo was criticized for putting his personal well-being before that of the party and the UGOCM. A split was avoided until 1967, but relations were inevitably strained. As the leadership of the PP became more and more divorced from the base, the UGOCM in Sonora and Sinaloa suffered setbacks in their struggle for land reform. As a result, it was unable to resist the offensive of the Right in the early 1960s and finally split into independent and progovernment factions in 1973.

Another major challenge to the government's agrarian policies came in 1963 with the formation of the Independent Peasant Confederation (CCI). This was the largest opposition confederation, and it brought together some of the most distinguished regional peasant leaders, including Ramón Danzós Palomino from the Yaqui valley of Sonora, Arturo Orona from the collective ejidos of La Laguna (Coahuila and Durango), and Alfonso Garzón from Baja California. More important, the CCI was not an isolated peasant movement, but formed a central part of the National Liberation Movement (MLN), a broad coalition led by Lázaro Cárdenas that united the major cardenista and communist groups that had been displaced from power in the previous two decades. Like the UGOCM, the CCI demanded the revival of land reform, an end to repression, democratization, and respect for the right to organize independently of the PRI and its affiliated unions.

In 1964 the government again used repression in an attempt to demoralize the CCI, imprisoning its most radical leaders, including Danzós Palomino. In the context of the Cuban Revolution and anticommunist propaganda from the Right, the MLN and CCI were soon forced onto the defensive, and their offices were ransacked by police. A split emerged in the CCI as the more moderate factions led by Humberto Serrano and Alfonso Garzón restated their support for the government and tried to expel the communist-affiliated faction (Moguel 1988:141–221). Serrano and Garzón gave their support to the administration of President Gustavo Díaz Ordaz (1964–70) while the communists remained independent but seriously weakened. Following the release of Danzós Palomino, the latter group renamed itself in 1975 as the Independent Confederation of Agricultural Workers and Peasants (CIOAC).[1]

The student movement of 1968 and the rise of liberation theology clearly influenced the transformation of peasant movements in Mexico. An influential current within the student movement argued that the Left's strategy of seeking socialism through parliamentary means was mistaken. The renamed Popular Socialist Party (PPS) and the PCM were criticized for their lack of organic links with workers and peasants and for their centralized internal structures. Instead these members of the student movement proposed turning the model upside down by building democratic mass organizations from the bottom up. In the early 1970s thousands of students went to live in rural communities and poor urban neighborhoods to put into practice Mao's theory of the "mass line." Socialism was conceived as something constructed through long-term politicization of economic demands, not as the seizure of state power. The failure of guerrilla movements in Mexico served to confirm this position. State power was to be gradually dismantled by an increasingly politicized mass movement, not overthrown in an instant. This strategy also allowed for concrete demands to be met in the process.

In the countryside, the student activists joined forces with new community leaders. In Chiapas, these included the catechists who had been trained by the Catholic diocese of San Cristóbal de Las Casas. In areas where the CNC had been dominant, this new generation criticized the corruption of the confederation's leaders and the lack of participation of the base in decision making. In areas where opposition parties had been active, peasants adopted a more critical stance. In general, two issues became central to the evolution of new peasant organizations. On the one hand, there was an increasing concern with gaining autonomy from political parties and, on the other, there were efforts to redefine the relationship between leaders and base. In most cases the demands of peasants remained the same, although issues of production, credit, and marketing became more nationally prominent after 1976.

The repression suffered by those peasant organizations most closely identified with PAOM, MLN, the People's Party, and PPS was one reason why the post-1968 movements adopted an independent position toward all political parties. More important, however, in most parts of Mexico in the early 1970s there were no opposition parties seeking to mobilize the rural masses. The PAOM and MLN had disappeared, and the PPS supported the government. The PCM, as the students argued, had little presence in the countryside. Nevertheless, the proposed strategy of the new leaders was not to build another party-movement alliance. Electoral struggle was considered a deviation from the main task of politicizing and resolving basic demands. This strategy was also facilitated by the revival of agrarian populism under President Luis Echeverría (1970–76). New resources were made available for rural development projects, reformist functionaries proved to be important allies for nascent regional producer organizations, and the expansion of the federal bureaucracy often provided a counterbalance to the power wielded by local caciques. Autonomy from parties coincided with the position promoted by the popular church, especially in areas of high indigenous population in southern states such as Chiapas.

A related criticism of past experience was that leaders tended to become divorced from the base and that they inhibited broad participation. This had not happened with Jaramillo and the PAOM, suggesting that a more regionally focused organization had a greater chance of reproducing itself over time if different political conditions prevailed. However, a gap between leaders and base was the case for most of the groups affiliated with the CNC and the official wing of the CCI. At the ejido level this critique was not made solely out of a concern for democratic accountability. Rather, in some regions, it was linked to the failure of leaders to resolve basic problems over land, water, and services. This was the context for various attempts to build politically autonomous and decentralized networks of regional peasant organizations. The two largest networks were the National Union of Regional Autonomous Peasant Organizations (UNORCA) and the National Coordinating Committee "Plan de Ayala" (CNPA).

Peasant Appropriation of the Productive Process

Whereas CNPA maintained a radical stance in favor of land reform, many other regional organizations opted for less confrontational tactics and instead sought government support for their proposals. This pragmatic strategy was clearly illustrated by the struggle to gain control of decisions regarding production and marketing. This shift in focus was influenced by a relative opening on the part of government toward non-PRI producer organizations during the late 1970s and early 1980s. These years saw the convergence of regional groups in a new network that culminated in the formation in 1985 of UNORCA.

In the case of UNORCA, relations between peasant organizations and the state have been shaped by what its leaders have called *cambios de terreno,* or "strategic shifts." The first of these was the transition from the struggle for land to the peasant appropriation of the productive process. This change was heralded by the formation in

1977 of the Coalition of Collective Ejidos of the Yaquí and Mayo Valleys (CECVYM) in Sonora following Echeverría's controversial land redistribution decision (Gordillo 1988; Otero 1989).[2]

The López Portillo government sought to replace agrarian reform with policies designed to increase productivity (Rubio 1987). The previous administration had introduced a new organizational structure for incorporating peasants into rural development projects. This involved the unification of two or more ejidos as second-level organizations, known as uniones de ejidos (UE). A third level was added with the creation of Rural Collective Interest Associations (ARIC), which brought together two or more UE. The first autonomous producer organizations broke with the old corporatist mechanisms by gaining control of these new second- and third-level organizations (Robles and Moguel 1990). This step allowed for a new type of peasant movement to emerge, one that was able not only to protest against government policies but also to put forward alternative proposals.[3] The goal was to achieve greater autonomy for peasant organizations in decisions concerning production, credit, and marketing, thereby challenging the control exercised by government institutions, particularly the Rural Credit Bank (BANRURAL) and the National Agricultural and Livestock Insurance Agency (ANAGSA).

The CECVYM promoted the first meetings and mobilizations of the new producer organizations. It commemorated its successful land struggle of 1976 by calling national meetings in November 1980, 1981, and 1982. It became the model for other uniones de ejidos to copy and invited regional leaders to spend several months studying how it functioned. Between 1980 and 1985 the network grew rapidly, and its character changed to reflect the presence of poorer southern regions in the struggle to appropriate the productive process. One of the most significant developments was the increasing activism of community-level food supply committees (CCAs), which had been established as part of the SAM initiative in 1980 to 1982. As had happened with the UE and ARIC, the CCA became a vehicle for transforming state-peasant relations as peasants sought greater accountability and control over their operation (Fox 1992). Another development was the autonomous organization of small coffee producers in the states of Chiapas, Oaxaca,

Table 5.1. Evolution of UNORCA membership, 1983–85

Organizations by region	1983	1984	1985
North			
Alianza Campesina del Noroeste de Chihuahua	X	X	X
Coordinadora de los CCA de la Laguna, Durango and Coahuila			X
Ejidos Colectivos Batopilas, Coahuila	X	X	X
UE Jesús Campos Mendoza, Durango		X	X
Northwest			
ARIC-CECVYM, Sonora	X	X	X
ARIC-Jacinto López, Sonora		X	X
Unión de Ejidos Independientes de Sinaloa (UEIS)			X
Center-west			
Comité de Agricultores Purépechas, Michoacán	X	X	X
UAE Artículo 27 Consitucional, Guanajuato	X		X
UE Lázaro Cárdenas, Nayarit	X	X	X
Center			
Cooperativa Agropecuaria Tosepan Titaniske, Puebla	X	X	X
UE Emiliano Zapata, Morelos			X
Unión de Productores del Altiplano, Tlaxcala		X	X
URECHH, Hidalgo	X	X	X
Southeast			
Coordinadora de CCA de Oaxaca		X	X
Sociedad Cooperativa Apicultores, Selva lacandona, Chiapas		X	X
UCI Cien Años de Soledad, Oaxaca		X	X
UE Alfredo V. Bonfil, Guerrero	X	X	X
UE Pueblo Maya, Campeche		X	X
Unión de CCA del Centro de Veracruz		X	
Unión de CCA del Estado de Tabasco			X
Unión de CCA del Estado de Yucatán			X
Unión de Productores de Café de Veracruz	X	X	X
Unión de Uniones de Chiapas	X	X	X
Unión Regional Productores de Café de Huatusco, Oaxaca		X	X
Total number of participating member organizations	11	19	24

Source: Costa (1989:77–153).

Guerrero, and Veracruz. This shift in the geographical presence of economic organizations can be seen in table 5.1.[4]

One of the main obstacles the new organizations had to face was the control of commodity prices exercised by the parastatal companies. Coffee producers in the southern states were among the most affected and between 1979 and 1982 they mobilized on several occasions to demand higher prices from the Mexican Coffee Institute (INMECAFE). This struggle was very wearing, and in 1983 the coffee organizations decided on a strategic shift (cambio de terreno) in the direction of autonomous appropriation of the productive process. In Chiapas and other coffee-producing areas, the new organization began to press the government to support their own economic infrastructure, including credit unions, processing plants, and retail networks (Fernández Villegas, 1991:32). The struggle over prices was continually fought on the terrain of INMECAFE and local intermediaries. The challenge now was to appropriate the productive process and neutralize the power exercised through state and private agencies.

The experiences of regional organizations such as CECVYM and Unión de Uniones were important in defining the political strategy of UNORCA. In its first bulletin UNORCA defined itself as a network of autonomous peasant organizations. As a network, it remained independent of all political parties but respected the decision of each member organization to support the party of its choice. However, its orientation has been more concerned with resolving economic demands than with furthering a specific political agenda. It therefore differed from CNPA (discussed in the following section) in that it did not criticize party affiliation. As a result, many of its regional organizations were able to support the PRI candidate in the 1988 presidential elections. This was in fact the position of the UE Quiptic in Ocosingo, whose leaders were able to open up negotiations with Salinas in 1986, when he was head of the Ministry of Budgets and Planning (see chapter 6).

Another distinction from the CNPA regarded strategy. The UNORCA promoted a less confrontational style and believed that there were spaces within the state that could be used to its advantage in resolving demands. It rejected the strategy of constant mobilization and denunciation of CNPA and CIOAC and placed its

Map 5.1. National Presence of the CNPA and UNORCA in 1985

faith in its capacity to get its proposals heard at the highest levels of the federal government. This strategy depended on maintaining linkages to those reformers who could help overcome the opposition of local elites and other functionaries within the state apparatus. Shifts within the federal bureaucracy, particularly in the Ministry of Agriculture and Water Resources (SARH), could therefore have far-reaching consequences for UNORCA-affiliated groups. Moreover, its negotiation strategy had been forged in the context of an interventionist state, one that between 1970 and 1982 saturated the legal and institutional terrain with new federal agencies and programs. After 1985 this terrain was rapidly transformed by the adoption of promarket, neoliberal policies. Unlike CNPA, UNORCA appeared to be in a relatively stronger position from which it could negotiate the pace and impact of the reforms, even if it was unable to contest their general direction (A. Bartra 1991;

García de León 1989). (See map 5.1 for distribution of the two organizations at that time.)

The National Coordinating Committee "Plan de Ayala"
(CNPA) and the Struggle for Land

During the first half of the 1970s new peasant organizations emerged in several states in response to the failure of agrarian reform and increasing pressure on the land brought about by the expansion of commercial agriculture, cattle ranching, and new state-financed projects such as oil exploration and the construction of hydroelectricity dams. The high point of a revived but limited agrarian reform, Echeverría's redistribution of prime irrigated land to collective ejidos in Sonora in December 1976 proved to be the last of its kind as the new government of President José López Portillo (1976–82) immediately moved to regain the confidence of the private sector. Land invasions, which occurred in almost every state in 1975, were no longer to be tolerated and instead met with repression (A. Bartra 1980). Between 1976 and 1979 the new movements were pushed into a defensive position in which confrontation with the government became common. Each movement then began to see the need for unity at the regional and national levels.

In 1979 various events were organized to mark the one hundredth anniversary of the birth of Emiliano Zapata and to discuss agrarian issues. In March a national meeting was held at the Autonomous University of Guerrero that was attended by representatives from several of the movements engaged in land struggles in Oaxaca, Puebla, Veracruz, and Guerrero. This meeting provided the space for the first contacts to be made between organizations and for the exchange of testimonies, ideas, and proposals for unity. The following month a national meeting of independent organizations was held in Morelos at the invitation of the Emiliano Zapata Union of Ejidos (UEEZ). Two main objectives emerged from this meeting. The first was to continue the struggle for land despite the government's insistence that agrarian reform had ended. The second was to oppose the government's plans to transfer the remains of Zapata from Cuautla, Morelos, to the Monument to the Revolution in Mexico City, where they would lie next to those of his assassin, Venustiano Carranza. This struggle to retain popular control over the symbolic importance of Zapata was supported by students, teachers, and peasants who blockaded the central square of Cuautla to prevent the removal of the remains. The struggle also helped to unify the independent peasant movement. Representatives from over forty groups from sixteen states met again in June at the National Peasant Meeting organized by the Autonomous University of Chapingo, where they called for the formation of a united front (Flores Lúa, Paré, and Sarmiento 1988:75–80).

In August, one of these organizations, the National "Plan de Ayala" Movement (MNPA) invited participants from earlier meetings to attend its first national congress. About thirty organizations attended, including some controlled by the PRI. The government's attempt to control the meeting and establish a new corporatist pact was rejected by many of the participants.

In October the first national meeting of independent peasant organizations was held in Milpa Alta, an indigenous community located on the southern edge of the Federal District. The meeting was marked by a struggle between progovernment organizations (led by the son of Zapata, Mateo) and those that favored an independent position. The former argued that it was necessary to support the government's new policies in favor of small producers embodied in the Mexican Food System (SAM). The independents countered that SAM did not offer any solutions to the problem of landlessness and that to support it would involve an alliance with the state. The independent movements saw the state as their enemy due to the repression of the land struggle. This latter position prevailed, and on October 14 CNPA was formed with eleven member organizations (see table 5.2).

The CNPA was mainly composed of indigenous comuneros, poor peasants, land petitioners, and agricultural workers. This makeup explains why the most important issues for CNPA were the defense of the lands and natural resources of indigenous groups and the implementation of agrarian reform. It also fought for recognition of rural unions and the defense of indigenous cultures. These positions were reflected in the resolutions of the Milpa Alta meeting

(CNPA 1980). Although its original slogan of "Today we fight for land, tomorrow for power" suggests that CNPA was not solely limited to sectoral interests, its main concern was winning solutions to problems of landlessness. By engaging in such struggles its member organizations necessarily confronted local power relations, but they did not propose a global strategy for the political transformation of Mexico. In this respect, CNPA maintained autonomy from all political parties, while allowing individual members the freedom to support whomever they wished as long as this did not contradict the principles of CNPA. This position was adopted in order to avoid incorporation into any single party and to favor a more genuinely grassroots movement with peasant leadership and a more democratic internal structure.

The internal organization of CNPA therefore emphasized broad participation from the base and the rotation of leadership positions. Among some of its regional organizations such practices had already been implemented during the 1970s (Gledhill 1988; Zepeda Patterson 1986). A critique of the role of leaders and organizational structure had been developed by peasants in alliance with outside advisers. Solutions were seen as dependent not on single leaders but on higher levels of community participation (Narro 1990:267). The general assemblies of member communities therefore elected representatives to a plenary assembly of their regional organization, which in turn elected delegates to the national assembly of CNPA. The national assembly elected a permanent commission to reside in Mexico City for one year with the task of implementing the assembly's resolutions. This commission was made up of one representative from each member organization. The national assembly also elected four other commissions responsible for press and propaganda, peasant women, relations with other organizations, and legal support. The regional organizations similarly divided their work among commissions to deal with the specific issues that most affected them.

The second national meeting of CNPA was called by the Emiliano Zapata Union of Comuneros (UCEZ) and held in Santa Fe de la Laguna, Michoacán, in April 1980. This Purépecha community had been engaged in a violent struggle in defense of its lands against the encroachment of private cattle ranchers. The meeting denounced

Table 5.2. Evolution of CNPA membership, 1979–85

Organization	Acronym	Region	1979	1981	1983	1985
Unión Campesina Independiente	UCI	Puebla, Veracruz	X	X	X	X
Comuneros Organizados de Milpa Alta	COMA	Morelos	X	X	X	X
Unión de Comuneros Emiliano Zapata	UCEZ	Michoacán	X	X	X	
Unión de Ejidos Independientes de Sinaloa	UEIS	Sinaloa	X	X	X	X
Alianza Campesina Revolucionaria	ACR	Guanajuato, Chiapas, Jalisco, Tamaulipas	X	X	X	
Central Independiente de Obreros Agrícolas y Campesinos	CIOAC	National	X			
Movimiento Nacional Plan de Ayala	MNPA	National	X			
Consejo Nacional Cardenista	CONACAR	National	X			
Coordinadora Nacional de Pueblos Indígenas	CNPI	National	X			
Coalición de Ejidos Colectivos de los Valles Yaqui y Mayo	CECVYM	Sonora	X			
Organización y Desarrollo de la Comunidad	ODECO	National	X			
Coordinadora Campesina Revolucionaria Independiente	CCRI	Sonora, Veracruz, Guerrero, and Coahuila		X	X	X
Coalición Obrera Campesina Estudiantil del Istmo	COCEI	Oaxaca		X	X	X
Unión de Pueblos de Morelos	UPM	Morelos		X	X	X
UE Lázaro Cárdenas	UELC	Nayarit		X		
Comité Coordinador Huasteco	CCH	San Luis Potosí		X	X	

Table 5.2. *Continued*

Organization	Acronym	Region	1979	1981	1983	1985
Frente Popular de Zacatecas	FPZ	Zacatecas		X	X	X
Comité de Defensa Popular	CDP	Chihuahua		X	X	
Organización Campesina Independiente de la Huasteca Veracruzana	OCIHV	Veracruz		X	X	
Organización Independiente de Pueblos Unidos de las Huastecas	OIPUH	Hidalgo, Veracruz, and San Luis Potosí		X	X	
Bloque Campesino de Chiapas	BCCH	Chiapas		X		
Organización Campesina Emiliano Zapata	OCEZ	Chiapas			X	X
Organización de Pueblos del Altiplano	OPA	Tlaxcala, Guanajuato, Hidalgo, and Puebla			X	X
Movimiento de Unificación y Lucha Triqui	MULT	Oaxaca			X	X
Movimiento de Lucha Revolucionaria	MLR	Guerrero			X	
Organización Regional Campesina de Occidente	ORCO	Jalisco, Nayarit			X	X
Organización para la Liberación	OPL	Oaxaca			X	X
Frente Campesino Independiente de Oaxaca	FCI	Oaxaca			X	X
Unión de Trabajadores del Campo	UTC	Guerrero and Oaxaca				X
Total Number of Participating Organizations			11	15	20	14

Source: Neil Harvey (1990:49).

the government's use of repression against CNPA organizations and agreed to support the newly formed National Front against Repression (FNCR), a coalition of human rights groups from throughout Mexico. In the face of repression, more regional groups joined CNPA, while more moderate organizations withdrew in 1980 (table 5.2). In November 1980 CNPA held its third national meeting in Tlapacoyan, Veracruz, at the invitation of the Independent Union of Peasants (UCI). Once again CNPA rejected SAM and the new Law of Agricultural Development and agreed to organize a peasant march to Mexico City to protest against government policy and the use of repression. It also agreed to establish closer ties with other movements, such as the National Coordinator of Education Workers (CNTE).

This moment marked the rise of CNPA as an independent popular movement. In May 1981 peasants from sixteen states joined teachers in a march to the Zócalo of the capital city to demand the release of imprisoned peasant leaders and the resolution of more than 300 claims for land redistribution. In July and August CNPA and FNCR organized a hunger strike that led to the release of several leaders. Furthermore, the successful mobilization of May 1981 prompted several new organizations to join CNPA prior to its fourth national meeting, called by the Worker-Peasant-Student Coalition of the Isthmus (COCEI) and held in Juchitán, Oaxaca, in August of that year. At the same time, repression became more common, and by the end of 1981 CNPA had been forced into a defensive position. Differences over strategy began to emerge as some organizations insisted on maintaining a high level of national mobilization while others argued that it was necessary to concentrate more on solutions at the local and regional levels.

In the face of these difficulties CNPA still succeeded in organizing its second national march to Mexico City in June 1982, although with less support than in the previous year. The following month it held its fifth national meeting at the Casa del Pueblo in Venustiano Carranza, Chiapas. This meeting drew up a more concrete program that included a broader range of demands concerning the rights of peasant women and indigenous peoples. Greater attention was also given to issues of production, marketing, and credit. It also articulated a clear class position in favor of "social change to destroy

1. "Free land for all, land without overseers and bosses, this is the war cry of the Revolution." — Emiliano Zapata (Banner of OCEZ-CNPA)

exploitation and social oppression." The CNPA also changed its slogan to "Today we fight for land and also for power," reflecting the politicization of its economic demands. At this meeting three more groups joined CNPA, bringing the number of member organizations up to nineteen, with representation from ten ethnic groups (table 5.2).

By 1983 CNPA had developed a capacity for mobilization far greater than its capacity for negotiation. Its actions succeeded in postponing the end of agrarian reform, but it was unable to articulate an alternative set of proposals to confront the impact of austerity policies such as the decline of guaranteed crop prices, the withdrawal of subsidies, and the reduction of public spending on health and education. There occurred a "regionalization" of CNPA as each group tried to focus on local-level mobilization, although national marches continued to be held to the capital each April.

The incorporation of the demands of diverse indigenous groups in the CNPA program also hindered effective national coordination. The struggles of indigenous communities for rights to land and natural resources first had to confront local and regional systems of power relations. This meant that the vulnerability of CNPA at the national level corresponded to the vulnerability of local organizations to repression and impunity. This lesson was learned by 1985 as CNPA members began to concentrate their efforts on building mass-based movements in their own regions. The time-consuming work of national coordination became an increasing burden for several organizations that were overstretched financially as well as lacking sufficient numbers of trained activists. Consequently, the impact of CNPA was felt more at the regional level, where its member organizations achieved their greatest degree of articulation with other popular movements, particularly the democratic currents within the teachers' union, student movements, and movements of the urban poor.

Regionalization was also the result of political struggles within the CNPA leadership over the role of political parties. The Trotskyist Revolutionary Workers' Party (PRT) was the most important party in CNPA due to its presence in the Independent Revolutionary Peasant Coordinator (CCRI), which coordinated land struggles in Veracruz, Guerrero, Coahuila, and Sonora. In the context of the 1985 federal elections to renew the Chamber of Deputies, CCRI leaders were accused of trying to manipulate other members of CNPA into voting for PRT candidates. This provoked a serious split during which several organizations left, denouncing the "reformism" of the PRT and CCRI and attacking participation in elections as falling into "a bourgeois game." This division had serious repercussions for CNPA. The PRT drew three other organizations away in 1986 to create its own peasant movement. As a national movement, CNPA never recovered from these divisions, its own lack of alternatives beyond land reform, and the incessant repression of its regional organizations. By the time Salinas came into power in 1988, CNPA was radically unprepared to resist his promarket reforms. Disputes over strategy and leadership also affected the regional organizations, including the OCEZ in Chiapas.

Divisions in the OCEZ

On his release from Cerro Hueco, Arturo Albores found that the OCEZ lacked an organizational structure that could allow it to consolidate its work beyond Carranza. During 1980 and 1981 new communities from the border municipalities of La Independencia, Frontera Comalapa, La Trinitaria, and Chicomuselo had joined the Coordinadora Provisional. Their initial contact was provided by catechists and marist nuns of the diocesis of San Cristóbal. The church had already created a new group of community leaders who began to work with Albores and the Casa del Pueblo in 1980. They supported the hunger strike in 1981 and the demonstrations to win the release of Albores. These leaders would become Albores's strongest allies in the internal struggles that eventually split the OCEZ.

At the same time, three communities in the municipality of Simo-jovel left CIOAC and joined the Coordinadora Provisional. Their main leader, who had been a Chol delegate at the Indigenous Congress, charged that CIOAC had accepted a program under which disputed lands were purchased from private owners by the state government and then resold to the land claimants over a period of ten years. He argued that the peasants should not be obliged to pay for land to which they had a legal right. He also alleged that CIOAC leaders took this decision behind the backs of the peasants and acted as caudillos instead of promoting consciousness among the base.

By the end of 1982, the presence of the OCEZ extended to three main regions: the Zona Centro (the Casa del Pueblo in Venustiano Carranza and a neighboring ejido, Flores Magón); Zona Fron-teriza (fifteen ejidos in the municipalities of Independencia, Fron-tera Comalapa, La Trinitaria, and Chicomuselo); and Zona Norte (four ejidos in the municipality of Simojovel). During 1983 the community of Lindavista in the oil-producing region of Ostuacán joined the OCEZ, establishing the base for the construction of the Zona Petrolera (map 5.2). This contact had been established be-tween one of the community's leaders and Albores when they were detained together in Cerro Hueco.

Prior to 1983 the leadership of the OCEZ did not reflect its re-gional composition. Instead, a group of seven activists within the Casa del Pueblo had simply assumed the main positions. This group prioritized the demands relating to Carranza. In 1983 Al-bores began to promote a broader and more formal leadership structure composed of representatives from each of the four zonas.

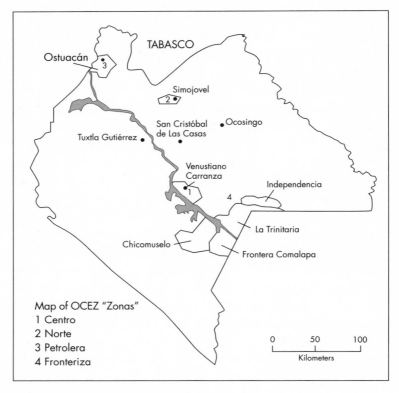

Map 5.2. OCEZ Zonas in 1987

This would also allow the OCEZ to fully address problems beyond those of Carranza. Leadership was now entrusted to an elected committee, the Comisión de Responsables, and three permanent committees were set up, to attend to land petitions (Comisión Jurídica), distribute communiqués (Comisión de Prensa), and collect and analyze information (Comisión Centralizadora). The selection of committee members was made through the general meetings, or *plenarias,* of the OCEZ. The organization began to function more effectively, and in 1984 a Finance Committee was added.

These changes created resentment from the previous leaders at the Casa del Pueblo. A division began to emerge as early as February 1983, making it impossible for Albores to even return to Carranza. Instead he began to work more intensely in the national leadership of CNPA, helping to unify a common popular front against the economic austerity measures of the de la Madrid government.[5] In Chiapas, he found strongest support in the Zona Fronteriza, and by 1984 a split had begun to appear between the latter and the leaders in Carranza.

The reorganization of the OCEZ in 1983 was not the only reason behind this division. In the same year the "group of seven" (which included the OCEZ leaders in Simojovel) had entered into contact with activists from the National Democratic Popular Front (FNDP). The FNDP was created in 1978 by Felipe Martínez Soriano, former director of the "Benito Juárez" Autonomous University in Oaxaca. It included several regional peasant organizations that simultaneously participated in CNPA and as a result were known to the leaders of the OCEZ. In fact, several of these organizations participated in the fifth national meeting of CNPA, held at the Casa del Pueblo in July 1982. The most important of these was the Independent Organizations of the United Pueblos of the Huastecas (OIPUH), comprised of Nahuatl and Otomí Indians from the impoverished Huastec region of Hidalgo, San Luis Potosí, and Veracruz. The leader of the Carranza faction was clearly impressed by the direct action tactics of the OIPUH, claiming that it was a model for the peasant movement in Chiapas.

The OIPUH was also extremely critical of all political parties and the electoral struggle. The political reform initiated by the PRI in 1977 had allowed several Left parties to gain legal registration. The PRI hoped that the reforms would help channel social dissent into an institutional arena that it clearly controlled. It proved to be highly successful as the main Left parties presented candidates in the 1979 and 1982 federal elections. With economic crisis undermining support for the PRI, the 1985 midterm elections appeared to offer opposition parties a good opportunity to increase their share of their vote and their presence in political life.

As discussed earlier with reference to the PRT split, CNPA was seriously debilitated by internal divisions over whether or not to participate in elections. In 1984 the most important positions within the national leadership of CNPA were held by PRT activists. Both Albores and the "group of seven" were opposed to the PRT, alleging that it was only concerned with using the mass organizations for the reformist goal of occupying a few seats in a PRI-controlled

Congress. As one of the latter's members said, "We don't want seats in the Congress. We want our land rights respected" (Interview, Casa del Pueblo, Venustiano Carranzo, Chiapas, June 13, 1987). However, whereas Albores argued that the OCEZ should remain within CNPA and continue to work for a truly independent politics, his opponents called for its withdrawal and for closer ties to the OIPUH. They began to propagate this position within the OCEZ, noting that, besides the OIPUH, two other respected organizations had split from CNPA because of the role played by the PRT *reformistas*.[6] The issue was debated at a plenary meeting of the Comisión de Responsables of the OCEZ in February 1986. Albores's position won out, and it was agreed to remain within CNPA. Nevertheless, the issue was not settled. In April 1986 CNPA held its annual march to Mexico City. The OCEZ agreed to participate, but the group that arrived did not join the main demonstration in the Zócalo but instead participated in a separate march with members of OIPUH, ACR, and UCEZ. This faction claimed that Albores was simply an opportunist who benefited personally from his leadership within CNPA and the OCEZ. By the end of 1986, the two factions had become clearly defined: Albores and his supporters in the Zona Fronteriza and the Zona Petrolera were attacked as reformistas because of their opposition to alliances with the OIPUH and FNDP. The "group of seven" in Carranza and Simojovel, on the other hand, were criticized for being divisionist. The Albores warned how the FNDP had infiltrated and divided popular organizations on many previous occasions. They also claimed that Martínez Soriano may even have been supported by elements within the Ministry of the Interior to help disarticulate independent movements. In their view, the *sorianistas* in the OCEZ and CNPA were only carrying out the work of the state, undermining genuine attempts to build an independent political project for social change.

During 1987 each faction tended to go its own way, although no formal division had yet been announced. In April the OCEZ participated in a hunger strike organized by CNPA in Mexico City to demand the release of political prisoners, including Victórico Martínez Hernández. In Chiapas, simultaneous actions were held in each of the four zonas in support of local demands. However, these actions were not well coordinated, as each faction carried out its own protests in the name of the OCEZ. One positive result was the release of Martínez Hernández in late April, but even this led to new problems. Due to his friendship with Albores, Martínez Hernández was soon seen in Carranza as a potential threat. He enjoyed great prestige within the community and could have formed a group more favorable to Albores's position. The fact that he began to accompany Albores on trips to the Zona Fronteriza and Zona Petrolera, as well as to Mexico City, created distrust among the opposing faction. This coincided with increasing criticism within the Casa del Pueblo concerning the level of disorganization and the failure of the leaders to promote broader participation. Their vulnerability was even more exposed when the only other participant in the Zona Centro (the ejido Flores Magón) withdrew from the organization in July 1987. In November they tried to expel Martínez Hernández from the community, claiming that he was a police spy. The attempt failed, but the divisions grew deeper.

Each group held their own political events, including two plenary meetings in July 1988. In May it had been agreed that the meeting would take place at the Casa del Pueblo on the condition that the Carranza faction attend meetings with the rest of the OCEZ. As this did not occur, the site for the plenary was switched to the ejido Buenavista in the Zona Fronteriza. The meeting in Carranza went ahead with only the participation of the Casa del Pueblo and the Zona Norte, which decided to formally break from the other zonas. Then, in September, the rest of the OCEZ announced its decision to break relations with the leaders in Carranza and Simojovel. This resulted in two organizations: OCEZ-*centro* in Carranza (supported by the group in Simojovel) and OCEZ-CNPA in the Zona Fronteriza and Zona Petrolera. Each faction pursued different alliances. The former continued to build ties to the FNDP. The latter worked more closely with CIOAC, Mactumatzá students, and sectors of the democratic teachers' movement in the creation of the Regional Front of Mass Organizations (FROM). The FROM organized four marches and demonstrations in Tuxtla during October and November 1988.

The divisions within the OCEZ were interpreted by Albores not simply in terms of personal rivalries but as political differences over strategy. In September 1988 the "group of seven" wrote a document denouncing Albores as an opportunist who lived off the back of the organization (OCEZ 1988). Albores was blamed for having deliberately divided the organization by gathering around him a group of leaders from other communities and publicly denigrating the leaders in Carranza: "On his release from prison he began to divide us. He used slander and misinformation to isolate other compañeros. Later he used corruption and bribes to create his own group of 'leaders' who had no following but ended up usurping the representation of our organization" (OCEZ 1988:2). The document accused Albores of acting as a caudillo, alleging that he took all the decisions and interfered with the different committees according to his own wishes. A significant point of conflict concerned the origins of the OCEZ. This group based its legitimacy on being the founders of the organization in July 1982 when Albores was still in prison and his wife was in Mexico City. Albores responded to this claim by arguing that the organization was created not by a small group of leaders but through an ongoing process in which many communities participated: "They [the Carranza faction] call themselves the 'founders' of the organization and feel that they have more rights than anyone who was not there at the beginning. They feel that they have the right to block the participation of others." (OCEZ-CNPA 1989:11).

For Albores, this issue was indicative of a lack of political maturity because it had the effect of putting sectarian goals before those of the organization as a whole. In his response to the accusations, Albores distinguished between the political practices of the two factions. These differences can be summed up by referring to three points. First, Albores believed in the capacity of the peasants to increase their political awareness and organizational skills to a degree where they would train other peasants and expand the level of participation in the OCEZ. He was critical of most popular organizations in Mexico for neglecting the tasks of political formation. He realized that this process may take longer but that "we have faith in the people because we know that it will decide its own history and choose its own leaders." Albores attempted to promote grassroots participation through cultural activities. During 1988 he worked with peasants and teachers in a project known as the Taller de Expresión Artística (TEA) Popular, a workshop to develop artistic skills in painting, music, poetry, and dance. After 1989 TEA-Popular produced several cassettes of songs by members of OCEZ-CNPA, which include the organization's anthem and invoke its history of struggle. In contrast, the Carranza faction believed that the people could be easily led as they lacked the knowledge and skills to make their own decisions. A small group of committed leaders could be more effective than futile attempts at political formation.

Second, the tactics of struggle differed between the two groups. Albores insisted on mass participation in mobilizations such as marches and demonstrations, combined with negotiations and the formation of alliances. The opposing faction instead argued for the use of surprise tactics, which could attract greater attention. It called these tactics *acciones de calidad,* where the "quality" of the action was more important than the number of participants. Examples were land seizures, hunger strikes, and the occupation of government buildings, including foreign embassies.

Third, Albores criticized the sectarianism of the Carranza faction, claiming that it was only concerned with its own localistic demands. Its unwillingness to work with organizations with different perspectives only served to isolate it further in its antidemocratic practices.

The divisions over leadership, tactics, and alliances proved irreconcilable. Albores worked to organize the first state congress of OCEZ-CNPA, scheduled to take place in Tuxtla in April 1989. However, on March 6 he was shot eight times in the back in the small stationery store he ran in Tuxtla with his wife. He died instantly. He was forty years old. Marisela González and other leaders of OCEZ-CNPA accused the opposing faction of having carried out the assassination. The latter denied the charges, alleging that it was the work of caciques and formed part of the pattern of repression in Chiapas. A former police officer from Carranza was indicted with the murder but the only eyewitness was not allowed to confirm his identity. Friends of Albores believed that the real culprit remained free, and they continued to call for a full investigation. A woman from the Zona Fronteriza remembered Albores with the following words:

When they shot him we really missed him a lot in our meetings and the congress. We felt alone, our leader had been taken from us, but then we saw how his ideals continued to live within the people and we had to make sure we kept them alive. So, when people say, "Zapata Lives," Arturo lives too, in the heart of the people and we see that he really left us strong and well prepared *[bastante instruidos]*. (Interview, member of OCEZ-CNPA, La Trinitaria, December 1991)

Chapter 6

FROM PLAN CHIAPAS TO

THE NEW ZAPATISMO

At the same time that peasant organizations were undergoing internal divisions or facing repression, the federal government began to give Chiapas greater attention on its policy agenda. In the period after 1982 Chiapas was defined as strategically important for national security, and new programs were created to ostensibly deal with a crisis on Mexico's southern border. This renewal of interest in Chiapas allows us to examine not only the intentions but, more important, the effects of government actions during the 1980s.

How are we to understand the actions of the Mexican state in Chiapas? Numerous programs have come and gone, but extreme poverty persists and land conflicts have not gone away. Part of the explanation (popular with federal bureaucrats) is that good, well-intentioned programs have consistently been subverted by local elites for their own personal gain. Indeed, there are many instances of corruption that diverted funds from their stated aims. But we need also to be clear when we talk of the failure of state intervention in Chiapas. The "failure" of "development" presupposes that the intention of political elites has been to create greater equality, despite a long history of evidence to the contrary (Escobar 1984, 1992; Esteva 1985, 1992; Ferguson 1990; Lummis 1996:45–78; Sachs 1992). We should not look to official intentions of "development" programs, plans, and projects, but to their concrete effects in the configuration of power relations. The power exercised through the state is not a commodity that one group possesses and another lacks. Instead, it is constantly affirmed, resisted, and transformed (Foucault 1980:93). The power of state discourses cannot be traced to some rational understanding of social needs but to the precise mechanisms (economic, institutional, and cultural) that allow them to assert a hegemonic position vis à vis other discourses. The power that diagnoses maladies and recommends cures is not a new form of power, but the fact that it is able to conceal itself so well behind apparently objective knowledge of scientific discourse is characteristic of the modern state.

Consequently, the intelligibility of state strategies is given not by the declared interests they pursue but by the relations of power they set in motion. Since the early 1980s these strategies have proceeded in Chiapas by defining the region as a problem for national security, as isolated from economic development, and as a threat to social stability. These policies may not have produced their supposed aims, but they did expand state power in Chiapas. They also provoked divisions within peasant movements over strategy and alliances. One of these divisions led to the emergence of the EZLN.

Securing the Border

In January 1982 the PRI "unveiled" a military man, General Absalón Castellanos Domínguez, as its candidate for state governor of Chiapas. This decision partly reflected a convergence of local and national political interests. On the one hand, the more conservative fraction of the local landowning class wanted one of its representatives to succeed Juan Sabines, whom they saw as an unpredictable populist. On the other hand, the PRI's presidential candidate, Miguel de la Madrid, and his team of advisers had decided to make the southeastern states areas of national priority. For both groups, General Castellanos was the ideal candidate. He came from the group of large ranchers and undercapitalized agriculture that had historically dominated economic and political life in Chiapas. His assumption of the position would only serve to continue that tradition.[1] His experience as commander of the Thirty-first Military Zone also made him an attractive candidate for the de la Madrid team, which was concerned about the traditional lack of attention given to the southern states and the possible threat to national security posed by the civil war in neighboring Guatemala. It should also be noted that conservative circles in both the United States and Mexico had begun to give prominence to the southern border. For example, in February 1982 the U.S. secretary of state, Alexander Haig, claimed in the *Washington Post* that "the arms destined for the Guatemalan guerrillas come from a variety of sources and part of the traffic passes through southern Mexico" (as cited by Aguilar Zinser 1983:168). In a similar tone, the president of the Employers' Confederation of the Mexican Republic (COPARMEX) complained in March 1982 about "guerrilla infiltrations on the southern border" and "undue flirtations with foreign ideologies" (Aguilar Zinser 1983:184). Despite the lack of evidence to support such allegations, it appears that they did have the effect of sealing the border, increasing the presence of the military, and making Castellanos Domínguez state governor.

Castellanos Domínguez became the PRI's favorite as early as August 1981 due to the expansion of the military's presence in Chiapas and the influx of refugees from Guatemala (Gracián and Sotomayor 1981:14).[2] At the same time, in campaign speeches the general clearly expressed the concern of his fellow landowners by insisting that he would not promote further land redistribution (Cruz 1982:42). In this regard his designation can also be seen as a response to the growing militancy of independent peasant organizations and to the failure of earlier corporatist and repressive strategies to contain the demand for land redistribution.

However, opposition to his selection came from within the ranks of the PRI in Chiapas, revealing a major division between the Castellanos-led fraction of large ranchers and coffee planters on the one hand, and, on the other, a sector of the peasantry that had benefited briefly from the new subsidies provided by the Mexican Food System (SAM) as well as from the support of the Sabines administration. This latter group was headed by the leader of the CNC in Chiapas, Germán Jiménez. These tensions and rivalries continued throughout the sexenio, even allowing for tactical alliances to be formed in 1986 between the democratic teachers' movement and a statewide union of maize producers, *maiceros,* led by Germán Jiménez (Castillo Burguete 1988; Foweraker 1993). The repression of both movements and the imprisonment of their respective leaders confirmed, in the case of the maiceros, the depth of divisions within the PRI between traditional, conservative elements and a new reformist wing.

The convergence of interests that brought Castellanos Domín-guez to power had serious implications for the independent peasant organizations and other dissident sectors in Chiapas, including church catechists, priests, students, teachers, and urban squatters. The new governor could count not only on the unity of the land-owning class and the weakness of incipient opposition within the PRI, but also on the modernization of equipment, an increase in troop numbers, and a new emphasis on professional training. As a result, the military's presence expanded into areas of land conflict within Chiapas, although the official goal was to strengthen the border against incursions by the Guatemalan army in search of guerrillas. In fact, soldiers were increasingly denounced for their intimidation of the indigenous peasants, particularly in areas of independent organization.[3] In line with the government's official policy, a second military zone was created in 1983 with its head-quarters in Tapachula, specifically to deal with border problems, while new units were deployed throughout the state (Sereseres 1984).[4] Finally, the increasing presence of the armed forces and police in the state followed maneuvers carried out in December 1981. Some 40,000 soldiers stayed behind in the military zone of Tuxtla Gutiérrez and Tapachula, while two new airstrips were con-structed in Comitán and Tonalá and the Terán airport in Tuxtla Gutiérrez was converted for military use (Cruz 1982:27).

Plan Chiapas: The Technocratic Response

The concern of President Miguel de la Madrid in Chiapas was immediately revealed by the announcement in early 1983 of two regional development plans. The Plan del Sureste revealed why the Southeast was a priority region for the new administration. The plan stated that because of the region's geographical isolation, it had not benefited from social and economic development. The plan was thus presented as a response to this traditional neglect (Mexico 1983a). More important, the Plan Chiapas was announced in May 1983. With a budget of 83 billion pesos, its stated goal was to "unify

Map 6.1. Marqués de Comillas and the Chiapas-Guatemala Border

the actions of federal and state government to rapidly improve the living standards of the *chiapanecos* and to strengthen the social and cultural integration of the state" (Mexico 1983b). The major areas of investment reflected the concern with border security and the lack of regional integration. For example, some 4.517 billion pesos were directed solely to road construction, including the completion of the Southern Border Highway linking Palenque and Comitán, which would effectively "seal" the otherwise open territory between Chiapas and Guatemala (see map 6.1). The economic strategy of the Plan Chiapas was based on resolving three problems: inadequate communications, environmental destruction, and land disputes.

The plan was limited by its failure to take into account the political nature of social relations. It was falsely assumed that local bosses would cooperate with federal agencies (Aguayo 1987:43). In fact, serious divisions existed between the latter and the state governor. These differences undermined de la Madrid's political goals of

strengthening the PRI through greater grassroots participation and
of cleaning up corruption in municipal and state government.

The border region clearly received the lion's share of investment
in communications and agriculture. Road construction was designed to facilitate border control, while 300 million pesos were
spent to increase the number of immigration posts (Paniagua
1983:53). In fact, the success of several components of the plan was
intimately linked to the road construction program. The goal was
to "advance in the completion of the Southern Border Highway, to
help develop the petroleum and tourism industries, the incorporation of the Marqués de Comillas region, the development of
the state and greater vigilance on the southern border" (Mexico
1983b:18). Furthermore, given that the Lacandon forest had a low
population density, the plan established a program to "increase and
substantially improve the immigration services, the border communications network and the training and development of human
resources" (Mexico 1983b:26). This was complemented by the
Plan del Sureste, which included a program to colonize the border
area in an orderly, rational manner. Marqués de Comillas, the
southeastern corner of the Lacandon forest, was seen as particularly
important because the inflow of Guatemalan refugees and the proximity of guerrilla activity in El Petén threatened the security of
Mexico's southern border. Although the colonization was presented as obeying a rational plan to protect the proper use of natural
resources, in effect the main objective (and result) was simply to
help establish the state's presence in the area. Colonization was not
orderly, nor did it lead to "rational" farming practices. The flow of
migrants doubled the population from thirteen ejidos with 10,000
inhabitants in 1984 to twenty-nine ejidos with 22,000 inhabitants in
1986. The lack of technical assistance, credit, and infrastructure led
colonists, ranchers, and loggers to deplete the forest's valuable mahogany trees. In addition, by 1985 the flow of refugees had significantly decreased and the road construction came to a halt, leaving
many of the new ejidos without any communication at all (González Ponciano 1995). It would take the Zapatista uprising for
the road construction to resume, this time for internal military
objectives.[5]

Subversion of Land Reform:
The Agrarian Rehabilitation Program

By 1983 peasant movements in Chiapas had succeeded in forcing land reform back on to the political agenda. A new program was in fact effective in distributing over 80,000 hectares of land to more than 9,000 peasants. However, the way it was implemented created more conflicts than it solved.

In 1984 the state government signed agreements with the Minister of Agrarian Reform to implement a plan to resolve land disputes in Chiapas. The plan, known as the Agrarian Rehabilitation Program (PRA), was designed to purchase land that belonged to private owners but which had been occupied by peasants whose claims for distribution had not been resolved by the SRA. These lands would then be officially given ejido status. The areas chosen for "rehabilitation" were obviously those with the greatest number of land invasions. Because the invasions tended to be led by the independent organizations, the CNC feared they would be strengthened, and it began to dispute ownership of the same lands, even carrying out its own land invasions in PRA-targeted zones. One of the most important areas for the PRA was Simojovel. With the announcement of the PRA, land in possession of CIOAC supporters and awaiting regularization was then invaded by CNC supporters. Violent conflicts between the two groups became inevitable and continued well into the following administration.

The PRA targeted forty-one municipalities (over a third of the state's total) grouped in six zones (the northern highlands, the border, the center, the coast, the Frailesca, and the Lacandon forest). The four municipalities that saw most redistribution were, as the program intended, those with a recent history of land conflicts: Simojovel and Bochil, Ocosingo and Venustiano Carranza. However, the independent organizations in each area did not receive the share of land corresponding to their demands or to their size. In Simojovel and Bochil CIOAC received title to sixteen ejidos, compared to thirty for the CNC. In Ocosingo seventeen ejidos were distributed among peasants without affiliation but promoted by

Table 6.1. Certificates of Nonaffectability Issued in Chiapas, 1934–87

Presidency	Period	Agricultural	Ranching
Cárdenas	1934–40	26	1
Avila Camacho	1940–46	82	0
Alemán	1946–52	315	57
Ruiz Cortines	1952–58	461	47
López Mateos	1958–64	107	6
Díaz Ordaz	1964–70	123	44
Echeverría	1970–76	5	46
López Portillo	1976–82	61	45
de la Madrid	1982–87	2,932	4,714
Total	1934–87	4,112	4,960

Source: SRA (1987).

the CNC, compared to only one for the Unión de Uniones. In Venustiano Carranza the OCEZ did not receive any land at all under the PRA. Rather than solve disputes, the PRA had the effect of transforming conflicts between peasants and landowners into conflicts between independent organizations and the CNC (Reyes Ramos 1992:113–18).

The principal beneficiaries of the PRA were the landowners and some agrarian reform officials. On the one hand, the former received payment for land they had resigned themselves to losing anyway. In the process, they were relieved of conflicts as different groups of peasants now battled with each other over land ownership. On the other, the program provided opportunities for corruption and personal enrichment. Landowners invented "land invasions" on their property, appealing to the state government to purchase the disputed land. Some officials colluded by paying out "compensation" for lands that were never to be distributed and, as part of the corruption, retained some of the money for themselves. The program was suspended in the summer of 1985, less than a year after it had begun, when the federal government ordered an investigation. In order to show that the PRA was still necessary, the state government began to evict members of the UU from allegedly disputed lands in Ocosingo. In August 1985 four communities were evicted by state police, leading to protests and a march by over 2,000 Tzeltal Indians to Tuxtla Gutiérrez. The UU was able to uphold its argument that the communities in question already had legal documents. However, the PRA did return in 1985 and continued until its U.S.$100 million budget expired in 1987.

The Castellanos Domínguez government also helped protect private landowners from possible expropriation by issuing more documents of nonaffectability (certificados de inafectabilidad) than all the previous state governors combined. The main beneficiaries were the private ranchers, who were issued with 4,714 certificados, equivalent to 95 percent of the total number distributed in the state since 1934 (see table 6.1). By the end of this administration at least 70 percent of the area used by cattle ranchers was legally beyond the reach of agrarian reform (Reyes Ramos 1992:119).

Dissent and Repression

The interventions discussed in the preceding sections did not reduce social and agrarian conflicts in Chiapas. On the contrary, they exacerbated them and led to repeated violent confrontations between peasant organizations and police. As we saw in earlier chapters, the peasant movement has constantly needed to use mass mobilization to force the authorities to negotiate and fulfill agreements. Between 1983 and 1988 both the OCEZ and CIOAC organized marches and demonstrations to Tuxtla Gutiérrez and Mexico City. In 1984 they also began to work together and with other popular organizations in a statewide network known as the Coordinator of Struggles in Chiapas (CLCH). The most common response was repression and persecution of independent leaders. Programs such as Plan Chiapas did not address issues of political domination, while the expansion of the military only strengthened the position of the governor, who proceeded to protect private landholdings from the threat of land redistribution. In fact, the PRA was implemented as a means to bolster the CNC and restrain the influence of independent organizations.

Between April 1984 and October 1987 the two factions of the OCEZ held eight marches, some to Tuxtla, others to Mexico City;

staged several hunger strikes; and occupied installations of the Mexican Petroleum Company (PEMEX), municipal palaces, and roads. They also published denunciations in the national press and extended the OCEZ's alliances with other sectors in Chiapas.

During 1983 both groups participated in local demonstrations against the austerity policies of the de la Madrid government. In April 1984 they participated in the national peasant march to Mexico City and demanded the release of four political prisoners, an end to repression, the withdrawal of 180 arrest warrants against the OCEZ's members, and the resolution of agrarian demands.[6] The mobilization failed to win any solutions. Three more members of the Casa del Pueblo were arrested in June, and the coras faction in Carranza obstructed a march by OCEZ supporters on August 1, 1984, to commemorate the death of Bartolomé Martínez Villatoro. Later that month, the four OCEZ prisoners and relatives participated in a hunger strike organized by the FNCR to demand the release of over sixty peasant leaders from prisons throughout Mexico. At the same time, it appeared that negotiations between the Casa del Pueblo and disaffected members of the coras group were leading to a solution of the conflict with the CNC in Carranza. However, any chance of a solution was destroyed by the murder of the leader of the coras, Bartolo Gómez Espinoza, on September 28. Although the involvement of the Casa del Pueblo was not proven, the killing led to the massacre on October 6 of nine members of the Casa del Pueblo at the hands of the CNC group.[7] The governor set up a committee to investigate the case, and a march by the OCEZ to Tuxtla Gutiérrez on October 20 won an agreement that the forty-nine families of the CNC group believed to have been responsible for the massacre would be resettled outside the municipality of Venustiano Carranza. According to Renard, in December 1984 the assassins of the coras leader were found to have been hired by the Orantes family who feared a reunification of the Casa del Pueblo and the growing influence of Gómez Espinoza in the municipal government (Renard 1985:199).

The government failed to implement the October agreement, and the forty-nine families remained and continued to threaten members of the Casa del Pueblo. This led the OCEZ to hold another march to Tuxtla in February 1985 to demand compliance with the resettlement order. This march also provided the first opportunity to carry out joint mobilizations with CIOAC, the urban popular movement in Tuxtla, students, transport workers, and teachers. Leaders of these groups had begun to meet in 1984 and had agreed to build an independent front of popular organizations in Chiapas, the CLCH. This broader action won negotiations and the release on February 20 of José María Martínez Hernández.

The strategy of forcing negotiations through mass mobilization began to define the OCEZ as one of the most combative organizations in Chiapas, despite its internal divisions. In October 1985 the CLCH held its second march and demonstration in Tuxtla, but it was broken up by security police who used tear gas and clubs to disperse protesters gathered in front of the palace of government (Amnesty International 1985). Two days later, with demonstrators once more in the central plaza, Castellanos Domínguez agreed to meet representatives and promised to implement the plan to relocate the forty-nine families of the CNC faction. These were finally moved to the ejido San Gregorio in Frontera Comalapa in 1986. In March and April 1986 the two factions of the OCEZ again marched to Mexico City and organized acts of solidarity in Chiapas through the CLCH (CLCH 1986). The CLCH was dismantled by the repression unleashed in 1986. In May the leaders of the teachers' union and the urban popular movement (Manuel Hernández and Gerardo Barrios, respectively) were arrested in separate protests (Amnesty International July 9, 1986). Further marches and hunger strikes in April and October 1987 won the release of Victórico Martínez Hernández and Agustín de la Torre, although no solution had been found to the agrarian demands of the Casa del Pueblo. The tactics of the OCEZ revealed the need to engage in simultaneous actions in Chiapas and Mexico City. For example, the mobilization in April combined a hunger strike outside the Metropolitan Cathedral, a demonstration in the central plaza of Tuxtla Gutiérrez, the seizure of PEMEX installations in Ostuacán, and the occupation of the municipal palace in Carranza.[8]

The CIOAC followed a similar strategy to that of the OCEZ between 1983 and 1988, combining mobilization with negotiations and seeking alliances with other political forces. Its most important mobilization was the March for Dignity and Freedom from Chiapas to Mexico City. This march began on September 24, 1983, as several contingents set out for Tuxtla from Simojovel, El Bosque, and Comitán. Their main demands concerned the release of CIOAC activists from prison, an end to repression, and land redistribution (*Uno Más Uno*, October 15, 1983, p. 2). They arrived in Tuxtla four days later. Despite earlier promises that they would be received by Castellanos Domínguez, they were told to return to their communities. A demonstration by over 2,000 peasants was held outside the palace of government on October 1, and a group of some 600 (including sixty-six peasants from Simojovel) decided to continue the march to Mexico City.[9] The state government failed to convince the marchers to return to Tuxtla for negotiations, and they arrived in the capital on October 17. The CIOAC leaders were able to press the federal government to establish an interministerial commission and begin negotiations.[10] The commission agreed to study the following demands:

1. Compensation and satisfactory relocation of peasant communities affected by the construction of the Itzantún hydroelectricity dam.
2. Resolution of fifty-two land petitions filed with the SRA.
3. Provision of agricultural credit to CIOAC-affiliated communities in Simojovel and Comitán.
4. Waiving of debts with the state government over eleven copropiedades that had been fraudulently sold to CIOAC-affiliated communities by the Sabines administration.
5. The granting of the CIOAC union with its official registro.
6. Intervention of the Ministry of Interior in securing the release of twenty-nine prisoners and the withdrawal of more than 300 arrest warrants.

The demonstration in Mexico City ended on October 20, and the marchers returned to Chiapas. The mobilization received wide coverage in the national press and, as with the OCEZ, obliged the state government to accept the presence of CIOAC as a legitimate representative of peasant communities in Chiapas.

In response to the emerging influence of CIOAC, local landowners and caciques stepped up the number of attacks against its activists.[11] The state government failed to comply with its promise to release CIOAC members from Cerro Hueco, and little advance was made on the other items the commission had agreed to study. As a result, CIOAC held another march and demonstration in Tuxtla in October 1984 (coinciding with that of the OCEZ) and won the release of seven of its leaders. Repression brought the attention of the national press, particularly *La Jornada,* which began circulation in 1984. CIOAC organized another march to Tuxtla in July 1985, which won the release of four prisoners and a commitment from the governor to speed up the accords of October 1983. The demonstration outside the palace of government was violently broken up by police. Several people were injured, including a photographer for *La Jornada*.[12]

One of the areas where CIOAC had begun to gain support was the municipality of Comitán, home of the politically influential Castellanos family. During 1984 and 1985 the governor's brother Ernesto Castellanos Domínguez incited attacks by CNC groups against members of CIOAC, culminating in the assassination on October 4, 1985, of Andulio Gálvez, a CIOAC adviser who had recently been elected to the local congress as a deputy for the Unified Socialist Party of Mexico (PSUM).[13] CIOAC responded immediately with a demonstration in Tuxtla, where it called for a full investigation into the crime. Again it coincided with a march by the OCEZ, which was still demanding justice for the massacre of nine members of the Casa del Pueblo a year earlier.[14] The lack of response from the government led CIOAC to call its fifth march in four years to the state capital in October 1986. Over 2,000 peasants from eight municipalities converged on Tuxtla on October 9 to once again demand respect for the agreements signed three years earlier and to commemorate the death of Andulio Gálvez.[15]

By the end of 1987 it was clear that political and social reforms in favor of indigenous and peasant communities could not occur without displacing local landowners and caciques. The latter's position in local and regional systems of power relations had come under sustained attack since the mid-1970s, but they had been able to count on the support of the state government and the apolitical interventions of federal programs. In the summer of 1987 both the OCEZ and CIOAC warned of an escalation of violence against their members. The CIOAC specifically denounced death threats against Sebastián Pérez Núñez, who had replaced Andulio Gálvez as a state deputy ("Denuncian PMS y CIOAC" 1987). Their warning was correct. In December 1987 state security police violently evicted several town halls that had been occupied by groups protesting the corruption of mayors in the handling of the funds provided by the Plan Chiapas. In the case of La Independencia, seven OCEZ members were killed during the eviction. In a related action, police ransacked the offices and home of Franciscan priests in Comitán who had allegedly supported the actions of the OCEZ. The contrast with the stated goals of Plan Chiapas could hardly be more striking. By the end of 1987 the majority of the state's 110 municipalities were marked by protests against corrupt mayors. A report published in December 1987 by the Mexican Academy of Human Rights denounced an average of two politically motivated killings per month in Chiapas since Castellanos Domínguez had been installed as governor in December 1982.[16]

Divisions within the State

Whereas the OCEZ and CIOAC continued to rely on mobilization to strengthen their position in negotiations, the Quiptic faction of the Unión de Uniones tended to avoid confrontations and was able to exploit divisions between the federal and state government to its own advantage. Its strategy of negotiations was not without its costs, including the co-optation of its leaders by Salinas.

One of these divisions was exemplified by the failure of the Agrarian Rehabilitation Program (PRA) to resolve land disputes. The PRA was funded by the federal government through the Ministry of Budgets and Planning, of which Carlos Salinas de Gortari was head. However, the money was handled by the state government and the regional office of the SRA. As noted earlier, the program allowed for corruption because landowners claimed compensation for lands that did not exist or that had already been granted as ejidos.

Landowners in the Ocosingo region saw the opportunity to profit from the new program. In December 1984 the regional association of private owners of the Segundo Valle of Ocosingo held a demonstration in Tuxtla Gutiérrez to denounce over twenty cases of land invasion. The UE Quiptic denied that these invasions existed and argued that the real motive for the protest was to gain access to the PRA funds. The Quiptic leaders were able to convince the SPP to investigate charges of corruption against representatives of the SRA and CNC. The charges were confirmed, and the program was suspended in July 1985 (Interview, adviser to the UE Quiptic Ta Lecubtesel, Ocosingo October 7, 1987). Landowners, backed by the state governor, responded with a campaign of evictions throughout Chiapas to show that the PRA was still necessary. For example, in August 1985 four groups of ejidatarios who had been falsely accused of occupying private land in the Segundo Valle were violently evicted by the state police *(seguridad pública),* their homes were burned down, and their crops destroyed. The Quiptic faction of the Unión de Uniones responded immediately by holding demonstration marches in Ocosingo and Tuxtla, publicizing the widespread corruption associated with the PRA and denouncing the evictions.

The Quiptic also sought to use divisions over environmental policy to propose a revision of the boundaries of the comunidad lacandona. The state government and the SRA had been reluctant to recognize the land rights of twenty-six ejidos located within this area. It was only after the demonstrations of October 1981 that the threat of eviction had been removed. Then, in January 1984, an agreement was signed with the SRA to respect the ejido titles of the twenty-six communities. This agreement was incorporated into a revised demarcation formalized by President de la Madrid in a titling ceremony with the Lacandon group in September 1984. However, the regional office of the SRA held up implementation of the accords, and further delays were caused by the loss of relevant documents when the SRA building in Mexico City was destroyed by the earthquakes of September 1985.

The reason for the delay was also political. The ejidos in question belonged to an independent organization, and a solution depended on their agreement to join the CNC. In order to maintain independence, the Quiptic leaders looked for allies within the SPP and the Ministry of Urban Development and the Environment (SEDUE).

The SEDUE was created in 1986, and one of its first priorities was the ecological crisis in the Lacandon forest. In June 1986 representatives of the Quiptic participated in a national meeting of UNORCA that was attended by the heads of the SPP and SEDUE, Carlos Salinas de Gortari and Manuel Camacho Solís, respectively. They met with Salinas and Camacho and explained how they were still threatened with eviction due to the delaying tactics of the SRA (Interview, administrative secretary of the UE Quiptic Ta Lecubtesel, Ocosingo, October 1987). Both officials responded positively, and Camacho promised to put pressure on the SRA in Chiapas to speed up the implementation of the 1984 accords. The Quiptic used the ecological concern to promote its position. It noted how peasant colonists were being identified in the media and policy documents as the principal cause of deforestation in Chiapas. Other agents, particularly ranchers and logging companies, received less attention. The Quiptic proposed an alternative based on the economic and social needs of the affected communities. It argued that due to the lack of credit, farm machinery, and other inputs, the peasant colonists were forced to bring more land under cultivation. Such inputs were necessary to support a more intensive form of agriculture, but access had been denied due to the lack of definitive land titles. With proper government support, the colonists would not need to clear more land. Conservation therefore depended on the full recognition of the land rights of the twenty-six ejidos.

This proposal appealed to SEDUE, a new institution with a clear interest in demonstrating its ability to deal with the ecological crisis in the Lacandon forest. Camacho took the initiative in setting up an Interministerial Commission for the Lacandon Forest and appointed a SEDUE official, Salvador Garcilita Castillo, as its coordinator. In October 1986 Garcilita organized a meeting in Palenque with the state governor and representatives from the SRA, SARH, SEDUE, the State Planning and Development Commission (COPLADE), and the UE Quiptic. The meeting agreed to recognize the land titles of the Quiptic, and SARH officials promised to provide it with financial and technical support. The Quiptic also agreed to participate in conservation and reforestation programs. As it became clear that the proposal offered a viable solution, the gover-

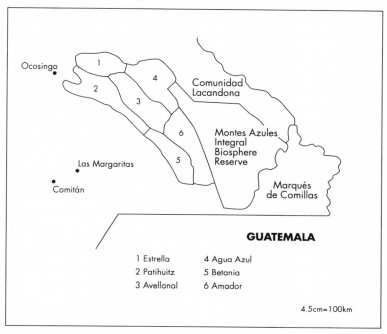

Map 6.2. Subregions of the Lacandon Forest. Source: Ascencio Franco (1995:366).

nor's position was undermined. He could not be seen to oppose a plan that was committed to protecting the forest at a time when public opinion was beginning to demand solutions to environmental destruction. A final agreement was signed in March 1987 by representatives of the Quiptic, SEDUE, SRA, SARH, COFOLASA, CFE, PEMEX, and the state government. This agreement established a special Coordinating Committee for the Preservation of the Lacandon Forest. Its provisions also included the unification of the various uniones de ejidos in the region in a third-level organization: the ARIC Unión de Uniones (see map 6.2 for the location of the constituent groups).[17] At the signing ceremony Camacho promised the Quiptic that it would have its land titles by the end of the year. The selection of Salinas as the PRI's presidential candidate augured well, and the Quiptic advisers looked forward to a productive alliance with the new government. The land titles were finally granted, some fifteen years after the struggle began, on August 25,

1988. The official act of land titling took place in January 1989 and was presided, as is custom, by the president of the republic. This was Salinas's first act of land titling and, paradoxically for him, it occurred precisely in the heart of the Zapatista base.

The negotiation strategy was not without its critics. The split in the Unión de Uniones in early 1983 seriously weakened the organization, and the pastoral workers of the diocese were unable to maintain the level of participation seen in 1979 to 1982. At the end of 1983 a new group of activists arrived, began to promote the armed option, and gained the support of several community leaders who had tired of the ineffectiveness of their legal strategy. The new activists included subcomandante Marcos and had their roots in an urban guerrilla organization known as the National Liberation Forces (FLN). However, they avoided imposing yet another political line or ideology on the indigenous communities. From the analysis so far, it should be obvious that many of these communities were tired of failure, manipulation, leadership rivalries, and ideological disputes. More important, they were tired of living in the same poverty and of facing the same repression as had existed prior to their organizational efforts of the 1970s. In the words of an adviser to the ARIC, the indigenous peasants of the Cañadas had been "vaccinated" against all forms of political organization. How was it, then, that the Zapatistas were able to overcome this history?

Finding New Words for Old Struggles

Marcos recounted that the Zapatista Army of National Liberation (EZLN) was born on November 17, 1983, out of the meeting of three indigenous people and three mestizos, including himself (EZLN 1995:131). The previous year had seen the violent evictions of peasants from three communities in the Lacandon forest: Flor de Cacao, Cintalapa, and Nuevo Progreso (see chapter 3). In the Cañadas of Las Margaritas, attacks had been carried out against Tojolobal communities. In both cases local CNC groups were responsible for the violence. The use of groups such as the coras in Venustiano Carranza and strikebreakers in Simojovel were part of this pattern of

local-level repression. The impunity with which these actions occurred, and their increasing frequency during the administration of
Absalón Castellanos Domínguez, did not go uncontested. Just as
earlier advisers had to find solutions to economic problems, the
EZLN had to respond to the need for self-defense in the face of
unrelenting repression. In fact, this appears to have been the initial
rationale for the formation of the EZLN. In Chiapas at least, it was
born not as a guerrilla movement with a clear revolutionary strategy
for taking power, but as a regional network of armed self-defense
units (García de León 1994:26–28). In interviews, Marcos recounted how the EZLN was born:[18]

I went to teach what the people wanted: literacy and Mexican history.
In 1984, I joined the first group of indigenous *guerrilleros* in the mountains. They had a lot of political experience already, having participated
in mass movements and they knew all about the problems of the left
political parties. They had also been in prison, suffered torture, all of
that. But they also demanded what they called the "political word" *[la
palabra política]* : history. The history of this country and of the struggle.
So that was the task I arrived with.

Marcos won people's trust by integrating fully into the armed
group that lived in the forest's harsh mountainous terrain, or *la
montaña*. He participated with this first group in making the area
habitable. It was here that the ideological discourse of Marxism ran
up against the distinctive cultural beliefs of the indigenous communities. To live in la montaña was to inhabit a respected and feared
place of stories, myths, and ghosts. Marcos began to appreciate
how indigenous notions of time and history were radically different
from those of Westernized mestizos: "You didn't know what period
they were telling you about, they could be recounting a story which
might have occurred a week ago just as easily as five hundred years
ago or at the time when the world began."

The source of historical knowledge was the culture itself, not the
scientific reasoning and laws of causality, which are familiar tools of
Western philosophy. This history was passed on by the elders, not,
of course, in written form but in the manner of stories. Communities chose certain members who would be responsible for memo-

rizing their history. They would become important figures because they represented a kind of "talking book." Over time, Marcos noted that they told history very precisely, describing the conditions during the Porfiriato or before the Spaniards arrived as accurately as any modern textbook. In adjusting to this culture, Marcos discovered the need to listen. He commented that the Latin American Left knew how to talk, but not always how to listen. Learning the indigenous languages and understanding their own interpretations of their history and culture led to an appreciation of the political importance of patience. Learning how to wait was, for Marcos, the most difficult exercise, but one that was now imposed by the indigenous leaders and their method of organization.

By 1986 the group had twelve members, eleven indigenous and Marcos, who was later joined by two more mestizos. Support began to spread as the word was passed on through kinship lines that stretched throughout the Cañadas. Activities such as the provision of food and the gathering of weapons were carried out at night, which caused some suspicion that people were engaged in witchcraft. The Zapatistas had to become more open, at least within the ejidos, in order to avoid such accusations. By the end of 1986, however, support had grown to an extent whereby the armed group could freely enter their first village, at the invitation of one of the indigenous founders of the EZLN, *el viejo* Antonio. In explaining the popular support for the Zapatistas at this stage, it is important to emphasize the cultural basis of their struggle. Instead of arriving directly from the city or the university, the EZLN emerged out of la montaña, that magical world inhabited by the whole of Mayan history, by the spirits of ancestors, and by Zapata himself.

Even so, the political discourse within which Marcos had been formed was not readily understandable. "Your word is very hard, we don't understand it," he was told. The political message required a new language, and it was found in the convergence of the Zapatistas' critical interpretation of Mexican history and the indigenous people's own stories of humiliation, exploitation, and racism. Crucially, this convergence allowed for the latter to gain political direction over the movement. Through the translation of la palabra política into the various indigenous languages, the support base of the

EZLN inverted the traditional leader-masses relationship and provided a distinctive model of popular and democratic organization. Marcos recognized that a process of "cultural contamination" of Marxist ideas was occurring. "It obliged us [the mestizos] to adapt our politics and way of viewing our own historical process as well as the national political process." (See also Le Bot 1997:142–52.)

This point is important in establishing not only the novelty of the EZLN in the history of the Mexican Left, but also in challenging our understanding of the history of political ideas. Rather than assume a single point of origin that can be uncovered by good detective work (the methodology that, in 1995, allowed the Attorney General's Office (PGR) to reveal the mestizo and Marxist identity of Marcos), the EZLN invites a more complex, culturally sensitive, and multistranded analysis. In fact, the political origins of Marcos lose their significance as they give way to the histories and spirits of la montaña. Marcos recognized this fact very clearly:

We had a very fixed notion of reality, but when we ran up against it, our ideas were turned over. It is like that wheel over there, which rolls over the ground and becomes smoother as it goes, as it comes into contact with the people in the villages. It no longer has any connection to its origins. So, when they ask me: "What are you people? Marxists, Leninists, Castroites, Maoists, or what?" I answer that I don't know. I really do not know. We are the product of a hybrid, of a confrontation, of a collision in which, luckily I believe, we lost.

This "defeat" proved to be decisive, and the EZLN grew rapidly as a result. Fathers recruited sons, sons recruited brothers, cousins, and uncles. During the year of 1988 to 1989, the number of armed combatants grew from 80 to 1,300. Many ejidos that had participated in the ARIC saw their members join the Zapatistas, who began to organize their own committees of clandestine government and purchase guns. Money that had previously been used for religious fiestas was redirected to purchasing arms on the black market. There was no massive or sudden sale of arms to the EZLN. Instead, they gradually and clandestinely built up their own collection of weapons and munitions. By 1992 support for the Zapatistas had spread throughout the Cañadas of Ocosingo, Altamirano, and Las

Margaritas. The armed group was subordinated to the clandestine committees and entrusted with organizing armed self-defense units. The political decisions remained under the control of the indigenous communities. The EZLN was their secret, the secret of la montaña, the secret that would reveal its new word on January 1, 1994.

Chapter 7

NEOLIBERALISM AND REBELLION

The Quiptic had maintained its struggle for land by using the divisions within the state, but at the cost of seeing its leaders co-opted by Salinas. The land titling, like many gains of popular movements, was a double-edged sword. Although it represented the victory of fifteen years of struggle with the SRA and state government, it also established closer ties between federal government agencies and the ARIC while virtually every other organization in Chiapas was feeling the heavy hand of repression. The strength of this alliance would also be undermined by Salinas's own policy reforms, leading to the desertion of the ARIC by almost half its membership between 1989 and 1993. It was also a highly contentious alliance in the context of the 1988 presidential elections. Salinas claimed victory with just over 50 percent of the vote. However, there was widespread fraud, including a computer crash when his main contender, Cuauhtémoc Cárdenas, was ahead in the count. Cárdenas, who had split from the PRI in 1987 and headed a multiparty coalition, the National Democratic Front (FDN), received support from peasants in regions where the memory of his father's land reform program of the 1930s was still vividly alive (Gilly 1989). In Chiapas, his strongest support came from some communities affiliated to CIOAC, but neither faction of the OCEZ paid him much attention. For their part, the leaders of the ARIC were now married, for better or worse, to a president whose legitimacy was questioned from the very start.

Salinas came to power promising to modernize the rural sector by eliminating bureaucratic paternalism and establishing a new understanding between peasants and the state. Central to Salinas's strategy was the policy of pact making, or *concertación*. In part this was an inevitable response to the crisis of the president's legitimacy following the fraudulent elections of 1988. Salinas had to make new alliances and drive a wedge between the popular movements and Cuauhtémoc Cárdenas. But it also corresponded to Salinas's view of state-peasant relations, which he had formed during his own doctoral research in rural Tlaxcala in the late 1970s. He found that peasant support for the regime did not correspond to higher government spending, but instead depended on the efficacy of programs that involved communities in their implementation. In the context of fiscal restraint, the government would need to build new linkages to communities through targeted, productive projects. The issue was to get results in the short term, with the hope of regaining credibility and thereby defusing potential or actual political opposition. The National Solidarity Program (PRONASOL) was established by Salinas in his first few weeks in office and became the main initiative for the attempted modernization of state-peasant relations.

The PRONASOL also accompanied the implementation of neoliberal economic reforms under Salinas. These reforms involved the privatization of state-owned corporations, trade liberalization, and restructuring of government agencies and budgets. Although each of these measures had begun under the de la Madrid administration, Salinas accelerated the process in the belief that Mexico needed to attract private investment from domestic and foreign sources in order to become internationally competitive and financially stable. The centerpiece of this strategy was the North American Free Trade Agreement (NAFTA), which united the economies of Mexico, the United States, and Canada in a single trading bloc. In the countryside, the neoliberal reforms implied a significant shift in state-peasant relations. The dismantling of government agencies, the reduction of credit, the removal of guaranteed crop prices, and the opening to cheaper imports were to have deleterious effects on the majority of peasants and their organizations. Constitutional reforms to legislation regarding land tenure also raised fears that the ejido sector would succumb to privatization and lead to a reconcentration of agricultural land. However, the ways these reforms have been implemented, resisted, and negotiated vary widely between regions. Local political conditions shape the perception and actions of those affected by the new laws and policies. In Chiapas, these conditions included continuing repression, the dislocations caused by the neoliberal reforms, and the limits of concertación. In this context, legal organizations such as the OCEZ, CIOAC, and

ARIC, already wracked by internal divisions and facing continued repression, were clearly unable to provide much resistance. That would instead come from the EZLN.

The Repression Continues

When a new governor took office in December 1988 many hoped that a more conciliatory approach would replace the repression. In his electoral campaign Patrocinio González Garrido echoed Salinas's call for the modernization of state-peasant relations. However, the first three months of his administration saw the assassination of several members of independent organizations, including two of the principal peasant leaders in the state: Sebastián Pérez Núñez of CIOAC and Arturo Albores of the OCEZ-CNPA. González Garrido denied government involvement, but human rights activists criticized the impunity of these and other actions. Nevertheless, the governor was forced to address the agrarian question.

In 1989 seven cases were targeted for negotiated solutions. These involved the return of communal lands in Venustiano Carranza, Nicolás Ruiz, and Villa Corzo and the titling of ejido land in El Carrizal (Ocosingo), San Sebastián Bachajón (Chilón), Unión Calera (Arriaga), and San Juan Chamula. Although these cases were partially resolved, there were another 547 cases still awaiting resolution in 1989, representing 22,598 land claimants (SRA 1989). Furthermore, although the governor had to deal with independent organizations in resolving these cases, once the agreements had been made no further opening was offered. On the contrary, as land conflicts continued to occur throughout the state, the governor reverted to the traditionally repressive tactics of his predecessors.

For example, several settlements in the municipality of Chiapa de Corzo were destroyed by state police and landowners on two separate occasions in April 1990 and April 1991. Members of the OCEZ-centro claimed the disputed lands were in fact covered by a presidential resolution in their favor. In June 1990 six people were injured when private gunmen shot at a crowd of over 100 cane producers who were demanding full payment for cane delivered to the Pujiltic sugar mill. In July of the same year women from the highland settlement of San Felipe Ecatepec staged a hunger strike in Mexico City's Zócalo to demand a hearing with the president. They protested the repression of their organization, the National Coordinator of Indigenous Pueblos (CNPI) at the hands of the state government. In October 1990 two members of OCEZ-centro were injured when unknown assailants opened fire on a peaceful march from Venustiano Carranza to Tuxtla Gutiérrez (Horizontes 1990, 1991a, 1991b). At the same time, thousands of mainly Tzotzil Indians in highland communities continued to be expelled by village caciques for their political and religious dissidence.[1]

In July 1991 a protest march by 300 peasants from Marqués de Comillas was broken up by police in Palenque using clubs and tear gas grenades. Seven leaders were arrested and forced to sign confessions linking them to Central American guerrillas and drug trafficking. They were protesting the confiscation of timber by state police and the corruption of municipal authorities. This protest gave birth to a new organization in Marqués de Comillas, the Independent Regional Peasant Movement (MOCRI), which subsequently affiliated with CNPA (Harvey 1992a). Finally, in September 1991 the parish priest of Simojovel, Joel Padrón, was arrested on charges of robbery, damages to property, and provocations. The roots of what became a political conflict between the state government and the diocese of San Cristóbal were to be found in the type of conflicts generated by the PRA. Peasants belonging to a CNC group claimed that members of CIOAC had evicted them from their land with the help of Joel Padrón. The state government attempted to condition the release of Padrón to a series of commitments from Bishop Ruiz to order the eviction of alleged land invasions and declare his opposition to actions against private property. Ruiz was also requested to drop charges against police for the illegal detention of Joel Padrón and to order Padrón to leave Chiapas upon Padrón's release (Aguilar Zinser 1991). Although these conditions were not accepted and charges against Padrón were eventually dropped, they were a clear indication of the governor's openness to the demands of ranchers and landowners. They also reaffirmed the active role played in the defense of indigenous people by the diocese and its human rights center, the Centro de Derechos Humanos

Fray Bartolomé de las Casas, formed less than six months after González Garrido had assumed office.

Political pressure against the church increased in 1993. In March of that year two soldiers were killed in the Tzotzil community of San Isidro El Ocotal in the Central Highlands. Members of the community feared that the clandestine use of local timber would be discovered by the army, and the two soldiers were mistakenly identified as forestry agents.[2] The Fray Bartolomé center denounced the killings but also denounced the abuse of human rights carried out by soldiers in the arrest of thirteen suspects who were allegedly subjected to torture. Police returned to the community on two further occasions, in April and May 1993, and carried out further illegal arrests and beatings. The original thirteen were eventually released without charges being brought against them (Minnesota Advocates for Human Rights 1993:10–16). During the rest of 1993 political pressure against the diocese of San Cristóbal increased, culminating in the efforts of the papal representative to remove Samuel Ruiz from his position in Chiapas. The outbreak of the rebellion frustrated this move as Ruiz became a key mediator in negotiations between the EZLN and the government.

The Rural Reforms in Chiapas

The analysis of Salinas's rural reforms in Chiapas must start with an understanding of the conditions of the social sector.[3] Tables 7.1 and 7.2 provide a general panorama for the state of Chiapas, using official data from 1988 (INEGI 1991). From this data we can gain a picture of the relatively poor level of development of ejidos and comunidades agrarias in Chiapas. Virtually all of the sector is dedicated to rain-fed agriculture. If we calculate that each of the almost 200,000 ejidatarios or comuneros has five or six dependents, the population we are referring to is over 1 million persons, occupying a little over 3 million hectares of land, of which only 40.8 percent is classified as good for agricultural use. Maize is clearly the principal crop for most ejidos and comunidades agrarias, followed by coffee (table 7.3). However, the figures do not indicate the combination

Table 7.1. The Social Sector in Chiapas, 1988

Number of ejidos and comunidades agrarias	1,714
Total number of ejidatarios and comuneros	193,515
Land surface in social sector (hectares)	3,130,892
Share of total land area in Chiapas	41.4%

Source: INEGI (1991). Note that the number of ejidos and comunidades agrarias in Chiapas increased by 358 to a total of 2,072 during 1989 to 1992 (PROCEDE, 1993:10).

Table 7.2. Land Use in the Social Sector

	Hectares	% of sector
Agriculture	1,278,147	40.8
Forestry	700,381	22.4
Pasture	923,182	29.5
Other uses	229,182	7.3
Rain-fed area	1,225,831	95.9
Irrigated area	52,316	4.1

Source: INEGI (1991).

of crops within each ejido. Survey data for 1990 also revealed that 44.6 percent of ejidatarios possessed between 0.1 and 4.0 hectares and 42.0 percent had plots between 4.1 and 10.0 hectares (SARH-CEPAL 1992:3). In the central highlands, the average plot size was 2 hectares.

In terms of opportunities to convert to new cash crops, it should be noted that the sixteen ejidos that produced soybeans were all located in the more developed Soconusco region. Ten percent of ejidos in the Soconusco also had access to irrigation. Regarding the limited use of inputs (see table 7.4), we can add that the category of "public services" tends to present a somewhat distorted picture of reality. This rubric includes electricity, drinking water, and paved and unpaved roads. The fact that three-quarters of the ejidos reported that they had unpaved roads (1,224) hardly constitutes access to public services. A more accurate indication is given by the

Table 7.3. Principal Crops in the Social Sector

Principal crop cultivated	Number of ejidos and comunidades agrarias
Maize	1,264
Coffee	349
Sugarcane	19
Soybeans	16
Beans	8
Green vegetables	8
Rice	3

Source: INEGI (1991).

Table 7.4. Availability of Inputs in the Social Sector

Inputs	Number of ejidos and comunidades agrarias	% of sector
Farm installations	495	28.9
Tractors	318	18.6
Agroindustrial equipment	206	12.0
Credit	951	55.5
Public services	1,390	81.1

Source: INEGI (1991).

low proportion that had paved roads (10 percent). Installation of electricity and drinking water was said to benefit 50 and 35 percent of ejidos, respectively.

According to the 1988 survey 62.5 percent of the rural social sector in Mexico received credit in 1988. In Chiapas the figure was given at 55.5 percent. The regions with the lowest proportion of credit were the central highlands and Lacandon forest (30 and 38 percent, respectively). However, the validity of these figures is contradicted by other sources. More recent data show that, at a national level, during the period of 1985 to 1989 only 22.2 percent of ejidatarios and comuneros had access to credit each year, falling to 16.3 percent in 1990. In fact, between 1985 and 1990, 62 percent of producers in the social sector had no access whatsoever to agricultural credit (SARH-CEPAL 1992:19). In Chiapas the number of producers with credit for planting fell from an annual average of 20.4 percent in 1985 to 1989 to 12.7 in 1990, while only 5.7 percent of producers received credit for machinery in 1985 to 1990. Similarly, the CNC claimed that in 1987 only 43 percent of ejidos in Mexico received credit (Equipo Pueblo/Instituto Maya 1988:49). Moreover, the INEGI survey gives us no indication of the amount of credit each ejido or comunidad agraria was said to have received.

At the same time that production in basic grains was left more and more in the hands of small farmers and ejidatarios, private sector commercial agriculture searched for new ways to maintain its profitability. Besides the coffee sector, elite agriculture was also in crisis during the 1980s in Chiapas. A small number of growers turned to new crops such as soybeans, peanuts, sorghum, and tobacco, but this represented only 4 percent of land under commercial cultivation (Thompson González, García Aguilar, and Castillo Huerta 1988:225–30). The cattle industry was also hit by the combined effects of price ceilings on beef, a reduction in the availability of bank credit, and increasing input costs. Ranchers responded by selling off as much cattle as they could, resulting in a steady decline in the size of Chiapas's herd between 1982 and 1990.

Reforming the Coffee Sector

For many years small coffee growers sold their crop to a state agency, the Mexican Coffee Institute (INMECAFE). The INMECAFE was established in 1958 to carry out research and provide technical support. As part of Echeverría's strategy to modernize small-scale production and increase the state's presence in regional markets, the functions of INMECAFE were expanded in 1973. It was given a central role in organizing and financing coffee production, as well as guaranteeing the purchase and export of the harvest. By the end of the 1970s it had managed to displace several important intermediaries and to have purchased half of domestic supply. In Chiapas, this conjuncture allowed for the emergence of new producer cooperatives and unions of ejidos in both the central highlands and Lacandon forest.

With the economic crisis of the 1980s the position of INMECAFE declined. Its share of the market fell from 44 percent in 1982 to 1983 to just 9.6 percent in 1987 to 1988 (Hernández 1991:62). Like many of the state agencies in this period, it suffered from internal inefficiencies, corruption, and mismanagement. By 1988 INMECAFE had an accumulated debt of approximately U.S.$90 million. The response of the Salinas government in 1989 was to begin the process of privatization. The INMECAFE immediately withdrew from purchasing and marketing and reduced its provision of technical assistance. Although the reform was originally designed to include the producer organizations in the transfer of infrastructure, the plan lacked the necessary political will and much of the infrastructure lay idle or passed into private ownership.

In 1988 there were 194,000 coffee growers in Mexico, cultivating over 560,000 hectares in twelve states. The skewed nature of production units in this sector is well known: 71.3 percent of growers have plots of fewer than two hectares. Another 20.6 percent have areas of between two and five hectares, whereas just 2 percent have over ten hectares (Hernández 1991:52). Chiapas, Mexico's principal coffee-producing state, presents a similar pattern. Here 73,742 growers occupy 228,264 hectares of land. Ninety-one percent of producers have fewer than five hectares, whereas 116 private owners possess 12 percent of the area under coffee cultivation (table 7.5). In the Lacandon forest, of the almost 17,000 producers, 93 percent have plots of fewer than two hectares (Hernández 1994b).

In June 1989 the International Coffee Organization failed to agree on production quotas, causing the world price to fall by 50 percent. In the ensuing period the Mexican government did not support efforts by other Latin American countries to reestablish a quota system and increase the price paid to producers. Another consequence of Salinas's macroeconomic reforms that hurt coffee producers was the overvalued peso. Potential export earnings, which might have offset lower world prices, were lost as a result. Between December 1987 and December 1993 domestic inflation increased by 89.3 percent while the exchange rate increased by under 50 percent. As a result, the cost of inputs rose faster than the principal source of income. In addition, in the absence of INMECAFE, marketing costs had to be absorbed by the producers

Table 7.5. Distribution of Coffee Producers by Plot Size

Plot size	Chiapas	Mexico
0–2 hectares	48,762	194,538
2–5 hectares	18,248	64,377
5–10 hectares	5,102	17,881
10–20 hectares	1,202	4,291
20–50 hectares	208	808
50–100 hectares	104	246
Over 100 hectares	116	178
Total	73,742	282,319

Source: INMECAFE (1992).

themselves, or alternatively through the reappearance of unregulated private intermediaries, or *coyotes* (Hernández 1994b).

Following the 1989 crisis it took over three years of negotiations and mobilizations by producer groups before the government agreed to an emergency support program. With less income and the simultaneous reduction of credit, thousands of growers were unable to invest in their crop. Both productivity and total output in the social sector fell by around 35 percent between 1989 and 1993. On average, small producers suffered a 70 percent drop in income in the same period (*La Jornada,* January 23, 1994, p. 47). Most producers were caught in a cycle of debt and poverty. Unable to repay loans due to the fall in prices and income, they became ineligible for new loans. The accumulation of debts in this sector reached approximately U.S.$270 million by the end of 1993. In these conditions thousands of small growers in Ocosingo, Las Margaritas, and highland Chiapas abandoned production in 1989 to 1993.

Basic Grains and Trade Liberalization

Another of the institutional reforms concerned the restructuring of state intervention in support of basic grain production and marketing. Chiapas is one of Mexico's largest maize-producing states, and it is the state that "exports" the most maize into the national market. The reform process began with the onset of the debt crisis in 1982. Under the administration of Miguel de la Madrid, governmental subsidies to the agricultural sector decreased on average by 13 percent annually, after having increased by 12.5 percent per year during the 1970s. Maize producers faced higher input costs and declining access to credit. By 1987 BANRURAL provided credit for only 37 percent of the area under maize cultivation and 43 percent in the case of beans. In contrast, it financed 52 percent of the land area dedicated to soybeans and 49 percent of sorghum cultivation (Robles 1988). Peso devaluation made inputs more costly, but producers were partly protected by the guaranteed prices that more or less increased in line with inflation in 1983 to 1986 (Hewitt de Alcántara 1992:10–12). Nevertheless, in order to pay their debts, most small producers had to sell their crops immediately after harvest. With inflation at over 100 percent and official prices adjusted only twice a year, this meant that, in practice, producers were forced to sell at 20 or 30 percent below the real value. It was this situation that led to producer protests in several states in 1984 to 1986, principally Chihuahua, Nayarit, and Chiapas (Equipo Pueblo/Instituto Maya 1988; Hernández Aguilar 1986).

This situation further deteriorated with the signing of the Economic Solidarity Pact (PSE) in December 1987.[4] The pact was primarily designed to control inflation, which reached almost 200 percent in 1987. The various renewals of the pact were aimed at controlling wages and prices, as well as limiting further devaluation of the peso. Although inflation was brought down to under 20 percent by 1991, the agricultural sector suffered disproportionately. The real value of guaranteed maize prices fell behind the rate of increase in input costs. As a result, the proportion of maize producers operating at a loss jumped from 43 percent in 1987 to 65 percent in 1988 (Hewitt de Alcántara 1992:13).

In Chiapas, the withdrawal of state support had a negative effect not only on output and productivity but also on the environment. In the Cañadas of the Lacandon forest many peasants, unable to capitalize their production, continued to clear forested land for subsistence needs. Tropical soils are notoriously unsuited for sustainable agriculture once the biomass has been destroyed. The land may be good for just three or four crops before it is turned into pasture for grazing and the process of deforestation begins anew. Thus, although the land area in Chiapas dedicated to maize increased by 20.6 percent between 1982 and 1987 (from 600,374 to 795,053 hectares), output of this crop in the same period fell by 19.6 percent (from 1.5 million to 1.25 million metric tons).[5] The same trend was observed for beans. Land area increased by 10 percent, but output dropped by 18 percent. Coffee displayed a slight increase in output, but this is probably explained by the performance of the large plantations (Thompson González, García Aguilar, and Castillo Huerta 1988: 225–30).

The Salinas administration accelerated these trends with a series of institutional reforms in 1989. These reforms were also closely related to the World Bank's prescriptions for Mexican agriculture. The bank conditioned the disbursement of new structural adjustment loans to a radical overhaul of the agricultural sector, recommending the privatization of state-owned enterprises and the gradual elimination of price supports and other input subsidies (McMichael and Myhre 1991; Robles and Moguel 1990).

On the positive side the reforms dealt a blow to corrupt functionaries and inefficient operating procedures. The new discourse of concertación was initially welcomed by peasant organizations, who had been complaining about bureaucratic delays and political manipulation for many years. However, the reforms were not accompanied by the type of financial and marketing support required to reactivate the rural economy. Instead, in most cases, they appeared simply as a means to abandon small-scale producers, all within the discourse of shared responsibilities and concertación.[6] As a result, although peasants were generally glad to see the disappearance in 1989 of the notoriously corrupt ANAGSA, it also left many without crop insurance. In the same year BANRURAL stopped all lending to producers in default. This decision particularly affected those maize producers who until the pact had managed to maintain productivity levels of the previous decade. New credit provided through PRONASOL (later known as Solidaridad) covered only half the production costs in this sector.

The transition to the free market in rural Mexico was governed by macroeconomic decision making far removed from the realities of the peasants. By the end of 1989 it was clear that the future of the agricultural sector would be subordinated to the economic goals of the Salinas administration: the reduction of inflation via wage and price controls, privatization of state enterprises, and trade liberalization (Otero 1996). After 1989 only maize and beans continued to receive a guaranteed price. For other grains, such as sorghum, soybeans, rice, barley, wheat, and safflower, guaranteed prices were replaced with a new scheme whereby prices were fixed through negotiations between the government, producers, and buyers. However, the new scheme was implemented at the same time that import licenses were removed. This had catastrophic effects for many ejidatarios. In 1990, for example, thousands of soybean and sorghum producers in Sonora, Guanajuato, and Tamaulipas were unable to sell their crops due to the sudden inflow of cheaper grains from the United States. Many of them protested by seizing government warehouses and blocking highways. In the case of sorghum, the final price that producers received was 20 percent lower than what had been agreed upon through the new scheme. Many switched back to maize production as all grain prices were depressed by the availability of cheap imports. This phenomenon extended to the entire agricultural sector (Interviews with representatives of UNORCA, Celaya, Guanajuato, September 1991).

The relative protection of maize and beans production was finally subordinated to the imperatives of free trade. Despite opposition from all national peasant organizations, the two crops were included in the negotiations leading to NAFTA. Recognizing maize and beans as "sensitive crops" in the new free trade area, NAFTA provided for a fifteen-year phaseout of tariffs and import quotas. The rationale for NAFTA was that each country and region should produce goods and services in which they have comparative advantages. This argument implied that over 2 million small producers in Mexico could not continue to survive as maize producers. Average yields in Mexico are 1.7 tons per hectare, compared to 6.9 tons in the United States. Disparities in terms of technological development, subsidies, infrastructure, and climatological factors also place Mexican producers at a great disadvantage (Calva 1993).

These points were obviously not lost on the Zapatistas, who timed their rebellion to coincide with the entry into effect of NAFTA on January 1, 1994.

In determining how many maize producers would lose from free trade, the crucial issue became the fixing of new pricing mechanisms. Under NAFTA the Mexican government decided that guaranteed prices would have to be phased out, allowing the international price to gradually take its place. After several months of debate, in October 1993 Salinas announced the Direct Rural Support Program (PROCAMPO), described by the SARH as "a new support program for the Mexican farm sector" (SARH 1993).

The PROCAMPO made over 3.3 million producers of seven crops eligible for direct payments on a per hectare basis.[7] All those who had planted one of these crops during the period between December 1990 and December 1993 and who had been included in a national directory compiled by SARH during 1993 could request payment of 330 new pesos (equivalent to U.S.$103) for each hectare cultivated during the autumn-winter crop cycle of 1993 to 1994. The first payments were due to be made at the time of harvest in March 1994. In fact, they were paid just a few days prior to the August 1994 national elections. One of the distinguishing features of PROCAMPO is that it included 2.2 million farmers who produce solely for their own family's subsistence needs and had been isolated from official support, especially credit.

At first sight it would appear that peasants in the highlands and Lacandon forest stood to gain from PROCAMPO. These are maize deficit areas and the lowering of maize prices should theoretically lead to a reduction of hunger, especially in the highlands where yields can be as low as 0.5 tons per hectare. The most negatively affected groups instead appear to be small and medium-sized ejidos in the Frailesca and Grijalva valley, who depend on maize sales for a significant part of their income. This is not a small sector. The proportion of total maize output in Chiapas that is sold on the market is twice as high as that consumed by the family unit. According to the Ministry of Agriculture and Water Resources–Economic Commission for Latin America and the Caribbean (SARH-CEPAL) survey, 67 percent of maize production within the social sector of Chiapas is sold on the market, while 33 percent goes to household consumption (SARH-CEPAL 1992:92). The North American Free Trade Agreement and lower maize prices will therefore have a direct effect on thousands of producers that until 1994 depended on the guaranteed price.

In the case of poorer producers in the central highlands and Lacandon forest, the potentially positive effects of falling prices were contingent on political factors. In many remote districts local caciques exercised monopolistic control over transportation and marketing. Prices in Ocosingo or Altamirano would not come to reflect international prices at all if local merchants continued to regulate the amount of maize available for purchase and at what price. In the absence of governmental regulation one possible alternative was to help grassroots organizations develop their own food purchasing and distribution cooperatives, but this required the types of political changes that have been so effectively resisted in Chiapas.

For its part, the PROCAMPO subsidy was generally seen as a palliative. The payments were simply used for any of several urgent necessities, such as obtaining food, clothing, or medical attention, rather than providing a stimulus for production. In this way the subsidy tended to find its way back into the hands of the local merchants and private intermediaries, who in turn controlled prices and the distribution of basic goods. In sum, without political change, the new pricing policy would benefit merchants more than rural producers or consumers.

Solidaridad and Political Control

The rural reforms were accompanied by the further expansion of PRONASOL, which in 1992 was incorporated by the Ministry of Social Development (SEDESOL). Although Chiapas received more funds from Solidaridad than any other state, several observers noted that the resources were insufficient to ameliorate extensive and increasing poverty. A central limitation was that support for the production and marketing needs of the social sector was not given sufficient emphasis within the program.

According to official figures, in 1990 over 50 percent of the population in Chiapas suffered from malnutrition, one of the highest

Table 7.6. Indices of Poverty in the Lacandon Forest

	Percentage of homes without		
	Electricity	Drinking water	Drainage
Republic of Mexico	12.5	20.6	36.4
State of Chiapas	33.1	41.6	58.8
Municipality of Ocosingo	67.9	49.2	60.2
Municipality of Altamirano	75.0	48.8	43.7
Municipality of Las Margaritas	66.4	72.7	38.5

Sources: Data for Mexico and Chiapas are from INEGI (1992). Data for Ocosingo, Altamirano, and Las Margaritas are drawn from the Consejo Nacional de Población (CONAPO) as cited in *La Jornada*, January 3, 1994, p. 11.

rates in the country. The state's illiteracy rate (30 percent) was three times higher than the national average, while the proportion of children who did not complete primary school was 62 percent, compared to 21 percent nationally. Overcrowded housing conditions affected around 80 percent of homes in the municipalities of Ocosingo, Altamirano, and Las Margaritas. Other services were equally lacking (table 7.6).

Solidaridad expenditure in Chiapas grew by 130 percent in 1989 to 1990, 50 percent in 1990 to 1991, 20 percent in 1991 to 1992, and a further 1 percent in 1992 to 1993. Most of the funding was designed to improve social welfare and public works, with only 12 percent going to support productive activities. This is especially important if we consider the impact of the rural reforms referred to earlier. In fact, according to the National Coordinator of Coffee-Growing Organizations (CNOC) the amount of credit that coffee growers received from Solidaridad in 1993 was 13 percent less than in 1988 when INMECAFE was still operating (Cano 1994:6).[8] Landlessness and unemployment, especially among the young, were not cushioned by Solidaridad. Each project had a low investment ceiling, allowing the government to reach a larger population with small projects but reducing their overall social impact. Proponents of a new antipoverty program argued that larger projects, comanaged with representative local and regional social organizations, should be designed to attack the structural roots of poverty rather than its symptoms. Such a strategy would also bolster peasant organizations as counterweights to local elites. The Zapatista rebellion lent weight to this position by demonstrating both the limitations of Solidaridad itself and the need for a political opening to the benefit of peasant organizations in the state.

Although Chiapas ranked first in the number of local Solidarity committees (8,824, or 8.26 percent of the national total), according to Moguel (1994) the figure was misleading because it included any type of group that received funds from the program. Most of these (7,474) participated in basic infrastructure and social welfare projects (Dignified Schools, Municipal Funds, and Children in Solidarity). These tended to either have a short time span between the disbursement of funds until the end of the project, or—as in the case of Municipal Funds—were very tightly controlled by local caciques. One of the factors that contributed to divisions and unrest within indigenous communities was precisely the manipulation of Solidaridad funds by municipal presidents loyal to the PRI and the state governor.

This manipulation was promoted by governor González Garrido. For example, one of the programs designed to support subsistence farmers was the Credit on Demand scheme (Crédito a la Palabra).[9] This plan involved the disbursement of interest-free loans on an individual basis (principally to maize and beans producers) that, when paid back, were meant to be recycled in the form of new loans and investment in community welfare projects. Chiapas had the distinction of being the state with the highest loan repayment rate. In 1992, 88 percent of loans were repaid and over 70 percent were recovered in 1993. However, the supposed benefits were not distributed equitably. Although loan repayment was highest in the central highlands and Lacandon forest regions, the share of the state's Crédito a la Solidaridad these regions received fell between 1990 and 1993 from 23 to 16 percent and from 17 to 6 percent, respectively.

Part of the explanation for this paradox was the governor's political control of the program. In other parts of Mexico the repayment of Solidaridad loans was used to generate new sources of financing for community projects. In Chiapas, by contrast, the governor created a state-level fund directly under his control. The disbursement of credit in this way favored political allies in the PRI and CNC, strengthening the control exercised by municipal presidents and marginalizing independent organizations. A state-level Ministry of Community Participation, staffed by loyal PRI and CNC leaders, was set up in early 1992 in an effort to institutionalize these arrangements.

The governor also dismissed officials who attempted to support local independent organizations. For example, in 1990 the regional director of the INI in Las Margaritas was forced to resign after assisting the Unión de Ejidos de la Selva in its efforts to gain Solidaridad funding to purchase a coffee-processing plant from INMECAFE. Then in March 1992 three top INI officials in Chiapas were arrested: the state director, and the regional director and treasurer for the Tzeltal area. They were accused of corruption in the use of funds to support small-scale livestock activities in Ocosingo and Chilón. Local peasant leaders came out in their defense, arguing that their only crime was to have supported the projects of independent groups. Although they were later released, none could return to their previous posts (*La Jornada,* March 21, 1992, p. 13).[10] The relative openness of Regional Solidarity Funds in Chiapas to independent organizations was also a source of irritation for González Garrido.

Solidaridad as a whole was not such a threat to González Garrido as he had feared. Yet his political aims compounded the program's own limitations and contributed to the anger that would be directed by the EZLN against municipal presidents. One of the immediate repercussions of the uprising was the resignation of the state delegate of SEDESOL in January 1994. The new interim governor, Javier López Moreno, also announced his intention to meet with municipal authorities to investigate the misuse of Solidaridad funds. During the first week of February 1994 several town halls were occupied by peasant organizations calling for the dismissal of municipal presidents.[11]

Ejido Reform in Chiapas

The most controversial of Salinas's reforms concerned the status of the ejido within Mexico's agrarian structure. In November 1991 he sent a bill to Congress entailing several modifications to Article 27 of the Constitution that were adopted just two months later. They were followed in late February 1992 by the passage of a new Agrarian Law to establish the new regulatory framework for the social sector. For the government the modifications were seen as necessary steps to attract private investment in agriculture and increase productivity and welfare. Four of the main changes embodied in the new Agrarian Law were the following:

1. Ejidatarios were given the legal right to purchase, sell, rent, or use as collateral the individual plots and communal lands that make up the ejido.
2. Private companies were allowed to purchase land in accordance with the legal limits ascribed to different crops. At a maximum, a company with at least twenty-five individual shareholders could purchase holdings of up to twenty-five times the size of the individually permitted limit.
3. The reforms also allowed for new associations between private investors and ejidatarios, the latter providing land as "T" shares in joint ventures.
4. In line with the reform's intention of guaranteeing security for private property, the sections of Article 27 that allowed for peasants to petition for land redistribution were deleted from the new law.

The debate surrounding the ejido reform raised several concerns. First, it was feared that the sale of ejido plots could lead to a reconcentration of land. Although the new law expressly forbids latifundios in Mexico, it also potentially allows for private companies of at least twenty-five individuals to own farms of up to 2,500 hectares of irrigated land, 5,000 hectares in the case of rain-fed areas, 10,000 hectares of good-quality pasture land, or 20,000 hectares of forested land. A company made up of twenty-five ranchers could also feasibly own an area equivalent to 12,500 hectares. In order for ejido land to be made available for private ownership, however, the assembly of ejido members must approve the measure by a two-thirds majority. Some commentators noted that the traditional control and manipulation of assemblies by ejido authorities could lead to forced votes in favor of privatization (Moguel 1992b:273). In Chiapas the potential for land reconcentration exists in the politically powerful ranchers' associations, representing over 12,000 *ganaderos* organized in sixty local associations. Ranchers applauded the reforms to Article 27, arguing that greater security in land tenure would attract foreign investors wishing to create new meat-processing plants in the region. The competition for land with indigenous peasants should be understood in this context (*El Financiero,* June 10, 1993:46).

Second, the use of land as collateral or in associations with private investors involved the risk of farm foreclosures and loss of land rights. The effective exclusion of much of the social sector from traditional sources of credit could influence the decisions of ejidatarios in putting land up as collateral. Women were placed at greatest risk because the male head of household could unilaterally decide how to dispose of what was family patrimony. The only special right women received was the first option to buy the ejido land their spouses decided to sell. In Chiapas it is possible that wealthier ejidatarios might concentrate land within communities as a result of foreclosures.

Finally, it was feared that most of the unresolved land petitions *(rezago agrario)* would simply be rejected. The government's claim that there was no more land to be distributed was contested by several organizations. Some called for an investigation into private holdings that allegedly exceeded the legal limits. It is significant that this demand was taken up by the peasant movement in Chiapas and reasserted in light of the Zapatista rebellion (*La Jornada,* February 1, 1994, p. 5). In fact, rather than providing for the immediate expropriation and redistribution of excess holdings, the new law gave private owners one year to sell off excess property (Moguel 1992b:271). The end of land reform in Chiapas and other states also canceled out the hope of a piece of land for thousands of peasants. In this respect, we should distinguish between effects that are directly measurable in terms of land purchases and those that operate more at the level of expectations, hopes, and fears. It seems clear that the end of land reform constituted a symbolic break with the past but one that offered no guarantees of improvement for the future.

As in most areas of rural Mexico, the immediate response to Salinas's announcement of ejido reform was one of fear and confu-

2. CNPA Protesting
the Reforms to
Article 27 in the
Zócalo, Mexico
City, December
1991

sion. Information about the precise nature of the reforms was
scarce and the immediate problems facing ejidatarios were increasing debts, falling prices for their crops, and the lack of credit. However, two demonstrations against the reforms were held in December 1991 and January 1992. The first was led by the OCEZ-centro in
Venustiano Carranza, the second by the ARIC Unión de Uniones in
Ocosingo. The members of the ARIC also made a formal commitment not to sell ejido land.

The diocese of San Cristóbal also invited different organizations
to reflect on the reforms at a special workshop held in January 1992.
The workshop concluded that the ejido reform was part of the
government's general strategy in favor of private capital; that the
spirit of the original law had been broken as the public interest was
subordinated to individual interests; that the reconcentration of
land in few hands was likely; and that the reform reflected the
objectives of the proposed NAFTA. In political, economic, and cul-

tural terms, the workshop saw only a deterioration of existing conditions. A more specific fear related to the deepening of divisions within communities as village caciques moved to buy up land from poorer neighbors (Taller de San Cristóbal 1992).

The impact of the ejido reform began to be felt during 1993. By the end of the year only 100 of the state's 2,072 ejidos had requested the assistance of the government's Program for the Certification of Ejido Land Rights and the Titling of Urban House Plots (PRO-CEDE) (Interview, representatives of the Registro Agrario Nacional, Mexico City, January 1994). The main problem with the reform concerned the lack of solution to the rezago agrario. Although in 1992 the state government announced that it would purchase land in order to deal with the rezago, the program did not advance. Peasant leaders blamed the delays on bureaucratic inefficiency, the reluctance of private owners to sell, and collusion between functionaries and landowners.

Crisis in the Lacandon Forest

In the Cañadas the lack of definitive titles was a major problem for many communities. Not only did the lack of legal definition increase the possibility of eviction by landowners or other peasant groups, it also restricted access to credit. This obstacle hindered those ejidos that began to devote more land area to livestock in the 1980s (Leyva Solano and Ascencio Franco 1993:274). The lack of secure titles further weakened the social organizations located in the area of rebellion.

The ARIC was particularly affected. During 1992 its leaders proposed several measures to deal with the agrarian problem. In addition to its existing legal petitions, the ARIC offered to buy land and asked for the redistribution of private estates that had been declared bankrupt. None of these proposals was taken up by the state government. For the president of the ARIC, the reason was a familiar one:

The agrarian authorities are friends of the landowners. They carry out their studies and reject our petitions. In this past year we have got nowhere. The landowners are refusing to sell and the Agraria says the ranchers all have documents protecting themselves from expropriation. This is the case in Patihuitz, Avellanal and La Estrella. (Interview, San Cristóbal de las Casas, January 1993)

It is no coincidence that the EZLN was able to recruit peasants in precisely these subregions of the Lacandon forest. The economic desperation of a new generation of young and landless Indians was the product of the lack of alternatives to colonizing more land. However, by the end of the 1980s the expansion of the agricultural frontier had reached its limits. These limits were imposed by three interrelated processes.

The first of these processes concerned the nature of the ranching in the Lacandon forest. Private ranchers in Ocosingo engaged in extensive livestock-raising techniques with little capital investment. The alternative of a more intensive form of ranching required credit, technical assistance, access to new technologies, and, from the ranchers' perspective, security of land tenure. Because none of these factors existed, the survival of the livestock economy depended on turning more land into pasture in a process similar to that seen in the central valleys in previous decades, thus placing a limit on the cleared land available for agriculture.

A second limitation resulted from the overcrowding of available ejido land. The population of Ocosingo, the region's largest municipality, more than doubled in 1970 to 1980 (from 34,356 to 69,757 inhabitants) and grew by another 56 percent in the following decade, reaching over 120,000 by 1990 (Ascencio Franco and Leyva Solano 1992:204). In addition, between 1980 and 1990 demographic growth in Ocosingo exceeded that for the state as a whole. Whereas the average annual rate for Chiapas in this period was 4.4 percent, the rate for Ocosingo was 5.6 percent.[12] This growth greatly increased pressure on available land, obliging new colonists, often the children from existing ejidos, to clear new land further into the forest. The lack of credit, marketing, and technical assistance prevented the ejidos from increasing the productivity of the land already under cultivation. Colonization was left as the only alternative, especially given the precariousness of land tenure and the delays within the agrarian bureaucracy in approving petitions

for the extension of ejidos *(ampliaciones)* that might have incorporated more of the young families and new colonists. As a result, the
subregions of the Cañadas of Ocosingo that suffered most were
those settled in the first wave of migration in the 1930s and 1940s.
This hardship was reflected in the growing inability of communities in the subregions of Pantihuiz and Estrella to maintain self-
sufficiency in maize and beans. Whereas the more recently colo-
nized subregion of Betania was able to produce small surpluses by
1990, in Pantihuiz, maize and beans production were 17 percent
and 24 percent lower than levels of consumption (Ascencio Franco
1995:371). Even worse, due to the unavailability of land elsewhere,
the older settlements were marked by higher rates of population
growth as the sons and daughters of ejidatarios remained at home
where they could at least survive through the support of extended
families and temporary migration. Overcrowding and disputes
over access to a dwindling land base created a growing sense of
desperation, particularly among younger members of communities. For them, the reforms to Article 27 ended any hope of gaining
access to land.[13]

A third limitation that affected these communities was the decision in 1989 to impose a ban on timber exploitation in the entire
Lacandon forest. This measure was taken by the state and federal
government in the face of pressure from environmentalists concerned by the alarming rate of depletion of the forest. The ban even
included the chopping of trees for domestic use, which led to several conflicts with police and forestry agents. The ban, although
understandable from an environmentalist perspective, was not accompanied by adequate programs to promote alternative sources of
income. The ban also involved the reduction of credit for cattle
raising, which, combined with trade liberalization, seriously undermined the livestock industry and, with it, the already limited employment opportunities it created for local peasants. What was lacking was a commitment to help the colonists make their land more
productive and allow them to retain enough profits to reinvest in
improving their social and economic conditions. The ARIC proposed a series of measures that potentially would have eased some
of the problems described. It saw the need for credit, technical
assistance, and improved marketing conditions to promote more

intensive agriculture, crop diversification, and job creation. It also demanded attention to the lack of teachers and doctors, the over-crowded housing conditions, and the poor sanitation. The inade-quacy of the government's response was partly why many became attracted to the armed option of the EZLN.

In the Cañadas of Las Margaritas the most important organi-zation prior to the EZLN was the Unión de Ejidos de la Selva, which had been formed after the split in 1983 within the Unión de Uniones. It maintained closer ties to the Quiptic than to the Pajal Credit Union and in March 1988 participated in the formal creation of the ARIC Unión de Uniones.[14] Nevertheless, it developed its economic strategy somewhat independently of the rest of ARIC and was probably the most successful in coping with the coffee crisis of the early 1990s, although its communities also became divided over the armed option presented by the EZLN.

The UE de la Selva survived the crash in coffee prices thanks to its ties with the Dutch alternative trading company, Max Havelaar. The contact had been made in 1988 through a sister organization in Oaxaca, the Union of Indigenous Communities of the Isthmus Region (UCIRI), which had begun to produce organically grown coffee for the European market. Max Havelaar began to work with the UE de la Selva in time for the 1988 to 1989 harvest. It offered to pay 40 percent above the international market price, which in effect cushioned the impact of the latter's collapse in June 1989. As a result, the UE de la Selva was able to repay both the principal and the interest on credit that had been given by BANRURAL and there-fore became eligible for new loans (Interview, representatives of UE de la Selva, Las Margaritas, January 1992).

The decision to repay the banks was not without costs for the organization. It involved a trade-off in which the coffee growers were paid less than they had been promised, the difference going to pay back the loans. This sacrifice led to a general loss of confidence and decline in participation in the UE de la Selva in 1989 to 1990, although those producers with better coffee orchards were able to take advantage of the market linkages opened up by Max Have-laar.[15] Lack of technical assistance, poor communications, and low productivity also hindered peasants' ability to appropriate the pro-ductive process. The orchards were thirty or forty years old, and their profitability depended on costly rehabilitation work. In response, the union encouraged producers to convert to organic production. This move offered four potential benefits. First, the international price for organic coffee was 30 percent higher than that paid for the nonorganic product. Second, production costs could be reduced by eliminating chemical fertilizers. Third, organic methods would result in healthier and more productive orchards. Finally, the preparation of organic fertilizers requires a higher level of participation and cooperation, which would thereby strengthen economic and social organization. The strategy was successful for those groups within communities who adapted to the new methods, but it also tended to create internal differentiation that, combined with the persistence of low coffee prices, discouraged community-based participation in new productive projects.

The union also helped to incorporate these producers into a regional organization, the Union of Coffee Producers of the Southern Border (UNCAFESUR), formed in April 1990 as an alliance with local affiliates of CIOAC, the CNC, and the Teacher-Peasant Solidarity Movement (SOCAMA). This convergence of independent and official organizations around economic concerns represented the new type of peasant movement promoted by reformers within the state and UNORCA. However, the political conditions in Chiapas were still not favorable to such an alliance. With the support of key figures within the Salinas administration, UNCAFESUR was able to purchase a coffee-processing plant from INMECAFE in 1990. The purchase was financed by a loan from INI-PRONASOL, whose regional director was promptly removed from his post at the request of González Garrido.[16]

Preparing the Rebellion

Until 1992 events in Chiapas had largely escaped national attention. However, that began to change with a march of 400 Indians from Palenque to Mexico City in early 1992. The catalyst was another violent eviction by state police, this time of members of the Committee for the Defense of Indigenous Freedom (CDLI) who had gathered in Palenque on December 28, 1991. Their protest was to draw attention to the corruption of municipal presidents, the imposition of village authorities *(agentes municipales),* the failure of the government to carry out promised public works, the lack of solution to the rezago agrario, and their opposition to the reforms to Article 27. Over 100 were arrested, and several people were beaten and tortured. The government used a 1989 reform to the state Penal Code in breaking up the demonstration. Articles 129 through 135 of this code classified participation in unarmed mass protests as threats to public order and liable to punishments of two to four years imprisonment.

The Xi'Nich march left Palenque on March 7, 1992, and arrived in the capital six weeks later.[17] The march received national coverage in the independent press and solidarity from communities in Tabasco, Veracruz, Puebla, and the state of Mexico. Its impact on national consciousness was to display the repressive nature of the state government in Chiapas. It also coincided with a growing awareness regarding the conditions of indigenous peoples in the country (Bellinghausen 1992; Cepeda Neri 1992; Reyes Heroles 1992). Yet, although Xi'Nich was able to gain promises of solutions from federal agencies, by the end of 1992 several of the demands had not been met. The state's Penal Code was not reformed; no police officers were ever brought to trial for alleged human rights abuses; and municipal presidents continued to impose agentes municipales. There were still thirty arrest orders out against CDLI members, and new public works had not begun.

It was in this context that the EZLN was formed in the Lacandon forest and central highlands. In late 1989 its public face was known as the Emiliano Zapata Independent Peasant Alliance (ACIEZ). Its strongest support was in the municipalities of Altamirano, Ocosingo, San Cristóbal, Sabanilla, and Salto de Agua. In early 1992 it changed its name to ANCIEZ by adding *Nacional* to its title, claiming member organizations in six central and northern states. However, it was clearly strongest in Chiapas and had extended its base of support in just two years among Tzotzil, Tzeltal, and Chol communities in the highland municipalities of El Bosque, Larráinzar, Chenalhó, Chanal, Huixtán, Oxchuc, Tila, and Tumbalá. The lack of solution to the economic and agrarian demands in the Cañadas de Ocosingo contributed to the radicalization of young peasants and their eventual support for the armed uprising.

The EZLN was particularly important for young women. In most of the communities, women occupied traditional roles of child rearing and caring for the home. Although some participated in cooperative projects established by the diocese, these tended to reinforce their position as providers of food, health care, and some extra income. Undoubtedly, this level of participation did create new ways of seeing gender roles within communities and made it possible for the EZLN to attract significant support from women. The most important factor was that the Zapatistas provided a space for women and young girls who appreciated the chance to learn how to read and write, to study Mexican history, and participate in the struggle. The way in which the EZLN recruited members also facilitated the incorporation of women. As male family members joined the armed group, mothers often encouraged daughters to do likewise. In an interview, Silvia, an eighteen-year-old Chol with the rank of captain in the EZLN, recounted her experience from childhood (Rovira 1997:63–64):

I had four or five brothers and sisters, more or less. I worked in the fields, I didn't study at all. In my community there was a school made out of wood, just *zacate*. The teachers came once but all they did was count the children and then they went away; they did not give any classes. My ejido is very poor, we have nothing. I helped my mother, my family lives in miserable conditions, with no money, with nothing. If the kids get sick, there is nowhere to go, there is no road or doctors. The sick have to be carried by someone walking for eight hours. They die. They die of fevers or sicknesses which can be cured. It is not just that they should die.

The women have nothing. They work at home, they carry firewood, they prepare tortillas and food, they help in the fields of their husbands and they attend to their children. Some, not all, participate in community meetings, those who come to understand.

I knew a while ago that there was an armed group, the EZLN. Someone told me, from a different place, not from my ejido. I began to think about the eleven points for which the EZLN fights. And so I felt very proud to be part of it. There is no one who just joins up for the fun of it. We are exploited by the government, by those who have power. . . .

I feel proud to be here in the EZLN, it is necessary to be here. Besides, you learn things here. In the home all you do is work, you prepare food and learn nothing, that is why it is better to join, for the good of our people, to take up arms. Before I didn't know any Spanish, just chol. Here they taught me everything. And now, well, I am moving ahead.

Those women who were unable to leave their homes to join the armed group provided support in other ways. They organized collective work projects; they met to study the problems of their communities and the history of popular struggles in Mexico. They became the civilian base of the EZLN and the providers of food to the combatants. In many cases, a woman's decision to leave her community for the mountains was seen as a violation of traditional norms. Whereas this decision was a source of tension for some, it was also one of liberation for others (Rovira 1997:107).

Between 1989 and 1992 the EZLN doubled in size, spreading throughout the ejidos that had formerly participated in the ARIC. By the time of Salinas's reforms to Article 27, the civilian Zapatistas controlled the majority of the communities in the Cañadas and had important bases in several highland communities, such as San Andrés Larráinzar, Oxchuc, and Chanal. The political leadership was held by the clandestine committees created in the previous six years, while the armed insurgents were entrusted solely with instruction and defense.

In the face of continual repression, increasing poverty, and worsening health conditions (including a cholera epidemic in 1991), the committees informed Marcos in 1992 of their readiness to fight. The reforms to Article 27 appear to have been the detonator. However, Marcos tried to explain that external conditions were not favorable. The collapse of communist states, the weakening of insurgent movements in Latin America, and the general crisis of socialism did not augur well, but the Zapatistas were firm in their decision (Castillo and Brisac 1995:140): "'We don't want to know what's happening in the rest of the world. We are dying and we have to ask the people. Didn't you say that we must do what the people say?'" "'Well, . . . yes.'" "'Well then, let's ask them.'"

Communities met during mid-1992 and discussed the armed option, finally voting in favor of initiating the armed struggle in October of that year to coincide with 500 years of resistance. They chose October 12 to "test the waters" and, under the guise of ANCIEZ, organized a peaceful march and mass demonstration in San Cristóbal de Las Casas. Marcos was there, videotaping the march and preparing for the "real" occupation of the city. During the march the statue of Diego de Mazariegos, the Spanish conqueror and founder of Ciudad Real, was pulled down (García de León 1994:27).

After the march, community assemblies met again and voted in favor of war. In January 1993 the supremacy of civilian over military power was formalized by the creation of the Indigenous Revolutionary Clandestine Committee–General Command (CCRI-CG, Comité Clandestino Revolucionario Indígena–Comandancia General). The CCRI-CG brought together the different regional committees that had formed during the previous ten years. The military leaders were ordered to prepare the uprising, but Marcos also recognized the political task of gaining legitimacy for the EZLN (Castillo and Brisac 1995:141–42):

As I was the military chief, they threw the ball to me and said: "You take charge." I asked for some time so that our army could readjust; we had to move from a defensive to an offensive structure, one that would be necessary in urban combat. To have a political impact we had to avert the likely accusation that we were a narco-guerrilla. We had to show our strength, our numbers, and take over county seats. So we were given one year, until December 1993. They [the members of the CCRI-CG] gave the military leaders freedom to fix the date and move people, troops and resources. The whole of 1993 was dedicated to this, with the probable dates of the uprising set for November 20th, then December 12th, 25th, or 31st. Due to logistical problems, November went by and we ended up with December 31st. Then began the last phase of our history. Well, I hope it is not the last one. I mean, the one we are in right now, the one that was born in January 1994.

Chapter 8

THE ZAPATISTA OPENING

The impact of the Zapatista uprising was clearly felt at both the local and national levels. Although it drew on earlier struggles, the rebellion also opened up many new spaces for popular mobilization. Its political significance can now be seen in terms of the openings it created for popular organizations to contest the meaning and scope of democracy and citizenship in Mexico. Rather than emerging with a preconceived plan for revolutionary change, the Zapatistas represented the antithesis of such a vanguard. The cry of *Ya basta!* was in fact a call for solidarity among all those Mexicans who had said "enough is enough." The precise nature of the demands could only arise from a broader dialogue to which all those who recognized the need for change were invited. The impact of the rebellion was therefore revelatory rather than programmatic. It focused attention on the social costs of neoliberal economic reforms and on the discrimination directed against two of the most traditionally marginalized sectors of Mexican society: indigenous people and women. However, in doing so, the EZLN also insisted on the centrality of democracy in articulating popular struggles against numerous forms of oppression. The EZLN looked beyond its own economic-corporate demands to the expansion of democratic political, social, and cultural practices in all spheres of Mexican life. Its strength therefore lay less with its own political and military resources and more in the changes that its presence affected in cultural understandings of democracy and citizenship. Without such changes, the EZLN would be condemned to fight defensive battles for particularistic goals and would eventually be dismantled as an alternative political force. However, the popular movements, including the peasant movements of Chiapas, had already created a democratic discourse through their insistence on respect for rights, associational autonomy, and the unfulfilled promises of the Mexican Revolution. The Zapatistas were able to draw on both the diverse and often contradictory elements of this political discourse, but they were also able to give them a new political meaning. The social exclusion of the indigenous peoples of Chiapas was seen as the most blatant violation of citizenship, the denial of the most basic human right, "the right to have rights." If citizenship in Salinas's Mexico was contingent on the economic competitiveness of each individual, then the indigenous had little hope of surviving, either as citizens or as peoples. A different concept of citizenship was required, but it was not readily available. It would have to be fought for by those who were resisting oppressive social relations, whether they were rooted in class, ethnicity, gender, or sexuality. The rebellion had created not only an opening for democratic change, but also for the very redefinition of democracy and citizenship in Mexico.

The Zapatista opening affected struggles in four main areas: the rights of Mexico's indigenous peoples, democratization in Mexico, land reform in Chiapas, and women's rights. These issues also reflected the themes of the peace talks between the EZLN and the government after their resumption in April 1995. The two sides agreed to present proposals and find negotiated solutions through four consecutive panels, or *mesas de diálogo*. These were to take place in the highland Tzotzil community of San Andrés Larráinzar. The first mesa, on indigenous rights and culture, began in October 1995 and reached a minimal accord (the first of the peace process) in February 1996. The second mesa, on democracy and justice, began in July 1996, but no agreements were reached and talks were suspended by the EZLN in September. The Zapatistas demanded that the government comply with several conditions if the talks were to resume, including fulfillment of the accords on indigenous rights and culture. The simultaneous presence of indigenous, democratic, agrarian, and gender struggles in Chiapas demonstrated the scope of the Zapatista opening, as well as the obstacles to articulating the struggles in a radical democratic discourse. These obstacles included unresolved conflicts between and within popular movements over the meaning of indigenous autonomy, perennial leadership rivalries, tendentious and sectarian interpretations of controversial decisions, poor communications, and disagreements over the scope of women's rights. However, on each of these points, the competing sides also made efforts to build bridges. If the basis of democracy is the recognition of antagonism, then, by 1996, the indigenous people of Chiapas were embroiled in an extremely fluid, unpredictable, and often threatening democratic revolution. This struggle was so threatening that their biggest obstacle was the constant use of violence against the potential bearers of radical change — the EZLN, indigenous and peasant organizations, opposition parties, and indigenous women.

The Struggle for Indigenous Rights

Several observers have noted that from the start of the 1980s, indigenous issues began to preoccupy the Mexican government and were particularly important during the Salinas administration (Díaz Polanco 1992; Fox 1994b; Hindley 1996; Sarmiento 1991). For example, the budget of the INI was increased eighteenfold during the first half of Salinas's sexenio (Fox 1994a:188) and local INI officers began to work more closely with independent grassroots organizations, such as the State Coordinator of Oaxacan Coffee Producers (CEPCO) and the Independent Front of Indian Peoples (FIPI) in Chiapas (Hindley 1996; Fox 1994a).

What factors explain this sudden interest in the most marginalized sector of Mexican society? More important, how did indigenous organizations transform this process through their strategic political interventions? According to Díaz Polanco, the shift in government strategy began in the early 1980s with the realization that it was better to simply absorb ethnic differences rather than suppress them. The techniques of power had to be more subtle and less violent, geared to a long-term project of remaking "national culture" in which indigenous people would take their place as *equals,* but *not as different.* Far from being an exclusionary ideology, the new *indigenismo* sought to include all peoples and provide them with the same rights and access to justice, irrespective of their ethnicity. However, as Hindley has argued, the new policies spoke of justice, not of rights, in the belief that rights were already established in law and the real issue was the procurement of justice (1996). This interpretation had the effect of not only ignoring the social and economic factors that prevented indigenous peoples from truly exercising their rights, but also reproduced the authority of the state (and specifically the executive branch) over the acceptable practices of indigenous peoples. Such neocolonial pretensions were fully consistent with neoliberal economics and, believing that the philosophical questions had been solved, Salinas immediately proceeded to implement a set of reforms that would alter the legal and institutional terrain for subsequent struggles, including the one that most reflected his administration's shortcomings — the Zapatista uprising.[1]

The most significant of these reforms turned out to be the modifications to Article 4 of the Constitution. The paragraph that was finally inserted and approved by Congress made reference, for the first time, to the pluricultural nature of the Mexican nation. It did not go beyond this to specify the collective rights that real indigenous people were demanding. In fact, the Consultation *(consulta)* the new INI organized was simply a sham exercise that excluded those voices not aligned with the government. Moreover, the reform to Article 4 generated much criticism from those people it was intended to assist. The issue would now be whether or not the debates on indigenous rights would be used to transform the political character of Article 4 and, subsequently, its regulatory law. This was a question that could only be answered in practice and depended on the strategic inventiveness of indigenous organizations and their leadership.

Prior to the Zapatista uprising, one of the most outspoken proponents of a "post-indigenista" Mexico was Margarito Xib Ruiz Hernández, a Tojolobal Indian from Chiapas and leader of the FIPI. Since the mid-1970s Ruiz had been an active member of one of the most important independent peasant movements in Chiapas: CIOAC. In 1988 he became a federal deputy of the Mexican Socialist Party (PMS) under Mexico's rules of proportional representation. In the Chamber of Deputies, Ruiz argued in vain for more far-reaching reforms to Article 4, concluding that what was at stake was not an "indigenous problem" but a problem with indigenismo as a set of assumptions, institutions, and practices (Ruiz Hernández 1993).[2]

Although Ruiz commended the openness of the Regional Solidarity Funds toward independent organizations in Chiapas (including the FIPI), he remained critical of the economistic approach and argued for broader, democratically managed regional development plans instead of numerous, disconnected microprojects. Interestingly, Ruiz also noted the speed with which the government responded to maintain the initiative in setting policy agendas. Almost in parallel with the independent activities of nongovernmental organizations (NGOs), he saw the emergence of new "governmental nongovernmental organizations" (GNGOs), such as the Fund to Support Indigenous Organizations and Peoples. Ruiz was also fully aware that the indigenous organizations were not automatically more effective instruments simply because of their social rather than their institutional origin. Many lacked the technical and administrative skills (not to mention the financial resources) the GNGOs commanded. Operating with these deficits constituted a central challenge for indigenous organizations if they were to increase their negotiating capacity while maintaining a distinctive set of political demands for autonomous, regional self-government.[3] The goal of the indigenous movements was therefore to establish an entire chapter of collective rights within a new Article 4. These rights would reflect the provisions of international laws to which the Mexican government is a signatory, in particular the Convention no. 169 of the International Labor Organization, which recognizes collective economic, political, social, and cultural rights of indigenous peoples (Hindley 1996:231–32).

The post-indigenista view was finally given its chance by the Zapatista uprising. Although the early communiqués did not specify the ethnic demands of the EZLN, it was not long before the question of autonomy was posed. Of the thirty-four demands presented to the government in February 1994 the following referred specifically to indigenous people: the creation of an independent indigenous radio station; the mandating of compulsory indigenous languages for primary through university education; respect for indigenous culture and tradition; an ending to discrimination against indigenous people; the granting of indigenous autonomy; the administration of their own courts by indigenous communities; the criminalization of forced expulsion from communities by government-backed caciques and allowing the expelled to be able to return; and, finally, the establishment of maternity clinics, day-care centers, nutritious food, kitchens, dining facilities, nixtamal and tortilla mills, and training programs for indigenous women.

The government's attempt to separate local from national reforms led the EZLN to reject the official response and instead turn its attention to building networks of grassroots support within civil society. It was in this context that the contacts with other indigenous leaders and organizations developed. Contesting Salinas's reform to Article 4 had provided a point of convergence indigenous organizations were now fully able to exploit. The economic struggles for land, credit, and fair prices, while necessary to build regional organizations, were increasingly articulated in a cultural-political discourse of indigenous autonomy. In Chiapas, the declaration of autonomous pluriethnic regions in late 1994 set the stage for a new period of mobilization to protest the illegitimacy of the new state government.

Democratization and the Mobilization of Civil Society

The mass protests against the government's use of military force in Chiapas helped to deepen the Zapatistas' appreciation of civil society as their most effective ally in the struggle for a peaceful solution. Civil society, then, would come to provide the bridge between the local and the national after the first round of peace talks in February and March 1994. As the EZLN delegates returned to their communities to discuss the government's proposals, they sent out a clear message: "Do not leave us alone." This call took on a new urgency in the aftermath of the assassination of the PRI's presidential candidate, Luis Donaldo Colosio, on March 23, which the Zapatistas interpreted as a sign that hard-liners within the government had taken the upper hand in reaction to the possibility of reforms favorable to the EZLN and the political opposition.

The mobilization of support groups such as the University students' Caravana de Caravanas and the national coalition of NGOs, Civil Space for Peace (ESPAZ), demonstrated the clear links to be established between Chiapas and national political reform. This goal became even more apparent when, in mid-June, the EZLN rejected the government's proposals and instead decided to deepen the dialogue with civil society. At the time of the "no" vote most commentators focused on the possible ramifications for the presidential elections scheduled for August 21, paying less attention to the Zapatistas' call for a National Democratic Convention (CND). Little by little, however, the idea of a citizens' assembly to unite the numerous opposition movements and groups began to catch on. An organizing committee was set up, and it began to work intensively over the next six weeks to assure the success of the convention.

In Chiapas, the Democratic State Assembly of the Chiapanecan People (AEDPCH) was born as a loose coalition of citizens' groups, peasant organizations, democratic union currents, and NGOs. Over sixty groups were represented at its first state convention in early July 1994. The convention supported the EZLN's call for a transitional government, a new Constituent Assembly, and new federal and state constitutions. The new coalition held a second convention two weeks later to prepare proposals of Chiapas delegates to the first meeting of the CND. This meeting was scheduled to be held two weeks prior to the national and gubernatorial elections, at a specially constructed site in Zapatista territory named Aguascalientes after the revolutionary convention of 1914 (Stephen 1995).

Democratic conventions were held in several other states during July, and delegates were elected. On August 6 more than 6,000 delegates, invited intellectuals, and observers descended on San Cristóbal de las Casas to begin deliberations in five miniconventions on the need for a transitional government, the adoption of peaceful strategies to achieve democracy, an alternative national project, the organization of a new Constituent Assembly, and the elaboration of a new federal Constitution. With this number of people it was impossible to reach more than general agreements in support of the EZLN. The major point of debate concerned the role of electoral participation in bringing about change in Mexico. Some groups on the far Left argued that only mass mobilization (possibly including armed insurgency) and not the elections could dislodge the PRI from power. However, the debate was constrained by the sheer number of delegates and the desire of the convention

3. Zapatista soldiers at the National Democratic Convention, Aguascalientes, Chiapas, August 1994

organizers to approve a common platform. As the EZLN had itself encouraged participation in the elections and in defense of the vote, the far Left groups were at a clear disadvantage.

The ensuing journey from San Cristóbal to Aguascalientes and the reaffirmation of unity behind the Zapatistas' demands served to demonstrate to the government and other sectors of society that the EZLN was indeed not alone. The EZLN displayed a great deal of political maturity by declaring that it would "step to one side" while it gave the newly constituted CND the opportunity to apply peaceful pressure for political change. In a major speech, subcomandante Marcos allayed fears of an imminent armed uprising following the national elections and instead called on the peaceful civic and popular movement "to defeat us," to make armed action unnecessary (*La Jornada*, August 10, 1994).

Mexico's presidential elections coincided with the election of a new governor in Chiapas on August 21. Although some observers declared that the national elections were relatively clean, the campaign of the PRI candidate, Ernesto Zedillo, benefited disproportionately from the use of public funds and media time. Hundreds of irregularities were also reported on election day, particularly the lack of sufficient ballot papers at special voting booths, the "shaving" of names from voting lists, and the violation of secrecy of the ballot (Fox 1996). In Chiapas, the PRI candidate, Eduardo Robledo Rincón, claimed victory in the governorship race in the midst of widespread protests against fraud (Friederlein 1995). The official result gave Robledo 50.4 percent of the vote, compared to 34.9 percent for Amado Avendaño Figueroa, candidate of the Party of the Democratic Revolution (PRD), and 9.2 percent for Cesáreo Hernández, of the National Action Party (PAN). The PRD claimed that Avendaño had in fact won and called for civic protests to prevent Robledo from taking office in December 1994. PRD supporters could point to several disturbing incidents during the election campaign, including the head-on crash of an unlicensed trailer into Avendaño's car just three weeks before election day. Although the candidate escaped with his life, three members of his campaign team were killed in what many people saw as a premeditated attack. The police investigation concluded that the crash was an accident and arrested the suspected driver. Following the elections another PRD leader was killed in the town of Jaltenango, near the Guatemalan border.

The PRD and PAN representatives also accused the electoral authorities of altering the voting results during the transit of the ballot papers from the individual polling stations to the offices of the State Electoral Commission (*Proceso,* August 29, 1994, p. 18). The EZLN issued a strong statement condemning the fraud and called on Robledo not to assume office, in order to avoid a potential "bloodbath." The government insisted that Robledo take office in December 1994, while the AEDPCH and EZLN recognized Avendaño as "rebel governor" and briefly occupied thirty-eight town halls in municipalities outside the declared conflict zone. At the same time, declining investor confidence in the new Zedillo government led to a 40 percent devaluation of the peso as Mexico found itself unable to service short-term debt coming due in January 1995. Faced with bankruptcy, the government agreed to stringent terms of a U.S.$50 billion bailout package sponsored by the U.S. government. Then, on February 9, 1995, Zedillo ordered a new military offensive against the EZLN. Believing that the operation would capture the

Zapatista leadership, the attorney general declared the identity of subcomandante Marcos to be Rafael Sebastián Guillén Vicente, a former university professor and leader of one of several regional cells of the EZLN. As in January 1994, Mexican citizens mobilized quickly to demand the withdrawal of troops from Zapatista communities, holding three mass demonstrations in Mexico City in the space of a week. Unable to capture Marcos, Zedillo called off the offensive, although troops remained stationed close to the communities suspected of supporting the EZLN. Human rights observers also denounced the destruction of domestic items, food, and farming implements by soldiers in villages suspected of supporting the EZLN. Thousands of villagers throughout the Cañadas fled into the forest in order to avoid arrest.

The February offensive clearly revealed the military weakness of the EZLN in the face of the Mexican army. Its future was increasingly linked to the political space it was able to create for its eventual emergence from armed struggle. In this regard, the Zapatistas decided to consult its allies within civil society on its political future. In August 1995 a national and international consulta was held, resulting in the decision to promote a civic, nonpartisan front, the Zapatista Front of National Liberation (FZLN). The front was officially created on January 1, 1996, as a means to articulate a wide range of popular struggles behind the banners of democracy, liberty, and justice. It was also seen as a response to the failure of the CND to unify these struggles in the period since August 1994. Internal leadership conflicts within CND threatened to squander a historic opportunity to reformulate the democratic tasks of the Mexican Left and the popular movements. However, the CND worked comparatively better at the grassroots level. In fact, it was through the local state conventions and an independent electoral monitoring group, Alianza Cívica, that the August 1995 consulta was organized. The Zapatistas responded by reaffirming their faith in the nonpartisan associations of civil society, a faith that was clearly articulated in their vision of the FZLN.

The political objective of the FZLN was defined not in terms of winning positions of power, but in demanding that those who govern, govern by obeying. This is the principle of mandar obedeciendo, which the EZLN drew from earlier practices within indigenous communities. In the Fourth Declaration of the Lacandon Forest, the political nature of the new front was spelled out:

Today, in the spirit of Emiliano Zapata and having heard the voices of all our brothers and sisters, we call upon the people of Mexico to participate in a new stage of the struggle for national liberation and the construction of a new nation, through this Fourth Declaration of the Lacandon Forest, in which we call upon all honest men and women to participate in the new national political force born today, the Frente Zapatista de Liberación Nacional, a Mexican civil and non-violent organization, independent and democratic, which struggles for democracy, liberty and justice in Mexico. The Frente Zapatista de Liberación Nacional is born today, and we extend an invitation to

The factory workers of the Republic,
the laborers of the countryside and the cities,
the Indigenous peoples,
the *colonos,*
the teachers and students,
the Mexican women,
the young people across the country,
the honest artists and intellectuals,
the responsible priests and nuns,
and all the Mexican people who do not seek power,
but rather democracy, liberty and justice for all of us
and for all our children.

We invite civil society, those without a party, the citizens and social movements, all Mexicans, to help build this new political force.

A new political dynamic which will be national.

A new political dynamic based in the EZLN.

A new political dynamic which forms part of a broad opposition movement, the National Liberation Movement, as a space for citizen political action where there may be a confluence with other political movements of the independent opposition, a space where popular wills meet and coordinate united actions with one another.

A political dynamic that does not aspire to take power.

A force that is not a political party.

A political dynamic that can organize the demands and proposals of those citizens and is willing to govern by obeying.

. . . A political dynamic not interested in taking political power but in building a democracy where those who govern, govern by obeying. (EZLN 1996)

This declaration, and the trajectory of the EZLN, can be seen as a novel attempt to articulate a new radical democratic imaginary within Mexican civil society. During 1996 the FZLN began to build itself from the ground up, through hundreds of civil dialogue committees. Their main task was to assist the EZLN in the formulation of proposals for the second round of talks on democracy and justice, scheduled to take place in San Andrés Larráinzar in July. A week prior to the talks, the EZLN organized a special forum on "The Reform of the State" in San Cristóbal, which was attended by thousands of delegates from the civil committees, as well as from popular movements, opposition parties, and universities. The forum came up with concrete proposals on political and electoral reform in Mexico, including the registration of nonpartisan, independent candidates in elections and the incorporation of referenda and plebiscites in a new Constitution. The government approached this round of talks with indifference and no agreements were reached, partly because it had already negotiated a more limited electoral reform with the political parties. The Zapatistas broke off talks in September 1996, calling on the government to replace its negotiating team and to comply with its commitment to implement the accord on indigenous rights and culture. The EZLN also continued to demand the unconditional release of all those detained as suspected Zapatistas during the police and military offensives of February 1995. Another factor was the government's response to the appearance of a new guerrilla organization, the Popular Revolutionary Army (EPR), in the state of Guerrero in June 1996. The EPR appeared less prepared than the Zapatistas to negotiate fundamental changes with the government and carried out several violent attacks on police stations. Zedillo attempted to portray the EPR as the "bad guerrilla" by speaking more kindly of the EZLN, a maneuver the EZLN rejected as an attempt to justify indiscriminate repression. The Zapatistas affirmed that they did not have any links with the EPR, whose existence was simply another indication of the desperation being felt by the majority of Mexicans in the face of a deepening economic crisis.

The Resurgence of the Struggle for Land

The rebellion also had the effect of reviving the independent peasant movements in Chiapas. The formation, in late January 1994, of the State Council of Indigenous and Peasant Organizations (CEOIC) opened up a period of peasant mobilization involving at least 8,000 land claimants belonging to eleven organizations.[4] During the first six months of the year some 340 private farms representing over 50,000 hectares were seized. In several cases the occupations led to violent confrontations and a CEOIC leader, Mariano López, was assassinated in March in Simojovel. The OCEZ-CNPA invaded more than 4,000 hectares of land in the border region, including three properties in La Trinitaria, which they renamed Arturo Albores, 6 de Marzo, and Albores de Zapata.

Given the already tense political situation created by the rebellion, the state government called on the leaders of CEOIC and the landowners' associations to find negotiated solutions. On April 14 the governor signed an agreement with both sides, promising to investigate case by case the claims of each group while offering not to order the eviction of those farms taken prior to that date. For their part, the CEOIC leaders agreed not to promote further land invasions. The government also offered landowners a monthly compensation of 45 new pesos (U.S.$13) per hectare of land they claimed as invaded. This measure obviously benefited larger landowners. For example, a holding of 300 hectares would be compensated for the sum of U.S.$3,900 per month as long as the invasions persisted.

The April 14 agreement did not hold. Ranchers accused CEOIC of continuing to carry out land invasions and in early July signed a new agreement with the state governor that threatened the imminent eviction of all the land seizures in the state. The fact that the government only proceeded to evict four farms was not only a source of irritation for the ranchers' associations, but more important an indication of the impossibility of removing thousands of peasant families by force in a political context that called for extreme caution. At the same time, CEOIC leaders claimed that the state government and the ranchers were responsible for breaking the April 14 accord, citing the eviction of several farms in the municipality of Teopisca in May; the arrest and imprisonment of Enrique Pérez López, a former leader of the OCEZ-CNPA and a human rights activist in Comitán; and the failure of the government to provide solutions to the claims presented since January 1 (Interviews with leaders of CEOIC, Ocosingo, July 1994).

The main obstacle to achieving a solution was the reluctance of landowners to sell. Some CEOIC leaders argued that the government should use its legal right to expropriate the land for the purpose of redistribution. The modifications to Article 27 did not delete the right of the nation to expropriate land "for the purpose of public benefit." This measure is often used to allow PEMEX to drill for oil or the Federal Electricity Company to construct a hydroelectricity dam. The negative response of the state government to the request for expropriation was predictable. In negotiations with CEOIC representatives in June, it claimed that the argument for expropriation was unfounded because "the decision to respect private property and the will of private owners is not open to negotiation." Illustrating a central ambiguity in agrarian legislation, the government added that "the constitutional order does not allow for exceptions" (Gobierno del Estado de Chiapas 1994). It concluded that expropriation is not the only way to solve land disputes and promised to search for alternative means. By completely rejecting this option the government revealed not only a lack of political will to oppose the interests of the landowners, but also a naive belief in the efficacy of other solutions such as the relocation of petitioning groups or support for productive projects in existing ejidos. The size of the problem was exposed by simply comparing the area that had been occupied (50,000 hectares) with the area that had been offered for sale (11,910 hectares). According to one CEOIC leader, the government set a ceiling of 20,000 hectares to solve the demand for land in Chiapas and its real objective was to begin evicting peasants from occupied farms after the August 21 elections.

Not all members of CEOIC adopted the same position. Since its

4. "If there is no solution, there will be revolution: Peasants Ready for War." — Graffiti, Tuxtla Gutiérrez, June 1994

inception, a clear division had existed between the independent organizations that called for expropriation and other moderate or PRI-affiliated groups that adopted different strategies. Among the latter, the three largest organizations were the Teacher-Peasant Solidarity Movement (SOCAMA), CNC, and ARIC Unión de Uniones. Each of these criticized the CIOAC, OCEZ-CNPA, and Xi'Nich for attempting to claim leadership of CEOIC and pursuing confrontational strategies for which there was no consensus.

This division became particularly apparent after April 14 during negotiations to resolve each organization's land claims. For example, SOCAMA elaborated an independent proposal that gained the government's approval in July. Under this plan, the federal and state governments would provide SOCAMA with 20 million new pesos for the purpose of obtaining a credit fund with 50 million pesos from the regional office of BANRURAL. This fund would be used to purchase the land SOCAMA members were claiming, and the credit would be paid back with the subsidies received from PROCAMPO over a period to be established by each individual beneficiary. Part of the interest on the credit would be covered by the interest generated by the initial 20 million–peso guarantee, and SOCAMA would request additional support from SEDESOL to make up the difference. Once the credit was paid back and the land fully paid for, the 20 million pesos would be used to support productive projects among the members. In the meantime SEDESOL agreed to provide infrastructure and interest-free credit. These measures were seen as necessary to include those peasants whose land claims had been turned down. One of SOCAMA's leaders explained that this approach was more likely to succeed than simply polarizing the issue between expropriation or maintaining the status quo (Interview, Mexico City, July 1994). The positive response the proposal received from the state government was seen by the radical wing of CEOIC as evidence of favoritism and an abdication of the commitment to the struggle for land in the future. The SOCAMA had negotiated independently of CEOIC and, in keeping with the reformed Article 27, agreed not to press for further land distribution once current claims had been settled. In addition, the use of PROCAMPO subsidies to purchase land was criticized as a diversion from their intended use, namely to support basic grain production.

In the case of the CNC the strategy was less innovative and more opportunistic. Although CNC groups invaded land as much as did CIOAC or the OCEZ-CNPA, it also accused the radical groups of politicizing CEOIC and supporting the opposition PRD candidacy for the governorship. Of the eighty-nine properties to be purchased for redistribution, the CNC was to receive seventeen, compared to forty-six for the CIOAC. However, the actual land area involved was not so different: 2,902 hectares for CNC and 3,565 hectares for CIOAC (SRA 1994). The CNC was therefore able to use the strength represented by CEOIC but participated less in its political struggles with the state government and tended to avoid confrontations over policy reform.

Finally, ARIC Unión de Uniones became an important part of the government's attempt to limit the radicalizing effects of the EZLN in Chiapas. Large amounts of new resources for productive projects and infrastructure were provided after the uprising. The effectiveness of this strategy was not entirely successful for either the government or the ARIC. Peasant support for the EZLN did not decline as a result of new government programs, while the increasing moderation of the ARIC leadership led to a split in July 1994 as several member organizations established a parallel leadership more clearly identified with the EZLN and the goals of the CND. One of the reasons for the split was the decision of the ARIC president to accept the PRI candidacy for federal deputy in the Ocosingo electoral district. His supporters recognized that the members should have been consulted more fully, but it is doubtful that the candidacy would have been approved. This division remained an important source of tension throughout 1995, leading to a struggle between the progovernment ARIC-*oficial* and the ARIC-*independiente* for control of the organization's office in Ocosingo and of access to communities in the Cañadas.

During 1994 the state government also tried to gather support for a new state-level agrarian law that was clearly biased against further land redistribution. The Law of Agrarian Justice and Promotion of Rural Development in Chiapas was designed to be the official response to one of the Zapatistas' demands regarding the need for land reform. However, the text did not add anything substantially different from the content of the 1992 federal Agrarian Law. Although it opened up the possibility of denouncing the existence of latifundio holdings, in reality it was highly unlikely that any latifundios would be detected, due to the practice of subdividing estates among family members and name lenders. At the same time, as with the federal legislation, landowners found to be in possession of properties exceeding the legal limits would be given the right to sell off the indicated properties within one year. There was no mention of the state's right to expropriate such extensions for the purpose of land redistribution.

Although the progovernment organizations supported these measures, there was clear opposition from a significant part of the affected population. The fact that the proposed law was drawn up hastily without proper consultation was also a source of tension. In response, the radical wing of CEOIC proposed that consultations with all peasant organizations in Chiapas be reopened and that the new law should be elaborated on the basis of proposals put forward in community and regional assemblies. In late December 1994 the Zedillo government announced that it would implement concrete steps against *latifundismo*. However, in the following month a cabinet reshuffle led to Arturo Warman's replacing Limón Rojas as head of the SRA. Warman had consistently declared that there were no latifundio holdings in Chiapas, denying many of the claims of the member organizations of CEOIC.

The government responded to the struggle for land in two ways. First, it implemented a program to purchase disputed properties from private owners and resell them to land claimants through the type of mechanism described earlier for the case of SOCAMA. The government supplied capital as credit in trust funds that peasants were then expected to repay with their PROCAMPO subsidies over a fifteen-year period. The second strategy was less institutional and consisted of the eviction of invaded lands with the support of private gunmen, or guardias blancas, at the service of landowners (see the following section). As a result, agrarian conflicts remained unresolved due to the corruption of the first strategy and the obviously violent nature of the second. According to data collected from official sources in August 1995, peasants in Chiapas were still awaiting the distribution of 1 million hectares of land that had presidential resolutions dating from before the 1992 ejido reform (Pérez 1995).

A Ministry of Finance report obtained by *La Jornada* in June 1995 revealed the extent of corruption and mismanagement in the land purchase program (Zúñiga 1995). According to this report, the state government issued 624 checks worth almost U.S.\$68 million in 1994 for the purchase of private properties in sixty-three municipalities. One case merits special attention. The 150 owners of a 22,000-hectare property known as San Isidro La Gringa, located in the Chimalapas forest on the Oaxaca-Chiapas border, were compensated with around U.S.\$4 million. Almost a quarter of this money went to one single owner for an unspecified amount of land. That individual was the head of the state government's Department of Agrarian Affairs.

If we leave this case out, 401 properties representing just under 40,000 hectares were purchased. Even if these properties had been distributed among CEOIC land claimants they would have still represented less than half the area in dispute. Several anomalies in the report indicated widespread corruption. Checks were made out to owners whose properties were not listed. Extensions of properties were not specified. One individual owner received U.S.\$3 million for seventeen properties. Although the average payment was calculated at just over U.S.\$1,000 per hectare, some owners received as much as U.S.$6,000 per hectare. Furthermore, just 6.6 percent of the owners received 31.7 percent of the compensation. Among these were politicians, government functionaries, and academics. The relatives of former governor Absalón Castellanos Domínguez figured prominently in the list.

The owners of many of the properties located within the area of military conflict received a rent from the state government. Between May and December 1994 a sum of approximately U.S.$15 million was paid to ranchers who claimed they were unable to use their properties due to the armed conflict. Because they retained their land titles, they could still sell their holdings in the future. The section of the report on rental payments was also deficient. Neither the names of the owners nor the properties in question were specified. These anomalies were reminiscent of the corruption that surrounded the PRA in 1984 to 1985, discussed in chapter 6.

Articulating Agrarian and Indigenous Struggles

The identification of sectoral and political goals became evident in CEOIC in June after the failure of talks with the state government to resolve land disputes. At a meeting held in Ocosingo in early July, leaders of the more independent organizations expressed their frustration at the time lost in negotiations. They also supported the EZLN in its call for a government of transition, a new constituent assembly, and the writing of a new Constitution. Those leaders who took a more official line rejected this position, and CEOIC effectively split into two camps: CEOIC-*oficial* and CEOIC-*independiente*. From this point on, CEOIC-*independiente* became an integral part of AEDPCH, and most of its leaders supported the candidacy of Amado Avendaño in the governorship race in August 1994.[5]

After the August elections the main goal was to prevent the PRI candidate for governor, Eduardo Robledo Rincón, from taking office. Land invasions now fitted into a more general civic insurgency that also included the occupation of town halls and the proclamation of rebel governments in "Autonomous Pluriethnic Regions" in several parts of the state (Burguete Cal y Mayor 1995). With the federal government's insistence on Robledo's inauguration, however, CEOIC (in line with the position of AEDPCH) refused to recognize the state government. In this situation the channels for negotiating land claims were restricted to the federal government, whose February 1995 offensive placed CEOIC and other Zapatista sympathizers at a clear disadvantage.

This period was marked by increasing violence against peasant movements associated with CEOIC. In September 1994 a PRD leader was assassinated in Jaltenango la Paz. In the same month police evicted peasants from private estates in Suchiate, carried out house searches in La Trinitaria, and impeded a meeting of the OCEZ-CNPA in Chicomuselo. The civic insurgency called for by AEDPCH began on November 20 with the occupation of nine town halls and five road blockades. A march in Comitán was violently dispersed by police fire and tear gas, leaving four people seriously wounded.

One of the most ominous signs was the presence of guardias blancas in evictions of land and town halls. In May 1995 the National Human Rights Commission called for an investigation into the killing of six people in southern Chiapas on January 10, 1995. On that date peasants taking part in the civic insurgency of AEDPCH peacefully occupied the town hall in Chicomuselo. They were violently evicted by police assisted by guardias blancas and local landowners. In addition to the six dead, several others were injured, including the parish priest and a nun who were shot at in their church. Further cases of violent evictions and killings were reported in April and May 1995 in the municipalities of Salto de Agua, Venustiano Carranza, Suchiate, and Jaltenango. The expulsion of three foreign priests from the diocese of San Cristóbal in late June was also in response to the unfounded allegations made by local caciques in Sabanilla, Yajalón, and Venustiano Carranza.

It was in this context that CEOIC began negotiations with Dante Delgado Rennauro, the representative of the federal government for social and development programs in Chiapas. The talks did not produce significant results and CEOIC leaders viewed Dante Delgado as part of the government's more general counterinsurgency plan for Chiapas. Access to resources and the solution of land disputes, which by May 1995 had increased to over 1,000 cases representing 90,000 hectares, were politically conditioned, forcing communities to make their allegiances known. The military presence in areas outside the zone of conflict, such as Marqués de Comillas, was also designed to intimidate oppositional movements from pursuing their agrarian and social demands. Not only were political activists identified as Zapatistas, but so were anyone associated with community organization, such as health promoters (Interview, members of Independent Regional Peasant Movement [MOCRI], Marqués de Comillas, June 1995 and July 1996).

The talks with Dante Delgado also created tensions within AEDPCH over whether to accept negotiations at a time when the EZLN was under attack. The Zapatistas needed to present the strongest negotiation position possible and feared that parallel agreements on something as fundamental as land reform in Chiapas could weaken their hand. Some leaders of CEOIC and AEDPCH argued that they wanted to coordinate their struggles with those of the EZLN but had not received replies to their requests for meetings with Zapatista comandantes. In any case, the peasants who were facing eviction from disputed lands could not wait until the government and the EZLN signed a peace accord. The EZLN and CEOIC obeyed different dynamics and, given the failed attempts to coordinate their respective struggles, AEDPCH went ahead and agreed to meet with Dante Delgado.

A related problem concerned the precarious status of the Autonomous Government in Rebellion led by Amado Avendaño. After the imposition of Robledo it became increasingly difficult to maintain the autonomous government as anything more than a symbol of resistance. The February 1995 offensive further weakened its prospects. The federal army now patrolled not only the Zapatista communities but also the Autonomous Pluriethnic Regions. Militarization encouraged landowners to increase their attacks on CEOIC members, leading to the evictions of April and May 1995 referred to earlier in the cases of Salto de Agua, Venustiano Carranza, Suchiate, and Jaltenango. In spite of these developments, Avendaño would not give up the fight to win recognition for the rebel government. He went on speaking tours in the United States and believed that he could draw on international solidarity to help rescue what was clearly an impossible situation. Back in Chiapas, especially in Suchi-

ate, Venustiano Carranza, and Sabanilla, the guardias blancas were
on the offensive and, with no solution in sight, CEOIC, in addition
to AEDPCH, decided (by a majority vote) to meet with Dante
Delgado.

The manner in which this decision was communicated to the
Zapatistas was typical of the worst of sectarian politics. What was a
highly complex and urgent situation was presented as a simple act
of betrayal. The leaders of long-standing independent organizations such as CIOAC, OCEZ-CNPA, and Xi'Nich, the largest movements within CEOIC and AEDPCH, were depicted as having sold
out to the government because of their decision to open the negotiations. Marcos wrote a damning letter in which he criticized these
elements of AEDPCH for surrendering to the government. Marcos
went on to admonish the "traitors" for thinking that "the struggle
would be easy, comfortable, full of photographers and big demonstrations. They forgot that freedom is won through sacrifice, that
defeats are normal for those who fight and that victory is not the
product of a banner or a declaration, but of organization, the combining of forces, political commitment and strength of convictions"
(Subcomandante Marcos 1995a:346).

This was like a bombshell for the leaders of AEDPCH, who had
spent their adult lives "combining forces" and dedicating themselves to their cause. The strength of their convictions was not
about to be dissipated by a federal bureaucrat, but, short of joining
the EZLN in the still pending peace talks, the options appeared to
be drying up. Offended by the content and tone of Marcos's letter,
the accused leaders sent a reply, explaining in detail the background
to their decision and the fact that they had on previous occasions
sought to coordinate with the EZLN and criticizing what they saw
as the frankly naive posture of Avendaño regarding the political
strength of the rebel government. Leaders of ARIC-independiente
also took the issue to the Zapatista comandantes and reminded
them that the EZLN would not have existed if it had not been for
the political commitment and sacrifice of many of its members over
the previous twenty years (Interview with AEDPCH and CEOIC
leaders, San Cristóbal de Las Casas, June 1995). Relations between
the two sides did not improve.

The difficulties faced by CEOIC were made apparent by another wave of violent land evictions in November 1995. This event coincided with the resumption of peace talks between the EZLN and the government in San Andrés Larráinzar. In early October, Interior Minister Emilio Chauyffet had met with leaders of the ranchers' associations and promised that land invaders would be evicted following the October 15 municipal elections. The negotiations at San Andrés Larráinzar were, in the words of one commentator, "the eye of the hurricane," as reports of detentions, beatings, and killings came in from around the state (Hernández 1995). Representatives of AEDPCH informed the negotiators gathered in San Andrés that their talks with Dante Delgado had broken down due to the lack of solutions to their agrarian demands. They also read out a long list of violent actions against members of popular organizations in 1995, which included 860 arrests, 50 evictions, and 40 politically motivated killings (Bellinghausen 1995).

In December 1995 judicial police violently evicted the three properties that had been taken over by OCEZ-CNPA peasants in March 1994. These were Arturo Albores, 6 de Marzo, and Albores de Zapata. Over 100 peasants were arrested and 200 homes destroyed.[6] Agreements to resolve over 2,000 land conflicts in Chiapas were signed between the federal government and sixty-nine peasant organizations (official and independent) in February 1996. The government agreed to distribute 60,000 hectares to the independent organizations represented in AEDPCH. However, according to a leader of AEDPCH, only 5,000 hectares had been distributed by July 1996. The February accord was immediately followed by the violent eviction of peasants from disputed lands in the municipalities of Pichucalco, Nicolás Ruiz, and Venustiano Carranza, in which several people were killed and others injured. In several areas violent attacks against pro-Zapatista groups were carried out by private paramilitary organizations in 1995 and 1996. These organizations were known as Brigada San Bartolomé de los Llanos, in Venustiano Carranza; Paz y Justicia, in Tila; and Los Chinchulines, in Chilón (see the concluding chapter).

The San Andrés talks on indigenous rights and culture reached a minimum accord on January 18, 1996, which was subsequently ratified by the EZLN bases and signed by the two delegations four weeks later. This was the first signed agreement since the January

1994 rebellion and was seen by the Zapatistas as a step toward the redefinition of Mexico as a pluriethnic nation. The accord recommended reforms to several articles of the Constitution (including Article 4) that would allow for the redrawing of municipal boundaries and the recognition of the right of indigenous people to compete for public office independently of national political parties. At the state level, similar reforms would be implemented with the goal of increasing political representation of indigenous people in the local congress. In addition, a state-level Law of Justice and Agrarian Development would be drawn up and a special committee would be created to discuss the agrarian problems in Chiapas, with the participation of representatives of the EZLN, other indigenous and peasant organizations, and government ministries. This body would also be responsible for drawing up a census of landholding in the state (*La Jornada,* February 15, 1996).

Although these agreements were seen by the EZLN as a step forward, other groups within the indigenous movement saw them as limited by the lack of legal recognition for the regional autonomy for indigenous peoples. Greater recognition would have permitted indigenous people increased control over the use of land and natural resources in their traditional territories by establishing pluriethnic autonomous regions as a "fourth level" of government alongside the current federal, state, and municipal levels. This limitation reflected not only the government's unwillingness to meet the demand for autonomy, but also the differences among sectors of the indigenous movement and Zapatista advisers over the extent to which the issue should be pressed in the adverse political climate of late 1995 and early 1996. The goal of regional autonomy remained a point of contention within the national indigenous movement during 1996. The idea of pluriethnic regional autonomy competed with several other understandings, such as community-level or municipal-level autonomy. Some advisers to the EZLN also warned against the possible reregulation by the state of indigenous norms and traditions under the guise of respect for autonomy.[7]

We must also bear in mind that the political context shifted significantly in the period between November 1995 and January 1996. During the first round of talks the government negotiators were more open to the idea of indigenous peoples' regional autonomy.

This position changed radically when the team of reformist advisers from the INI was replaced for the second round by hard-liners from the Chiapas state government. Military maneuvers close to Zapatista bases in late December were another ominous sign of a shift in the government's position prior to the final round of talks. During 1996 many observers feared that the continued militarization of Chiapas and the hardening of the government's position on each of the issues to be negotiated at San Andrés would lead to a breakdown of the entire peace process. By December, no progress had been made in reinitiating peace talks. In that month, the multiparty commission entrusted with mediating between the EZLN and the government presented Zedillo with a new proposal for the implementation of the accords on indigenous rights and culture. This proposal was based on the original text of the February 1996 agreement and was accepted by the leadership of the EZLN. However, Zedillo chose to reject the document and submit a counterproposal that bore little relation to the existing accords. It was clear that this would be unacceptable to the Zapatistas, who immediately denounced the government for going back on its commitments and for undermining the entire peace process (Hernández 1997).

Women's Rights

The Zapatistas also provided the space for indigenous women to demand equal participation in their homes, communities, organizations, and nation. Although the peasant movements discussed in this book tended to restrict women's participation to supportive roles, the participation of women in community life did create the conditions for a reappraisal of gender relations in the wake of the rebellion. This change was most evident in the Lacandon forest, where three interrelated processes helped indigenous women to assert their own demands during 1994 to 1996. The first of these was the very fact of colonization itself, which required women to adopt nontraditional roles in the new lowland ejidos. Due to the lack of government assistance in providing adequate infrastructure, the migrants were left to clear the forest on their own. Women carried out as much of this work as the men, as well as caring for

5. Zapatista Women, Oventic, Chiapas, July 1996

children and the elderly. The second process was the incorporation
of women into grassroots agricultural cooperatives and health and
education programs by the diocese of San Cristóbal and a number
of NGOs. These programs began when the diocese adopted its preferential option for the poor in the 1970s. It was deepened in the
1980s by new projects initiated by university researchers, students,
NGOs, and craft cooperatives located in San Cristóbal. The third
process was the creation of the EZLN itself. Male-dominated community assemblies were transformed by women's demands for
equal participation in the struggle. This was reflected in the Zapatistas' Revolutionary Women's Law, which states that all women
should have the right to a life free of sexual and domestic violence,
the right to choose one's partner and number of children, and the
right to political participation on an equal footing with men (Hernández Castillo 1994).[8]

During the first quarter of 1994 indigenous and mestizo women
from independent organizations (including CIOAC, the OCEZ-
CNPA, the OCEZ-centro, and the ARIC-independiente) began to
construct a common platform in support of the Zapatistas. In preparing their proposals for the National Democratic Convention,
they met in San Cristóbal in late July 1994, where they formed the
Chiapas State Women's Convention. This meeting issued a list of

demands that reflected the spirit of the Zapatistas' revolutionary law. They included the right of women to participate in the making of laws that relate to indigenous people and women, the right to be elected to positions of responsibility within their organizations and communities, and the right to choose the number of children that they want and can maintain (Convención Estatal de Mujeres Chiapanecas 1994). They also addressed gender discrimination within indigenous communities by demanding an end to the practice of exchanging girls for money, animals, or objects, and the establishment of the right to choose marriage partners. Some of these proposals inevitably implied conflictual relations between indigenous men and women, between daughters and parents, and between women and the various churches, including the Catholic diocese. The issue of contraception is particularly sensitive, and during 1996 some feminists openly criticized amendments to the Zapatistas' women's law that would restrict the use of contraceptives to married couples only. These amendments appeared to have been heavily influenced by a sector of the diocese that accepts the right of *married* women to contraception as a means to uphold its teachings on the sanctity of the family rather than as an affirmation of the rights of women *as women*.

The Chiapas State Women's Convention gradually consolidated itself during 1995, despite internal disputes over its understanding of feminism and women's goals. Against the universalist perception of some intellectual feminists, the indigenous women appeared to be demonstrating the validity of their own particular struggles as women within a patriarchal society. Analytical distinctions made by outside feminists between the "practical" and "strategic" gender interests of women were seen by some observers as reflecting the ethnocentric views of feminists in North America and Europe. The actions of women in Chiapas, whether in the EZLN or the state-level convention, were considered to be simultaneously practical and strategic in that they sought solutions to material problems and, in doing so, challenged the gendered power relations that had traditionally subordinated women to men (Stephen 1996). Indigenous women became active participants in organizing acts of civil resistance against the imposition of PRI mayors during the fall of 1994. They also participated in protecting the Zapatista delegates at the peace talks and in building the EZLN's bases of support throughout the highlands and Lacandon forest. Women also drew attention to the use of sexual violence against indigenous women. Although a number of cases of rape by soldiers and police were denounced by human rights groups in the national and international media, the majority of abuses were covered by a blanket of silence. By 1996, many grassroots activists were perplexed by the weakness of the Zapatistas' own response to this issue. Despite the opening created by the Revolutionary Women's Law, indigenous women still felt alone in their struggle for respect and dignity (Hernández Castillo 1996).

CONCLUSIONS

One of the goals of this book has been to establish the novelty and significance of peasant movements and the Zapatistas. By restating the main points of analysis, this chapter attempts to underline the importance of the rebellion while noting some of the obstacles to a peaceful and democratic outcome.

One of the advantages of taking a historical approach is that it allows us to observe the evolution of peasant resistance over time. There is obvious continuity between the EZLN and earlier movements. The symbol of Zapata and the centrality of agrarian demands are clearly part of a long history of rural movements in Mexico. Nor is the struggle for autonomy without precedent. The revolts of 1712 and 1867 can be seen as similar attempts to set limits on the colonial and neocolonial pretensions of ladino elites. They also resulted in the redrawing of boundaries between indigenous and ladino society. Finally, the struggles against local bosses and corrupt municipal government have precedents in both the nineteenth and twentieth centuries, as the pattern of state formation in highland Chiapas created resistance to the gradual institutionalization of caciquismo.

This history reveals not only the contested nature of state formation, but also the impossibility of any social order ever fully constituting itself. In the case of Chiapas, this means the inability of colonial and neocolonial structures to absorb conflicts into a stable order. This is not unique to Chiapas; it is inherent to neocolonial forms of domination, which, by definition, cannot allow indigenous people to freely represent themselves as equal members of a political community. Here we can bring out the novelty and significance of the Chiapas rebellion. Unlike previous struggles that sought to win concessions from the state, the EZLN aims to open spaces for the gradual dismantling of authoritarian (and specifically neocolonialist) politics in Mexico. Whereas the Unión de Uniones became caught in an overly economistic strategy, the EZLN calls for the type of political changes that are the precondition for gaining autonomous control of the productive process. Whereas the OCEZ became embroiled in sectarian disputes between rival factions, the EZLN offers the possibility of solidarity and respect for different political traditions. Whereas the CIOAC suffered from caudillismo, the Zapatistas organized their rebellion through consensual decision-making of hundreds of communities. The novelty of the EZLN is therefore to be found in its political organization, strategy, and objectives, rather than in its social base or material conditions.

If we refer back to the discussion on the significance of popular movements, we can now see that it is precisely their political nature that is of most importance. By recognizing the contingency of all forms of domination, we also affirm their political and transitory nature. Our methodology is therefore directed toward the numerous conflicts and contradictions (referred to here as "antagonisms") that actually give shape to political processes. By documenting the ways peasant movements have acted upon these antagonisms, we have been able to reveal the highly contested forms of political order in Chiapas. The particular dislocations that appeared in the 1970s and 1980s can be seen as creating the conditions of possibility for the emergence of new movements and, eventually, the EZLN. By this we mean the limits placed on land redistribution, the impact of economic modernization on peasant agriculture (the loss of land to hydroelectricity dams, oil exploration, logging, and ranching), the shifts within the Catholic Church, the education of bilingual teachers and catechists, the activism of students in the aftermath of 1968, and the gradual liberalization of the party system at the national level. Popular movements, such as those in rural Chiapas, played an important part in this process of political change, although there was no single direction to this activism. In general, however, we can say that more spaces for oppositional voices were opened up, creating the potential for a new, democratic politics or new "imaginary."

In this regard, the key innovation of the EZLN has been to make recognition of the rights and cultures of indigenous peoples an integral part of democratization in Mexico. It is likely that the indigenous peoples will play a fundamental role in the future transformation of Mexico. They are already the subject of competing discourses that range from the right to self-determination to the affirmation of the indivisible nature of the Mexican nation. This is an arena in which various currents of thought intervene, representing a remarkable shift in political debate at the end of the twentieth century. As a result, the significance of the peace talks on indigenous rights and culture goes beyond Chiapas, revealing the contingency of neocolonialism and pointing to a potentially historic transformation of ethnic relations in Mexico, with lessons for the rest of Latin America.

Each of these points undoubtedly requires further empirical investigation and conceptual elaboration. Nevertheless, we can say that things political have changed as a result of the Chiapas rebellion and that it is impossible to return to the status quo ante. We should expect future outcomes to be diverse, complex, and unpredictable but, above all, different. With these considerations in mind, we can turn to some of the obstacles facing the Zapatistas in their attempts to forge a democratic and peaceful outcome, focusing on how issues of power and responsibility must be addressed by local, national, and international actors.

The Costs of Rebellion

Establishing the right to have rights is no easy task. Effective citizenship does not inevitably flow from economic development or from the adoption of new cultural traits. In fact, it only exists to the extent that people are able to organize and open spaces for political representation. In Chiapas, this process was intimately linked to recurring patterns of resistance in which the struggle for land was central. The construction of citizenship grew out of local experiences of confronting caciques, landowners, and government officials. It was the impossibility of affecting change through legal channels that led to the decision to take up arms. The Zapatistas were prepared to risk their lives in an attempt to be heard, to open up a dialogue with others, to be treated as equals, to be respected for their differences, and to win the right to have rights. At least 145 people, mostly Zapatistas, died in the first days of January 1994 as federal troops attempted to crush the rebellion. More than 20,000

Zapatistas were forced to flee their homes in order to avoid another military confrontation when President Zedillo ordered the February 1995 offensive. After January 1, 1994, military camps and maneuvers became a constant source of intimidation and threat for Zapatista communities. It is clear that the cost of opening new spaces for political participation in Chiapas has been borne mostly by the men, women, and children who make up the EZLN.

Other groups have also been attacked because of their support for the EZLN. In February 1995 over a dozen people were arrested and charged with conspiracy because of their suspected identification with the EZLN. Priests and catechists of the Catholic diocese of San Cristóbal have been accused of fomenting the rebellion and of organizing land invasions. Several priests have been deported from Mexico on the basis of allegations made by local landowners. The offices of nongovernmental organizations who support a peaceful solution in Chiapas have been broken into, ransacked, and set alight. Their staffs have been issued death threats, and some have been kidnapped and tortured. Delegations of international solidarity groups and human rights observers have been fired at.

At the same time, however, thousands of Zapatista sympathizers have visited Chiapas to participate in a wide variety of activities, from the National Democratic Convention, to the establishment of peace camps, to the national forum on indigenous rights and culture. Spaces have indeed been created and have been used to build stronger linkages between local and national movements for political change. Civil society has responded with caravans of aid, street protests against military action, national consultations, and the protection of Zapatistas during peace talks.

The construction of citizenship is a double-edged sword. The creation of political space requires that communities search for alliances with new outside actors and political forces. Not all community members may be in agreement. Some may feel threatened or fear that existing notions of community are being undermined. The rebellion itself was not universally accepted in the Cañadas, and several thousand Indians decided to abandon their homes and seek refuge in urban centers rather than be caught between two armies. Most were settled in government-run camps in Comitán and Ocosingo, returning under the auspices of the military to "repopulate" communities abandoned by the EZLN following the February 1995 offensive. The rebellion also deepened existing conflicts within highland communities between pro-Zapatista and pro-PRI factions. In some cases, these divisions have been exacerbated by the emergence of paramilitary groups supported by government officials. With the failure of peace talks to bring about new institutional reforms, many communities became battlegrounds for the control of municipal government. While the EZLN continues to press for recognition of indigenous rights, highland Indians must also contend with new levels of intracommunity violence.

Much of the conflict stems from the crisis of existing institutional linkages between the federal government and indigenous communities. This crisis was revealed by the emergence of alternative forms of social, economic, and political organization in Chiapas during the 1970s and 1980s. The experiences documented in this book attest to the search for new forms of representation of peasant and indigenous groups. Grassroots support for the EZLN was facilitated by the actions of community leaders who had decided that traditional forms of political engagement were ineffective. Due to their position as intermediaries between indigenous and ladino society, these individuals played a crucial role in determining the subsequent development of opposition struggles in Chiapas. As in the rebellions of 1712 and 1867, dissident leaders would have to leave their communities in order to establish a new base from which they could issue their call for support. In the mountains surrounding the ejidos of the Lacandon forest, indigenous rebels formed their alliance with the urban rebels of the EZLN. It was the breakdown of earlier patterns of integration of indigenous society that again led to the creation of new bases of resistance. However, in many highland communities the same crisis of representation did not lead to the emergence of a fully consolidated alternative, but to a protracted struggle to fill a political vacuum. It is for this reason that control of municipal government has become such a contentious issue. In some cases, the base communities of the EZLN have simply declared autonomy from the "official" institutions, refusing even the scant public services that are still provided by the federal government. In these conditions, there is a tendency toward the polarization of antagonistic groups and organizations. This pattern is evident in

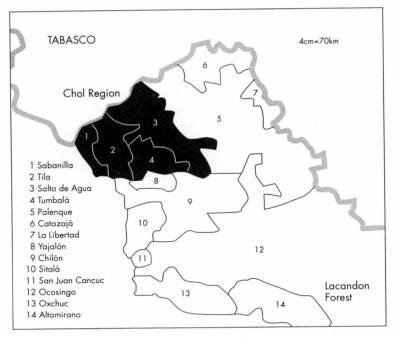

Map 9.1. Chol Region and the Lacandon Forest

most of the central highlands but became particularly pronounced in the northern Chol region during 1995 and 1996 (map 9.1).

The Other War:
Paramilitary Violence in Northern Chiapas[1]

The conflicts in the municipalities of Tila, Sabanilla, Salto de Agua, and Tumbalá have their own specific history, but they also reflect the kind of issues that continue to prevent peaceful solutions in Chiapas. The problems stem from the activities of a paramilitary group supported by the PRI, named Paz y Justicia. This group is led by Samuel Sánchez Sánchez, former leader of a faction of the teachers' union in Chiapas and, since October 1995, PRI deputy in the Chiapas state congress. Sánchez Sánchez is accused by human rights organizations of using his political office to obtain arms and other supplies for Paz y Justicia. The group's main objective is to forcibly destroy Zapatista base communities in the Chol region. In most cases, these communities have also participated in elections by supporting PRD candidates against incumbent PRI authorities.

Zapatista strength in this region is not negligible. Even prior to 1994, support for the rebellion had been organized through the ANCIEZ (see chapter 7). The radicalization of Chol Indians in 1989 to 1993 followed a similar pattern to that observed in the Lacandon forest. Prior to 1989, most of the ejidos were members of the Unión de Uniones. They were also hit by the fall in coffee prices and the simultaneous reduction or withdrawal of institutional support. Feeling abandoned by the government, many people rejected any linkages whatsoever with the regime, marking a clear and radical break with the institutionalist strategies adopted by most popular movements in the 1980s. The form in which the government responded to the coffee crisis led to further polarization. As discussed in chapter 7, the main program that attempted to fill the gaps created by neoliberal restructuring was PRONASOL. As in other regions of Chiapas, the state government sought to centralize control over the distribution of Solidarity resources for productive projects. In general, the local leaders of the CNC and PRI became the key intermediaries in this process. In the Chol region, however, the government sought to co-opt a new organization, the Teacher-Peasant Solidarity Movement (SOCAMA), an alliance of one faction of the teachers' union and some peasant leaders tied to the Orive wing of the Unión de Uniones. The SOCAMA developed strong relations with President Salinas and fitted in perfectly with the discourse of concertación. This relationship created tensions within ejidos as PRONASOL funds were channeled to only those members who supported the leaders of SOCAMA. In the midst of rising debts and depressed coffee prices, many small producers felt excluded and turned to the more radical alternative presented by the ANCIEZ and, later, the EZLN.

Another source of tension resulted from the elections in August 1994. According to investigations carried out by an independent tribunal of electoral observers, irregularities were reported at 57 percent of polling stations in Chiapas. In the Chol region, there was majority support for the PRD's gubernatorial candidate Amado Avendaño. Irregularities — including violations of secrecy of the

ballot—were reported at more than 70 percent of polling stations
in Tila and over 61 percent in Sabanilla. The failure of the electoral authorities to recognize the occurrence of fraud led dissident
groups to abstain from participating in the mayoral and local congressional elections in October 1995. In Tila, abstentionism rose by
24.4 percent between the two elections, from 41.6 percent in August 1994 to 66 percent in October 1995. A similar trend was observed in Salto de Agua, Tumbalá, and Sabanilla. The absence of
guarantees for free and fair elections continued to prevent the opposition from competing for office though legal channels. Instead,
many abandoned the electoral arena completely, as revealed by the
high rate of abstentionism, but also by the search for greater autonomy in the use of traditional means for selecting community representatives. The goal of indigenous autonomy can therefore be seen
as a response to the crisis of the institutional sphere and the continuing absence of democratic guarantees in Chiapas. In these conditions, despite the euphoria of democratic participation in Mexico
City, the national congressional elections in July 1997 continued to
be seen as a sham in Chiapas. The Zapatistas destroyed polling
stations in several districts in an attempt to have the elections nul-
lified. In explaining its position, the EZLN pointed to three factors:
the militarization of indigenous areas, the failure of the government
to recognize and implement the San Andrés accords on indigenous
rights and culture, and the lack of interest shown by all political
parties toward the problems of indigenous peoples. Countering
those who criticized the EZLN for its abstentionist position, subcomandante Marcos encouraged people to exercise their right to
vote where the conditions allowed, but added:

Who is responsible for the decision of indigenous communities [to
participate in the elections]? How is this decision to be made? On what
basis can Indians be called on to vote if they are not even able to live
under normal conditions? Can they be asked to pretend that they live in
a normal civic order for one day, and then return to daily terror the rest
of the year? (Cited in López Arévalo, 1997:17).

Divisions within Chol and other indigenous communities were
not created by the rebellion. They existed prior to January 1 and
were exacerbated by electoral fraud and intimidation of govern-

ment opponents. What the rebellion did, however, was to bring those divisions into sharper relief as SOCAMA leaders sided with the federal army, the state government, judicial police, the PRI, and the local ranchers' associations in defining a strategy of containment and eventual destruction of the Zapatista movement in the Chol region. Since 1994, the main objective of the federal government has been to prevent the spread of the EZLN beyond the area it successfully occupied on January 1, seeking to restrict it primarily to the Cañadas region of the Lacandon forest. It has deployed a strategy of low-intensity warfare in which military patrols and constant harassment of Zapatista sympathizers are combined with the provision of food, roofing materials, and health care to factions allied with the government (Global Exchange 1997; López Astrain 1996).

In this context, the Chol municipalities are of great strategic importance. To the North, they border the oil fields of Tabasco. To the West lies the Grijalva river with its complex of hydroelectricity dams. To the East is the main line of communication to the Yucatán peninsula. Finally, the ladino ranchers and merchants of Palenque and Salto de Agua have their own interest in limiting the advance of pro-Zapatista organizations. The Chol Indians are separated from the Cañadas by only a handful of municipalities that belong to the Tzeltal region. The most important of these is Chilón, where a similar polarization of community factions occurred in 1994 to 1996. In this case, the progovernment group, known as the Chinchulines, attempted to prevent the election in May 1996 of a new comisariado in the municipality's largest ejido, which also happened to be the strongest base of support for the Zapatistas and the PRD. The Chinchulines provoked a violent reaction and their leader was killed, many people were injured, and buildings were destroyed. The State Judicial Police intervened and arrested supporters of both groups, but the Chinchulines were unable to prevent the PRD from consolidating its control of the municipal government and subsequently saw their influence decline rapidly. This placed SOCAMA leaders in Tila on red alert. In Paz y Justicia they had a significant armed presence that had been supported by the PRI and local ranchers since its formation in March 1995. Attacks were carried out against PRD supporters in the summer of that year, but the events in Chilón increased the stakes even more. In June

1996 several ambushes and assaults took place between *priístas* and *perredistas* in Tila and Sabanilla, in which over twenty people were killed and many others injured. Paz y Justicia, with logistical and material support from the police and army, succeeded in terrorizing the opposition and was able to establish control over the principal roads that connect Tila with surrounding municipalities. Freedom of movement was restricted by the presence of its members. In August 1996 a delegation of human rights observers to the region was stopped and threatened, and the state police did nothing to intervene.

The lessons to be drawn from this case are essential for understanding the complexity of intracommunity relations in Chiapas and for finding peaceful solutions to the region's problems. The Zapatista rebellion has led to the formation of new, pan-Indian alliances. However, this process is inevitably limited by the type of divisions created prior to 1994. These divisions are not therefore a product of the rebellion. They are the product of institutional abandonment and the conscious manipulation by outside elites of internal disputes in the midst of severe economic strain. This point cannot be emphasized enough. Although any form of outside intervention is likely to affect the configuration of power relations within communities, some forms are clearly more destructive than others. Deciding to support candidates registered with an opposition party is one way of involving outside actors. It also happens to be a democratic right. On the other hand, arming paramilitary groups to terrorize local populations certainly disrupts community life, but it has no basis in legality whatsoever. This seems to be an obvious point, but it is striking how official responses to intracommunity violence sidestep issues of power and responsibility. The resulting impunity with which groups such as Paz y Justicia are allowed to operate is probably the major obstacle to achieving peaceful change in the region.

Zapatistas and Democratization

The consolidation of new spaces for democratic citizenship is also a matter of national political significance. The Zapatistas forced the

Mexican government to recognize the need for more far-reaching reforms in the electoral arena than it had been prepared to concede prior to 1994. Of particular importance was the package of reforms approved just three months prior to the August 1994 elections. These reforms allowed a greater role for national and international observers, enhancing the capacity of political parties and independent groups such as Alianza Cívica to monitor voting irregularities and contribute to the eradication of the most blatant forms of fraud. The Zedillo government's main political goal became the negotiation of a "definitive" reform in time for the 1997 national congressional elections. This would allow Zedillo to isolate the EZLN by demonstrating his willingness to pursue political reform through talks with the established political parties. Indeed, the mayoral election in Mexico City in July 1997 was seen by many international observers as a triumph for Zedillo. Despite the fact that the PRD candidate Cuauhtémoc Cárdenas won the election, Zedillo benefited from the low incidence of voting irregularities, enabling the media to praise him as a great reformer. The residents of Mexico City were finally able to participate in a free election and did so in favor of the opposition. At the same time, the PRI, in the midst of the worst internal crisis in its history, lost its majority in the Chamber of Deputies and must seek alliances with other parties in order to pass new legislation.

It is clear that the dominant-party system in Mexico is breaking down, but what type of system will replace it? Furthermore, what role will the EZLN play in this process? Three points should be apparent from the discussion in this book. First, the goals of the EZLN are not restricted to local issues of land, democracy, and justice in Chiapas. The rebellion addressed national problems that will remain on the political agenda irrespective of the distribution of votes among political parties. Among these is the ongoing debate regarding the social and environmental costs of neoliberalism and NAFTA for the majority of Mexicans. The EZLN will continue to dialogue with the nonpartisan organizations of civil society in an effort to extend the parameters of debate beyond the Chamber of Deputies and the party system. Second, if the transition to democracy in Mexico is to be inclusive of all sectors, it cannot be restricted to the mainly urban constituencies of the major political parties.

There is a danger that the democratic euphoria unleashed by the July 1997 elections will once again marginalize indigenous peoples and rural areas where civil and political rights continue to be violated on a daily basis. The increased military presence in the states of Guerrero, Oaxaca, Hidalgo, and Veracruz represents a constant source of intimidation and human rights violations of indigenous communities. Will the new, pluralistic party system be willing or able to restrain the tendency toward militarization of rural communities? The EZLN and its supporters will continue to pose this question. Finally, the Zapatistas have sought to open up spaces for new forms of political participation in Mexico. Their view of democratization is one rooted in the indigenous practice of governing by obeying, but it is also applicable to the wider society. Rather than restricting participation to the right to vote in elections, the EZLN favors the extension of that right to all areas of social, economic, political, and cultural life. This is akin to Norberto Bobbio's observation that democracy is not solely about who can vote but where one can vote (Bobbio 1989). The most important area in this respect concerns indigenous rights. The various currents within the national indigenous movement may have different notions of autonomy, but they are united in their opposition to any form of political system that continues to deny them full and equal representation. The party system may now appear to be a pluralistic one, but the absence of channels for indigenous peoples' representation will constitute a serious limitation on the nature of democracy in Mexico. The construction of a truly inclusive political system cannot ignore the historical exclusion of indigenous peoples, while new efforts at institution building must take account of the multicultural nature of Mexican society. All those engaged in building democracy in Mexico must also recognize that their actions cannot be divorced from questions of power and responsibility.

U.S. Military Assistance

In a June 1996 report entitled "Drug Control: Counter-narcotics efforts in Mexico," the United States Government Accounting Office (GAO) wrote that "In the past, the Mexican government has misused some US provided counter-narcotic helicopters. For example, during the 1994 uprising in the Mexican state of Chiapas, several US-provided helicopters were used to transport Mexican military personnel to the conflict, which was a violation of the transfer agreement."[2] Should we be surprised that the Mexican government could feel free to use this equipment against the Zapatistas? When it comes to impunity, what differences are there between Paz y Justicia and the Mexican military? Who can hold them accountable? In the first case, accountability is a task for Mexican civil society, political parties, and government institutions. In the second case, it pertains to the provider of military equipment, the U.S. government. However, end-use monitoring of U.S. helicopters in Mexico is ineffective. The U.S. embassy relies heavily on biweekly reports submitted by the Mexican government that typically consist of a map of specific operational records. U.S. personnel have little way of knowing if the helicopters are being properly used for counternarcotics purposes or are being misused. Despite the lack of effective monitoring, the U.S. government continued to supply Mexico with helicopters in 1996. President Clinton's 1998 budget proposal also included over U.S.$21 million for programs in the Pentagon and State Department to support anti–drug trafficking and military training in Mexico. This package included $1 million for the International Military Training and Education program, administered by the State Department, to train Mexican military officials (*La Jornada,* February 8, 1997).

Official U.S. policy toward Mexico has traditionally favored stability over the more unpredictable consequences of political reform. Stability has been seen as essential for national security and for protecting U.S. investments in Mexico. The Clinton administration's response to the Chiapas rebellion has been to avert a full-scale military confrontation, in the belief that this would produce further violence and instability of greater proportions. It has therefore backed the Mexican government's strategy of containing the rebellion. As mentioned above, the use of low-intensity warfare in Chiapas is designed to destroy support for the EZLN and to prevent communication between different regions of Zapatista influence. This strategy consciously seeks to avoid attracting international attention. Unlike the massacres of entire villages perpetrated by the

Guatemalan army in the early 1980s, low-intensity warfare involves a much longer-term plan to wear down communities and groups who have been identified as pro-Zapatista. By 1997, there was little sign that this political objective was being achieved, although the effects were apparent in the rising incidence of disease and hunger in Zapatista villages. Women were particularly affected by sexual abuse, rape, and humiliation at military checkpoints located along the roads that connect EZLN communities. Due to its role in the provision of military aid and in the training of Mexican officers, the U.S. government must also recognize its power and responsibility in Chiapas.

The construction of democratic citizenship in Mexico does not depend solely on the EZLN. In opening spaces for the assertion of political rights, the Zapatistas have subverted oppressive social relations. In doing so, they have raised important questions about the social impact of neoliberal economics, the future of indigenous cultures, the transformation of gender relations, and the scope of political reform in Mexico. These questions remain open and inspire many nonindigenous people to act in solidarity, providing hope and strength in the face of cynicism, despair, or indifference. In the context described in this work, solidarity requires a degree of patience and determination that, by necessity, has become the hallmark of the Zapatistas.

The Lessons of Don Durito

In a letter to a ten-year-old girl, Marcos told the story of a black beetle, Don Durito, who lives in the Lacandon forest, smokes a pipe, and steals his tobacco (Subcomandante Marcos 1994). One day, Marcos tracked Durito down and confronted him about the missing tobacco. Durito said he had to take some because it is so hard to get hold of in the forest. Durito was wearing his reading glasses and was studying intensely.

"What are you studying?" asked Marcos.

"I am studying about neoliberalism and its strategy of domination in Latin America," replied Durito.

"Why would a beetle be interested in that?" Marcos inquired.

Durito, offended by such a question, said that he needed to know how long the struggle would go on and if the Zapatistas would win or not. "Besides," he continued, "a beetle should make the effort to study the situation in the world, don't you agree?"

"I don't know," Marcos replied. "I still don't see why you need to know this."

"So that we beetles might know how long we must avoid you all trampling on us with those big heavy boots!" explained Durito, despairingly.

"Ah," said Marcos, "and what conclusions have you come to from your studies?"

Durito pulled some notes out from his desk, thought for a moment, and said, "you will win."

"I knew that already," said Marcos, "but how long is it going to take?"

"A long time," Durito sighed with resignation.

"I knew that too. But do you know how long exactly?" persisted Marcos.

"We can't put an exact time on it. Many things have to be taken into account: the objective conditions, the subjective conditions, the balance of forces, the crisis of imperialism, the crisis of socialism, etc., etc."

Marcos pondered on this analysis for a moment and then said he had to leave. He let Durito know that he could help himself to the tobacco whenever he wanted.

"Thanks, captain."

"Thanks, Durito. Now I am going to order my compañeros that it is forbidden to tread on beetles. I hope that this will help," offered Marcos.

"Thanks, captain. Your order will be of great use to us," replied Durito.

"In any case, be careful because our people can be a little distracted and they don't always look where they tread," warned Marcos.

"I'll be careful. Come back and chat whenever you want. Goodbye," said Durito.

"Yes I will," said Marcos, returning to the command post. "Goodbye."

Appendix A

CHRONOLOGY OF PEASANT

MOVEMENTS IN CHIAPAS

1965   Presidential resolution recognizing land claims of comuneros
       in Venustiano Carranza
1971   Resurgence of land invasions in Simojovel
1972   Presidential resolution creating the comunidad lacandona
       published in March
1974   Indigenous Congress held in October in San Cristóbal de Las
       Casas
1975   Left-wing faction of Independent Peasant Confederation
       (CCI) renamed Independent Confederation of Agricultural
       Workers and Peasants (CIOAC)
       Assassination of Bartolomé Martínez Villatoro in Venustiano
       Carranza in August
1976   Federal troops attack Casa del Pueblo and arrest leadership in
       Venustiano Carranza in May
       Formation of Unión de Ejidos Quiptic Ta Lecubtesel in
       Ocosingo in December
1977   Participation of CIOAC advisers in land struggles in Simojovel
       Federal troops used to evict land claimants from coffee
       plantations
1978   Participation of Maoist advisers in struggle against the
       comunidad lacandona
       Release of imprisoned leaders in Venustiano Carranza
       Division within Casa del Pueblo in February
1979   Formation of National Coordinating Committee "Plan de
       Ayala" (CNPA) in Milpa Alta
1980   Formation of Provisional Coordinator of Chiapas in July
       Formation of Union of Ejidal Unions and United Peasant
       Groups of Chiapas (UU) in September

Formation of "Miguel de la Cruz" Agricultural Workers'
Union (SOA) in Simojovel in October

1981 Arrest and imprisonment of Arturo Albores Velasco and
Victórico Martínez Hernández in Venustiano Carranza in
April
Mass demonstration by CNPA and democratic teachers'
movement in Mexico City in May
Hunger strike organized by CNPA in August for release of
peasants imprisoned because of land disputes
CIOAC organizes strikes on coffee plantations in Simojovel to
demand recognition of local union
Mass demonstration by UU in Tuxtla Gutiérrez in October

1982 Division between the main rival factions in Unión de Uniones
Provisional Coordinator of Chiapas renamed Emiliano Zapata
Peasant Organization (OCEZ) in July

1983 Plan Chiapas announced in May
CIOAC march from Chiapas to Mexico City in October
Arrival of members of National Liberation Forces (FLN) in
Lacandon forest in November

1984 State government announces Agrarian Rehabilitation Plan
(PRA)
Splits within OCEZ over leadership and alliances
Nine members of Casa del Pueblo killed in ambush in
Venustiano Carranza

1985 Formation of National Union of Regional Autonomous
Peasant Organizations (UNORCA)
Split in CNPA over role of political parties in the peasant
movement

1986 Protests by maize producers in alliance with democratic
teachers' movement

1987 Agreement to create the Coordinating Committee for the
Preservation of the Lacandon Forest in March

1988 Formalization of Rural Collective Interest Association (ARIC)
Unión de Uniones in March

1989 Creation of "Fray Bartolomé de Las Casas" Center for Human
Rights in San Cristóbal de Las Casas
Crash in world coffee prices. Restructuring of Mexican Coffee
Institute (INMECAFE)

Formation of Emiliano Zapata Independent Peasant Alliance
(ACIEZ)

1991 Arrest of Joel Padrón, parish priest in Simojovel, in September
Salinas government announces reforms to Article 27 of the
federal Constitution in November

1992 New Agrarian Law enacted by Mexican Congress in February
Xi'Nich march from Palenque to Mexico City in March–April
ACIEZ renamed National Emiliano Zapata Independent
Peasant Alliance (ANCIEZ) and led protest march in San
Cristóbal de Las Casas on October 12

1993 ANCIEZ becomes Zapatista Army of National Liberation
(EZLN)
Clash with federal troops in May

1994 January 1 uprising by EZLN
Salinas deploys troops
145 killed in fighting
Formation of State Council of Indigenous and Peasant
Organizations (CEOIC) in January
Land invasions carried out in several parts of Chiapas
Dialogue held between EZLN and government representatives
in Cathedral of San Cristóbal de Las Casas in February
EZLN bases reject government's proposals for reforms in
Chiapas
National Democratic Convention held in August

1995 New military offensive against EZLN ordered by President
Zedillo in February
Peace talks resumed in San Andrés Larráinzar in October

1996 San Andrés Accord on Indigenous Rights and Culture signed
by representatives of the government and EZLN in February
EZLN suspends participation in peace talks in September,
pending implementation of San Andrés Accord and other
demands
Paramilitary groups organized and supported by PRI in
northern and central Chiapas

1997 45 Zapatista sympathizers massacred in Acteal, Chiapas, by
paramilitaries on December 22

NOTES

1. The Right to Have Rights

Throughout this book all English translations of Spanish quotations are my own unless otherwise noted.

1. For the Zapatistas' account of the first days of the uprising and their military tactics see EZLN (1994) and Le Bot (1997:189–238). See also Reygadas, Gómezcesar, and Kravsov (1994) and Ross (1995). An independent, Mexican video company, Canal 6 de Julio, produced several documentaries on the rebellion, including *La Guerra de Chiapas,* which portrays the armed conflict in the highlands and the bloodiest confrontations in Ocosingo. Communiqués, letters, interviews, and other EZLN documents were translated to English and published in *Shadows of Tender Fury* (Subcomandante Marcos 1995b) and in *Zapatistas! Documents of the New Mexican Revolution* (Autonomedia 1994).

2. Tello's detailed description of the history of the EZLN, complete with names, made no reference to the sources of his information. It is unlikely that he pieced together such a complex history from a small number of interviews during 1994. The story has no gaps or contradictions, no competing evidence, and no citations at critical points in the text.

3. The term *imaginary* is used here to refer to the development of a myth that can successfully create and maintain a meaningful set of ideas, institutions, and practices. New social movements can be said to be "new" to the extent that they break with dominant imaginaries such as Marxism-Leninism and different forms of populism. In the case of Chiapas, we can say that the creation of a new myth around the figure of Zapata reveals both continuity with past agrarian struggles and novelty in the articulation of these struggles with specifically democratic struggles.

4. Similarly, Susan Eckstein (1989) stressed that the impact of popular protest cannot be reduced to social movements alone, but is instead contingent on elite responses, class alliances, and geopolitical forces. Despite the broader perspective of Arturo Escobar and Sonia Alvarez, who stressed the impact of social movements on cultural practices and everyday life, these authors were also forced to recognize the need for

institutional analysis. They concluded their volume by recommending
that "As students of social movements, we must direct more of our
attention to the terrain of formal democratic institutions because it
now intersects the terrain of quotidian politics so crucially expanded by
social movements during the 1980s" (Escobar and Alvarez 1992a:329).
5. In outlining his methodology, James C. Scott explained that "given
the choice of structures explored here, it is apparent that I privilege the
issues of dignity and autonomy, which have typically been seen as secondary to material exploitation. Slavery, serfdom, the caste system,
colonialism, and racism routinely generate the practices and rituals of
denigration, insult, and assaults on the body that seem to occupy such a
large part of the hidden transcripts of their victims. Such forms of
oppression . . . deny subordinates the ordinary luxury of negative reci-
procity: trading a slap for a slap, an insult for an insult. Even in the case
of the contemporary working class it appears that slight to one's dignity
and close control of one's work figure as prominently in accounts of
exploitation as do narrower concerns of work and compensation"
(1990:xi–xii).

2. Colonialism, State Formation, and Resistance

1. In Chiapas, the term *ladino* refers to the people of European
descent.
2. The imagery of inversion of the social world was not unique to
Chiapas. Scott discusses the popularity of world-upside-down prints
among peasants in eighteenth-century Europe. In what could easily be
a reference to Chiapas in 1712, he cites the description of one revolutionary print showing "peasants disputing with learned theologians,
ramming the scriptures down the throats of priests and pulling down
the tyrant's castle" (1990:171).
3. According to Antonio García de León, these figures represented the
largest percentage increase in private landholdings in Mexico during
the porfiriato (García de León 1985, vol. 1:167). By 1910 around 1
percent of the population possessed approximately 70 percent of all
arable land in Mexico, and in most states nearly 95 percent of the rural
population had no land (Huizer 1982:12).
4. "To keep the acquiescence of those over whom they ruled, the caciques were patriarchal figures. They administered justice in their own
way, favoring those who were loyal to them. They would distribute
some land or protect people from having to pay taxes to the govern-

ment. Even in San Cristóbal, in spite of the [liberal] Reform Laws, the Church continued to have an influence in government affairs." (García de León 1985, vol. 1:171–72).

5. Robert Wasserstrom cited how these landowners saw the Mexican Revolution: "In view of the vandalism to which the Chiapanecan family has been subjected by the armed bands sent by the Carranza government, which have invaded Chiapanecan soil with no other purpose but to trample on our political institutions, we have resolved to rise up in arms in defense of society" (1983:158). On the 1914 to 1920 counterrevolution in Chiapas see J. Casahonda Castillo (1974), M. T. Castillo Burguete (1985), García de León (1985, vol. 2:41–100), Alicia Hernández Chávez (1979), and Prudencio Moscoso Pastrana (1960).

6. The term *mapache* (raccoon) was adopted by the counterrevolutionaries because they moved at night and ate uncooked maize in the fields (Benjamin 1989:124).

7. In comparison to the mapaches and Pineda's Brigada las Casas, the zapatistas made up a much smaller force in Chiapas. They were led by Rafael Cal y Mayor, the son of a landowner in the lowland town of Cintalapa, who had made contact with Emiliano Zapata in Morelos and had proposed the formation of a front in Chiapas in 1916. According to Marion Singer, the zapatistas sought alliances with the mapaches and Pineda in a common struggle against the Constitutionalist army of Carranza. However, Cal y Mayor was never able to establish leadership over this struggle and, as a result, the agrarian demands of Zapata remained clearly subordinated to the political goals of the Chiapanecan elites until the 1930s (Marion Singer 1988:81–82).

8. For clear, succinct accounts of the place of corporatism in Mexican politics see Roderic Camp (1993) and Wayne Cornelius (1996).

9. "Mexican agrarian reform has institutionalized the peasants' desire for a piece of land. They soon learn that obtaining a plot is legally conditioned and regulated. They also know that they need the CNC to 'represent' them in their demands and to facilitate all the necessary institutional procedures. There are other peasant confederations which carry out this function but none can open doors, jump interminable queues, gain access to private offices or consult documents and archives with the same ease as the CNC can" (Hardy 1984:177–78).

10. As Wasserstrom noted, their function was both economic and political. "Not pure coincidence, it would seem, but rather conscious design inspired state authorities to create a group of local leaders, beholden exclusively to the governing party, who would ensure the flow of seasonal laborers to their appointed destinations." (1983:178).

11. Similarly, George A. Collier (1987) argued that the new brokers furthered the state's goal of maintaining political acquiescence in the highlands until the onset of agrarian crisis in the 1970s.

12. Eight ejidos were formed in Simojovel between 1934 and 1940, seven of which were granted to former tied peons. However, most of these lands were of poor quality due to their location on steep, rocky slopes or within areas of uncleared scrubland (Pérez Castro 1982:216).

13. The most complete historical accounts of migration and population in the Lacandon forest have been provided by Jan de Vos (1988a; 1988b; 1993; 1995). The first studies were carried out by Frans Blom and Gertrudis Duby Blom in the 1940s and 1950s. See Frans Blom and Gertrudis Duby (1955).

3. Leaders and Base in the Lacandon Forest

1. Caudillismo is derived from the term caudillo, which is an adaptation of an Arab word meaning "leader." The caudillo tradition can be traced back as far as Viriatus, who led local resistance in the final stages of the Roman conquest of the Iberian peninsula. It is based on the combined principles of loyalty to place and chieftain, honor, and leadership in battle. In Spain, the caudillo reappeared in the form of military leaders in the war against the Moors and in the conquest of the New World. The tradition became implanted in the armies of Spanish America, where the wars of independence were often led by caudillos (Fuentes 1992:38, 61, 263).

2. Lehmann describes how conservative elites and the United States Agency for International Development (USAID) supported literacy programs in the northeastern Brazilian hinterland to offset suspected communist organizing in the late 1950s. The governor of Rio Grande do Norte state invited Paulo Freire, then a professor of social work in Recife, to set up a radio station that would facilitate the literacy programs. Although Freire and the lay preachers went much further than the governor or USAID had originally intended, their efforts at consciousness-raising (concientización) among the poor can also be interpreted as part of the modernizing thrust of development thinking in postwar Latin America. That is, for many years, the practices of a liberatory pedagogy remained dismissive of popular cultures and tended to reproduce the vertical power relations between teacher and pupil (Lehmann 1990:98–99).

3. This point is discussed in greater detail in chapter 8. See the EZLN communiqué "Mandar Obedeciendo," dated February 26, 1994, pub-

lished in (EZLN 1994 vol. 1:175–77). See also Enrique Dussel (1995) for an analysis of the centrality of dialogue in Mayan society.

4. The priest had asked the people to make a communal confession. They replied by asking him to be patient, "because there are many problems and we are divided." Everyone spoke, argued, and asked for forgiveness from each other. Then, after three days, they said to the priest, "Now we can celebrate the Holy Eucharist. Now we can give ourselves the embrace of Peace." (Diócesis de San Cristóbal de Las Casas, 1978:9). Note how this event illustrates not only a contrast between communal and individual acts of confession, but also the effect the awareness of this difference has on creating community identity and cohesion. The members first sought peace with each other, and only then could they seek peace with the divine.

5. According to Ana Bella Pérez Castro, the participants in this project "gained an appreciation of the need to organize in their places of origin, as well as a broader vision of the situation they confronted." (Pérez Castro 1981:225). See also Pérez Castro (1995). One of the first academic studies of the conditions of indigenous women in this period was written by the director of the INI's School for Regional Development in Simojovel, Mercedes Olivera (1979).

6. "The tied peons live in extreme poverty. This is due to the harsh work conditions, starvation wages, company stores and alcoholism. We work from sunup to sundown for wages below seven pesos a day. As soon as they are seven years old our children must begin working for two pesos a day. Wages are not paid in cash, but in alcohol or tokens to be exchanged at the company store. On Sundays we must work for no pay and during the harvest women and children are expected to work the same as men. There are no medical services on the plantations. The Labor Department is unaware of this situation because of the lack of roads in our region" (Congreso Indígena 1974:6). This was not an isolated phenomenon in Chiapas. In 1970, tied peons still made up approximately 30 percent of the agricultural workforce (García de León, 1979:87).

7. The SRA replaced the DAAC in 1975.

8. For a detailed, albeit uncritical, self-appraisal of its strategy, see Unión de Uniones (1983).

9. "Al pueblo de México. Al gobierno federal y al del estado de Chiapas. A las organizaciones de masas," *Uno Más Uno*, February 13, 1981, p. 5. For the more oppositional stance of the National Coordinating Committee "Plan de Ayala" (CNPA), see *Punto Crítico*, (1981:22) and Graciela Flores Lúa, Luis Paré, and Sergio Sarmiento (1988:79).

10. See "Denuncian el secuestro de indígenas," *Uno Más Uno,* Au-

gust 17, 1982, p. 6, and "Queja de ejidatarios por enfrentamiento," *Uno Más Uno,* August 20, 1982, p. 6. In a similar case in July 1982, representatives of the UE Lucha Campesina in Las Margaritas accused the regional secretary of the CNC, Aarón Gordillo Noriega, of coordinating attacks on members of the ejido "20 de noviembre" because they had refused to join the CNC. Gordillo was also accused of creating divisions between rival peasant groups over disputed land and of directing illegal logging on the communal lands of Tojolobal Indians. See Rubio López (1985:55).
11. The credit union was called the Unión de Crédito Pajal Ya Kac'Tic. Its offices were installed in San Cristóbal de Las Casas. "Concesión a campesinos para una unión de crédito," *Uno Más Uno,* May 22, 1982, p. 4.

4. Mobilization and Repression in Simojovel and Venustiano Carranza

1. Information on the land struggles in Simojovel is drawn from interviews carried out in the summer of 1987 and from the analyses of Marie-Odile Marion Singer (1984), Pérez Castro (1981), Ovalle Múñoz and Pontigo Sánchez (1983), and Pontigo Sánchez (1985).
2. It should be noted that the revival of agrarian populism in Sonora in 1976 did not pass unnoticed in Chiapas. For example, landowners in the coastal and central Frailesca regions threatened to paralyze production, banking, and transportation if the state government failed to use security forces to evict invaded lands in Arriaga. At the end of May 1976 ranchers supported judicial police in the violent eviction of invaded properties. See "Junta Permanente de Ganaderos en Chiapas, por el temor a invasiones," *Excélsior,* April 20, 1976, p. 27; "Amenazan con paralizar a todo Chiapas si los invasores no desalojan predios," *El Universal,* April 28, 1976, p. 14; "Incendiaron un pueblo en el municipio de Arriaga, Chiapas," *El Día,* June 4, 1976, p. 2; and "Desalojar a invasores fue 'último recurso' para preservar el orden," *Excélsior,* June 16, 1976, p. 32. The "Sonora factor" was held to be partly responsible for the fear of expropriation among landowners. See *El Día,* June 16, 1976, p. 2.
3. For testimonies of these evictions see Marion Singer (1984:39). See also "Indigenas de Chiapas denuncian graves agresiones y atropellos," *El Día,* October 3, 1977, p. 23, and "Varios ejidos de Chiapas protestan por graves atropellos a campesinos," *El Día,* October 10, 1977, p. 14.
4. Miguel de la Cruz was a local leader killed during the repression of 1977.
5. For a detailed account of the repression, including the arrest of

seventeen strikers at El Vergel plantation in December 1981, see the series of articles by Juan Balboa published in *Uno Más Uno* on January 4, 1982 (p. 7), January 6 (p. 6), and January 8 (p. 8).

6. "Marcha de campesinos contra la CFE y la SRA," *Uno Más Uno,* December 17, 1981, p. 5.

7. In 1965 the municipal center *(cabecera)* of Venustiano Carranza consisted of seven neighborhoods, or barrios, San Pedro, Señor del Pozo, del Carmen, El Convento, San Sebastián, El Calvario, and Guadalupe. The indigenous population made up approximately half of the 16,000 residents of the cabecera.

8. Arturo Albores and Marisela González represented a new form of political engagement in the 1970s. The student movement had revealed a deep dissatisfaction with how university education tended to reproduce authoritarianism and elitism in Mexican society. At the UNAM, one of the foremost struggles to reform the curriculum and internal governance occurred at the School of Architecture. In 1972 students and professors united to gain greater autonomy over the content and purpose of the school's programs. The new direction was clearly oriented toward meeting the needs of the poor majority. The school was also restructured to allow for greater independence from the university's central administration. It advocated self-government *(autogobierno)* and the integration of theoretical knowledge and technical skills with the needs of the popular sectors (Albores and González 1983).

5. National Movements, Local Factionalism

1. As its new name suggested, CIOAC emphasized not only the land struggle but also the need to organize rural wage workers for better conditions. In 1977 activists from CIOAC began to organize indigenous workers on coffee plantations in northern Chiapas. The CIOAC remained formally independent of the Mexican Communist Party (PCM), although, in practice, many of its activists were identified with the party and its evolution into the Unified Socialist Party of Mexico (PSUM) in 1981, the Mexican Socialist Party (PMS) in 1987, and the Party of the Democratic Revolution (PRD) in 1989.

2. This change did not represent a complete break with land struggles; nor was it the first time that credit and marketing issues had been taken up by peasant organizations. The point here is to note how those organizations that converged in UNORCA were born out of agrarian struggles and, once they had received land titles, began to press other demands instead of continuing the struggle for further land reform.

3. Besides CECVYM the first of this new type of organization were the Federation of Workers and Peasants of Durango State (FOCED); Federation of Workers and Peasants of Chihuahua State (FOCECH); Regional Union of Ejidos and Communities of the Hidalgo Huasteca (URECHH); Union of Ejidal Unions and United Peasant Groups of Chiapas (UU); Unión de Ejidos Artículo 27 Constitucional, Jerécuaro, Guanajuato; and Ejidos Colectivos Francisco I. Madero, Coahuila; and some uniones de ejidos in Veracruz, Michoacán, and Campeche (Costa 1989:19–74). Fernando Rello (1990) provides a general analysis of second- and third-level organizations.

4. Table 5.1 presents a synthesis of the participation of 25 peasant organizations in six national meetings held between September 1983 and March 1985. Note that these meetings were different from those called by CNPA (see later discussion in the text on the evolution of CNPA), although some organizations participated in both.

5. Albores was instrumental in the formation of the National Assembly of Workers, Peasants, and Popular Sectors (ANOCP) and the organization of two national civic strikes in July and October 1983. On the ANOCP and other responses of the Mexican Left to the economic crisis, see Semo (1986).

6. These were the Revolutionary Peasant Alliance (ACR), with supporters in Chiapas, Guanajuato, Jalisco, and Tamaulipas, and the Emiliano Zapata Union of Comuneros (UCEZ), located in the Purépecha region of Michoacán. The OIPUH and ACR rejoined CNPA in 1987 after several organizations closely linked to the PRT decided to leave and form a new confederation, the General Union of Peasants, Workers, and Popular Sectors (UGOCP).

6. From Plan Chiapas to the New Zapatismo

1. The Castellanos and Domínguez families have been, and continue to be, important landowners in several areas of the state, particularly in the municipalities of Comitán and Las Margaritas. See J. A. Cruz (1982).

2. Between 1980 and 1983 over 100,000 refugees arrived in Chiapas as a result of the counterinsurgency campaigns unleashed by the Guatemalan military in the northern highlands. See Sergio Aguayo (1988) and Coordinadora de Ayuda a Refugiados Guatemaltecos (1984).

3. Such was the case in Simojovel in 1983 and 1984, where army units intimidated those communities affiliated with CIOAC or the OCEZ. Interview, OCEZ leader, Simojovel, August 3, 1987.

4. Sereseres claimed that despite the increase in support to the military, the border was not militarized and that soldiers kept a low profile, something OCEZ and CIOAC peasants would dispute.

5. By summer of 1996 the Southern Border Highway still had not been completed, although the Mexican military had quickly improved the 200-kilometer stretch linking Palenque to Benemérito de las Américas on the northern edge of Marqués de Comillas. The journey time had been cut from twelve to just four hours. Transit along this road came under military control in the aftermath of the rebellion. During 1994 and 1995 the army established checkpoints at intervals of twenty-five to thirty kilometers between Palenque and Benemérito de las Américas. Checkpoints were also established between ejidos within Marqués de Comillas. The surveillance and harassment of community organizers in this region is discussed in chapter 8.

6. In March 1984, one of Victórico's brothers, José María Martínez Hernández, was accused of murder and imprisoned in the municipal jail in Carranza. The three other prisoners at this point were Victórico and Agustín de la Torre (both from Carranza) and Gustavo Zárate, an economics professor at the Autonomous University of Chiapas who sympathized with the peasant movement. See "Vienen tres marchas campesinas al DF: denuncian represión e irregularidades en la tenencia de la tierra," *El Universal,* April 3, 1984, p. 18, and the interview with OCEZ members published in *Boletín Agro* (Instituto de Investigaciones Sociales 1985:333–35).

7. See the report of Amnesty International (1986:68–69) and "Nueve campesinos muertos y varios heridos, saldo del choque entre comuneros," *El Día,* October 8, 1984, p. 2; "Corre de nuevo la sangre en Chiapas" *El Día,* October 9, 1984, p. 3; and, on page 6 of the same edition, "Acusan a la CNC de propiciar actos violentos en Chiapas."

8. Interview, OCEZ members, San Cristóbal de Las Casas, Chiapas, July and September 1987. See also "Campesinos chiapanecos inician ayuno en la Catedral el lunes," *La Jornada,* March 29, 1987, p. 12; "Miembros de la OCEZ iniciaron un plantón indefinido en Chiapas," *La Jornada,* April 2, 1987, p. 11; and "Toman campesinos de la OCEZ el ayuntamiento de Venustiano Carranza, Chiapas," *La Jornada,* April 10, 1987, p. 6.

9. The march received solidarity from peasant organizations in Oaxaca and Puebla as it proceeded toward the capital. It also began to raise awareness among Mexico City's intellectuals concerning the repression and poverty of peasants and Indians in Chiapas. For example, Rolando Cordera interpreted the march as a struggle for effective citizenship and respect for basic rights. See "¿Se escuchará a los campesinos?" *Uno Más*

Uno, October 15, 1983, p. 3. Similar reactions were generated almost a decade later when Chol Indians marched from Palenque to Mexico City to protest the repressive actions of governor Patrocinio González Garrido (see chapter 7).

10. The ministries which participated were Budgets and Planning (SPP), Labor and Social Welfare (STPS), Agrarian Reform (SRA), and the Federal Electricity Commission (CFE). The state government of Chiapas was also represented.

11. "Se agudiza la represión contra los organismos independientes de campesinos en Chiapas: CIOAC," *El Universal,* March 2, 1984, p. 23.

12. See the following articles in the July 24, 1985, edition of *La Jornada:* "Mitin reprimido en Chiapas; 15 heridos" (p. 1); "Los campesinos llegaron en orden a Tuxtla Gutiérrez" (p. 8); and "Brutalidad contra el fotógrafo Fabrizio León Díez" (p. 8).

13. Andulio Gálvez was a lawyer who specialized in agrarian law and had worked as an adviser for CIOAC. He also worked for the release of peasant leaders in Chiapas and was the defense attorney for Arturo Albores during 1981 and 1982.

14. "Culpa la CIOAC al gobernador de Chiapas de la muerte de uno de sus dirigentes," *Uno Más Uno,* October 6, 1985, p. 12; "Protesta el PSUM por el crimen de Andulio Gálvez," *La Jornada,* October 6, 1985, p. 5.

15. "Tierra pa'vivir, sólo pa'vivir," *El Observador de la Frontera Sur,* October 7, 1986, p. 4; "Se sumarán a la marcha indígena que se dirige a Tuxtla," *La Jornada,* October 8, 1986, p. 5.

16. "El temor alcanza récords" (1987:14–17). See also Burguete Cal y Mayor (1987).

17. That part of the Unión de Uniones, which split from the leadership of Adolfo Orive in 1982, was formalized as a third-level organization, or ARIC, on March 24, 1988. Henceforth, it was known as the ARIC Unión de Uniones. The ARIC Unión de Uniones was established with the participation of six uniones de ejidos and two rural production associations (SPR). Member organizations are located in the different subregions of the Cañadas of Ocosingo (see map 6.2). The UEs were Quiptic Ta Lecubtesel (Betania), Junax Betic (Amador), Pajal Yacoltay (Avellanal), Agua Azul (Agua Azul), and Relámpagos de Agosto (Estrella). The SPRs were Snopel Ayotic (Estrella) and Junax Cotantic (Patihuitz). The other member organization, UE de la Selva, represented twenty-three communities in the municipality of Las Margaritas (see chapter 7). The use of ARIC in the rest of this book refers to the ARIC Unión de Uniones.

18. Information in this section is taken from the interview conducted

with subcomandante Marcos by Carmen Castillo and Tessa Brisac, Aguascalientes, Chiapas, November 24, 1994, and published in Adolfo Gilly, Subcomandante Marcos, and Carlo Ginzburg (1995:129–42).

7. Neoliberalism and Rebellion

1. Expulsions had begun in 1974 and reached their peak during the early 1980s. Such dissidents had been settling on the periphery of San Cristóbal or joining the colonists in the Lacandon forest, where they created new settlements and adopted the organizational and religious practices of several Protestant churches. Many of these communities supported the EZLN, although the precise level of participation by religious creed is not known. In the highlands, those expelled from Chamula and nearby villages began to form independent organizations in the late 1970s. A decade later, these groups had become significant actors in the struggle for agrarian and political rights (Morquecho 1994).

2. Despite a 1989 ban on exploitation of forestry resources in Chiapas, this activity has continued due to the lack of adequate alternative sources of income. Moreover, the ban has led to several conflicts with the police and army. The July 1991 protests in Marqués de Comillas, referred to in the preceding text, originated in application of the 1989 decree (Interview, representatives of MOCRI, Mexico City, September 1991).

3. The "social sector" comprises lands distributed under Mexico's agrarian reform. It includes ejidos, which the state formed through the breakup of large private estates and the distribution of areas of unused "national lands." It also includes *comunidades agrarias,* or the lands and resources that were returned to indigenous communities.

4. The PSE was renamed Pact for Economic Growth and Stability (PECE) after Salinas came into office in 1998.

5. It should be noted, however, that not all of this increase in maize cultivation was due to the incorporation of land in the Cañadas. Traditional maize-growing areas in the central valleys witnessed a significant increase, while highland Indians turned back to maize in the wake of the 1982 crisis and the decline in off-farm sources of income (Collier 1990; Collier and Quaratiello 1994, ch. 4).

6. One piece of anecdotal evidence is the remark made by a peasant leader following a meeting with BANRURAL officials in Durango in the fall of 1991. "It's funny," he said, "before we didn't know each other but there was always some money. Now we can talk face to face, but there is nothing!" The peasants were requesting a loan to finance marketing of

maize and beans. BANRURAL was in the process of pulling out of Durango. (Interview, member of UNORCA, Durango, September 1991).

7. These were maize, beans, sorghum, soybeans, rice, wheat, and cotton.

8. The CNOC emerged as an independent response to the collapse in the international price in 1989, although its origins lay in the regional movements of the early 1980s (Moguel 1992a). By the end of 1993 it represented almost 60,000 small producers from seven states, including approximately 20,000 growers from Chiapas. Most of its member organizations were independent of the PRI and other political parties. According to its own census compiled in December 1993, in Chiapas there were forty local organizations participating in the CNOC (Interview, representatives of CNOC national office, Mexico City, January 1994).

9. Information contained throughout the rest of this section is drawn from Cano (1994). In Chiapas the program was renamed Crédito a la Solidaridad by González Garrido.

10. It is significant that Salinas failed to support the INI-PRONASOL personnel in their confrontations with the governor. Instead of removing González Garrido for his obstructive and repressive politics, Salinas preferred to trade autonomy for loyalty and votes. In fact, the governor was such an impressive hard-liner that Salinas appointed him minister of the interior in January 1993. It would have been his task to oversee the 1994 elections had the Zapatista uprising not forced Salinas to demand his resignation.

11. The announcement in August 1993 of a further U.S.$55 million for social projects in the border region of Chiapas obviously came too late to forestall the rebellion. Solidaridad moneys were also allegedly used for such nonpriority works as the construction of hundreds of basketball courts, a sumptuous convention center in Tuxtla Gutiérrez, and the refurbishment of central parks and town halls (Hughes 1994).

12. The annual rates for Las Margaritas and Altamirano were 7.4 percent and 3.4 percent, respectively (Ascencio Franco and Leyva Solano 1992:204).

13. In the words of subcomandante Marcos: "The thing that most radicalized our compañeros were the changes to Article 27; that was the door that was shut on the Indian people's ability to survive in a legal and peaceful manner. That was the reason they decided to take up arms, so that they could be heard, because they were tired of paying such a high blood tax." (*La Jornada,* February 7, 1994).

14. The UE de la Selva represents 800 families of mestizo and Tojolobal peasants from twenty-three ejidos in the municipality of Las Margaritas.

15. In 1989 the UE de la Selva paid its members an advance of 2,750 pesos per kilogram and promised to pay the remainder after sale to bring the total to 3,500 pesos. This was the price that had been expected prior to the crisis of June 1989. Even with the price paid by Max Havelaar, the union was unable to fulfill its promise, and its advisers tried to convince members that it was better to repay the banks rather than be cut off from future loans. One indication of the impact of this decision was the fall in production in the following cycle. In 1989 to 1990 the UE de la Selva collected only 2,890 sacks, compared to 3,950 in the previous year.

16. Interview, adviser to UE de la Selva, Comitán, January 1993. For a critical view of PRONASOL in Chiapas, see "La resistencia cafetalera en Chiapas. Habla José Juárez, dirigente de la UE de la Selva y de la Unión de Cafetaleros del Sur (UNCAFESUR)," *Campo Uno* (supplement of *Uno Más Uno*), March 23, 1992, pp. 4–5.

17. *Xi'Nich* is a Chol expression meaning "march of the ants." One of the leaders of the march explained how the government had tried to stamp out the Palenque demonstration but had only succeeded in disturbing an "ant's nest."

8. The Zapatista Opening

1. Salinas's reforms are discussed by Héctor Díaz Polanco (1992:164–70) and Jane Hindley (1996). Besides the increase in the INI's budget, the reforms included the appointment of the prominent anthropologist Arturo Warman as head of the INI (January 1989), the creation of a new Comisión Nacional de Justicia para los Pueblos Indígenas (April 1989), and ratification of the International Labor Organization Convention no. 169 (August 1990). Salinas also saw that there were easy short-term benefits to be gained from portraying his government as a defender of indigenous rights. International fora, such as the first Iberoamerican Summit in Guadalajara in 1991, were ideal opportunities to present an internationally agreeable picture leading up to the quincentenary and, of course, NAFTA.

2. Ruiz was also a member of the coordinating committee of the Mexican Council of 500 Years of Indigenous, Popular, and Black Resistance (Consejo Mexicano 500 Años de Resistencia Indígena, Popular y Negra), which coordinated protests and demands of a wide range of indigenous and popular organizations in the context of the quincentenary in 1992. Until the 1980s the ethnic dimension of rural movements had been subordinated in theory and practice to the peasant or class

dimension. This orthodoxy began to be challenged by the specifically
ethnic demands of new indigenous organizations in the mid-1970s,
some of which participated in CNPA and other national movements.
The most complete account is provided by M. C. Mejía Piñeros and
S. Sarmiento (1987). For an analysis of the historical evolution of anthropological debates on peasants, class, and ethnicity in Mexico, see
Hewitt de Alcántara (1984). For a clear reminder of the indigenous
presence in contemporary Mexico (and a call to action), see Guillermo
Bonfil Batalla (1990).

3. In an interview in January 1992, Ruiz explained to me how post-
indigenista thinking was indispensable for a true process of democratization in Mexico. Although, as Díaz Polanco noted (1992:148), national political parties and movements had begun to see the democratic
value of pluralist respect for difference, in practice there was still a long
way to go in overcoming racism or ethnic-blind structures and practices. Similarly, the electoral system did not allow for the true representation of Mexico's pluriethnic composition.

4. The state government promoted the formation of a coalition of
peasant organizations in the hope of isolating the EZLN through the
co-optation of influential leaders of independent movements. The
founding of CEOIC was attended by the interim governor, Javier López
Moreno, and included both CNC-affiliated and independent organizations. To the government's dismay, the independent organizations
quickly moved to express their full support for the Zapatistas' demands
and openly criticized Salinas when he visited Tuxtla in early February.
By this time the most active organizations within CEOIC were the
OCEZ-CNPA, CIOAC, and Xi'Nich.

5. Avendaño had been initially postulated as the independent candidate of "civil society" but, due to the electoral code in Chiapas, was
obliged to register with a political party in order to run. The PRD met
this requirement, and Avendaño formally ran on the PRD ticket.

6. See "Violento desalojo de 5 predios en Chiapas; al menos 100 de-
tenidos," *La Jornada,* December 13, 1995.

7. These debates have been developed within the National Plural Indigenous Assembly for Autonomy (ANIPA), a grouping of various
regional organizations of indigenous people that drew up proposals for
constitutional reforms during 1995. The January 1996 forum gave birth
to a broader initiative to continue the debates beyond constitutional
issues and to ensure implementation of the San Andrés accords. This
initiative became known as the National Permanent Indigenous Forum
(Foro Nacional Indígena Permanente). The first National Indigenous
Congress was held in October 1996 in Mexico City and called on the

government to respect the accords reached with the EZLN. The congress slogan "Never again a Mexico without us!" revealed the main thrust of the meeting, which was also attended (with the escort of the FZLN and other members of civil society) by EZLN comandanta Ramona.

8. For the most complete account of women's participation and the gender-specific impact of the militarization of Chiapas, see the two volumes compiled by Rosa Rojas (1995; 1996).

Conclusions

1. The discussion in this section draws on the detailed report of events in this area elaborated by the Centro de Derechos Humanos Fray Bartolomé de Las Casas (1996).

2. Excerpt from a letter to U.S. Secretary of State Warren Christopher, September 20, 1996, signed by fifteen members of the U.S. House of Representatives. Cited in National Commission for Democracy in Mexico (1997:5).

BIBLIOGRAPHY

Primary Sources

Interviews

June–August 1987	Members of the Central Independiente de Obreros Agrícolas y Campesinos (CIOAC), Simojovel, Chiapas.
June–September 1987	Members of the Organización Campesina Emiliano Zapata (OCEZ), Venustiano Carranza, Simojovel, and San Cristóbal de Las Casas; and of the OCEZ–Coordinadora Nacional Plan de Ayala (CNPA), Lindavista, Independencia, La Trinitaria, Chiapas.
September–October 1987	Members of the Unión de Ejidos Quiptic Ta Lecubtesel and Unión de Uniones, Ocosingo; and of the Unión de Crédito Pajal Ya Kac'Tic, San Cristóbal de Las Casas, Chiapas.
June 1990	Members of the national leadership of the CNPA and Unión de Organizaciones Regionales Campesinas Autónomas (UNORCA), Mexico City.
July 1990	Representatives of the Secretaría de Agricultura y Recursos Hidráulicos (SARH), Mexico City.
July–November 1991	Representatives of UNORCA, Mexico City, Guanajuato, Durango, and Chiapas. Representatives and members of Coalición de Ejidos de la Costa Grande de Guerrero, Coordinadora Nacional de Organizaciones Cafetaleras (CNOC), Atoyac, Guerrero.
September 1991	Representative of Movimiento Campesino Regional Independiente (MOCRI), Mexico City.

December 1991	Representatives and members of OCEZ-CNPA, Mexico City, Comitán, La Trinitaria, and Frontera Comalapa, Chiapas.
January 1992	Representatives and members of Unión de Ejidos de la Selva, Las Margaritas and Comitán, Chiapas.
April 1992	Representatives of OCEZ-CNPA, Mexico City.
January 1993	Representatives of Asociación Rural de Interés Colectivo (ARIC)–Unión de Uniones, San Cristóbal de Las Casas, Chiapas.
	Representatives of Unión de Ejidos de la Selva, Comitán, Chiapas.
January 1994	Representatives of the Consejo Estatal de Organizaciones Indígenas y Campesinas (CEOIC), San Cristóbal de Las Casas, Chiapas.
	Director of Registro Agrario Nacional (RAN), Mexico City.
	Representatives of CNOC national office, Mexico City.
July 1994	Representatives of CEOIC, Tuxtla Gutiérrez and Ocosingo.
	Representatives and members of OCEZ-CNPA, Frontera Comalapa, La Trinitaria, Chiapas.
	Representatives and members of Asamblea Estatal Democrática del Pueblo Chiapaneco (AEDPCH), Tuxtla Gutiérrez, Chiapas.
	Director of Procuraduría Agraria, Tuxtla Gutiérrez, Chiapas.
	Representatives of Solidaridad Campesina Magisterial (SOCAMA), Tuxtla Gutiérrez, Chiapas, and Mexico City.
August 1994	Members of Ejército Zapatista de Liberación Nacional (EZLN), Convención Nacional Democrática, Aguascalientes, Chiapas.

February 1995	Members of communities affected by military actions of the federal army and Misión Civil de Observadores por la Paz, Las Margaritas, Chiapas.
June 1995	Representative of AEDPCH and CEOIC, San Cristóbal de Las Casas, Chiapas.
June 1995 and July 1996	Representatives and members of Movimiento Campesino Regional Independiente (MOCRI), Marqués de Comillas, Chiapas.
August 1996	Members of EZLN, Encuentro Intercontinental contra el Neoliberalismo y por la Humanidad, La Realidad, Chiapas.

Documents, Pamphlets, and Communiqués

Albores Velasco, Arturo. 1981–82. Personal correspondence with Marisela González.

CIOAC (Central Independiente de Obreros Agrícolas y Campesinos). 1983. "Pliego petitorio de la marcha campesina de Chiapas." *Textual* (Universidad Autónoma de Chapingo), 4 (13) (September):130–50.

CLCH (Coordinadora de Luchas de Chiapas). 1986. "22 días de movilización de la Coordinadora de Luchas de Chiapas." Leaflet. April.

CNPA (Coordinadora Nacional Plan de Ayala). 1980. "Documentos de la CNPA." *Textual* (Universidad Autónoma de Chapingo), 1 (3) (April–June):104–26.

———. 1981. "Manifiesto de la CNPA." *Textual* (Universidad Autónoma de Chapingo), 2 (7) (April–June):124–41.

CNPA and FNCR (Frente Nacional Contra la Represión). 1981. "¡Alto a la represión en Chiapas!" Flyer. April.

Congreso Indígena. 1974. *Acuerdos del Primer Congreso Indígena "Fray Bartolomé de Las Casas."* San Cristóbal de Las Casas, Chiapas.

Convención Estatal de Mujeres Chiapanecas. 1994. *Escribiendo nuestra historia.* San Cristóbal de Las Casas, Chiapas.

EZLN (Ejército Zapatista de Liberación Nacional). 1994. *Documentos y comunicados.* Vol. 1. Mexico City: Era.

———. 1995. *Documentos y comunicados.* Vol. 2. Mexico City: Era.

———. 1996. *Fourth Declaration of the Lacandon Forest* (January 1,

1996). Translation in *Dark Night Field Notes* (Chicago: Dark Night Press) 7 (Winter):33–40.

OCEZ (Organización Campesina Emiliano Zapata). 1988. "Documento de aclaración." Unpublished document. Venustiano Carranza, Chiapas, September.

OCEZ-CNPA (Organización Campesina Emiliano Zapata–Coordinadora Nacional Plan de Ayala). 1989. "La OCEZ: su historia y su lucha." *Boletín de Información y Análisis de la OCEZ-CNPA*. (8) (January).

Subcomandante Marcos. 1994. "Durito" (letter to Mariana Moguel, April 10, 1994). Pp. 217–19 in EZLN. *Documentos y comunicados*. Vol. 1. Mexico City: Era.

———. 1995a. "Critica la negociación de un sector de la AEDPCH con el gobierno." (May 30, 1995). Pp. 345–47 in EZLN. *Documentos y Comunicados*. Vol. 2. Mexico City: Era.

———. 1995b. *Shadows of Tender Fury: The Letters and Communiqués of Subcomandante Marcos and the Zapatista Army of National Liberation*. Translated by Frank Bardacke, Leslie López, and the Watsonville, California, Human Rights Collective, with an introduction by John Ross and afterword by Frank Bardacke. New York: Monthly Review Press.

UU (Unión de Uniones). 1983. "Nuestra lucha por la tierra en la selva lacandona." *Textual* (Universidad Autónoma de Chapingo), 4 (13) (September):151–63.

Unpublished Papers and Reports

Albores, Arturo, and Marisela González. 1983. "La vinculación popular y el encuentro con la realidad." Paper presented at the School of Architecture, UNAM, Cuarto Congreso de Arquitectura–Autogobierno, August.

Amnesty International. 1985. Urgent Action Bulletin. AMR 41/14/85.

———. 1986. "Reported killings, detentions and torture in the state of Chiapas." Urgent Action Bulletin. July 9.

Coordinadora de Ayuda a Refugiados Guatemaltecos. 1984. "Los refugiados son verdaderos y numerosos." *Boletín de la Coordinadora de Ayuda a Refugiados Guatemaltecos*. San Cristóbal de Las Casas, Chiapas.

Diócesis de San Cristóbal de Las Casas. 1978. "Líneas básicas para entender donde estamos." Report. San Cristóbal de Las Casas: Comisión Encuentro Diocesano.

Global Exchange. 1997. "Analysis of Violence in Chiapas." Report distributed on World Wide Web (Archives of Chiapas-1 mail list).

Horizontes. 1990. *Boletín del Centro de Derechos Humanos "Fray Bartolomé de Las Casas"* (2) (November), San Cristóbal de Las Casas, Chiapas.

———. 1991a. *Boletín del Centro de Derechos Humanos "Fray Bartolomé de Las Casas"* (3) (March), San Cristóbal de Las Casas, Chiapas.

———. 1991b. *Boletín del Centro de Derechos Humanos "Fray Bartolomé de Las Casas"* (4–5) (September), San Cristóbal de Las Casas, Chiapas.

Minnesota Advocates for Human Rights. 1993. *Civilians at Risk: Military and Police Abuses in the Mexican Countryside.* North America Project Special Report 6. New York: World Policy Institute.

National Commission for Democracy in Mexico. 1997. "U.S. Military Aid in Chiapas." Report. El Paso, Tex.: National Commission for Democracy in Mexico.

Taller de San Cristóbal. 1992. *Reformas al artículo 27 constitucional.* Workshop proceedings, San Cristóbal de las Casas, Chiapas.

Government Documents

Gobierno del Estado de Chiapas. 1994. "Comunicación a los dirigentes del CEOIC." Unpublished correspondence. Tuxtla Gutiérrez, Chiapas.

INEGI (Instituto Nacional de Estadística, Geografía e Informática). 1991. *Atlas ejidal del Estado de Chiapas. Encuesta nacional agropecuaria ejidal, 1988.* Aguascalientes: INEGI.

———. 1992. *XI censo general de población y vivienda, 1990.* Aguascalientes: INEGI.

INMECAFE (Instituto Mexicano del Café). 1992. *Censo cafetalero.* Mexico City: INMECAFE.

Mexico. 1983a. Gobierno de la República y Gobiernos de los Estados de Campeche, Chiapas, Oaxaca, Quintana Roo, Tabasco, Veracruz y Yucatán. 1983a. *Programa de desarrollo de la Región del Sureste.* Mexico City: Poder Ejecutivo Federal.

———. 1983b. Gobierno de la República y el Gobierno del Estado de Chiapas. *Plan Chiapas.* Mexico City: Poder Ejecutivo Federal.

PROCEDE (Programa de Certificación de Derechos Ejidales y Titulación de Solares Urbanos). 1993. *Documento guía.* Mexico City: Procuraduría Agraria.

SARH (Secretaría de Agricultura y Recursos Hidráulicos). 1993.

"PROCAMPO: A new support program for the Mexican farm sector." Mexico City: SARH.

SARH-CEPAL (Secretaría de Agricultura y Recursos Hidráulicos and Comisión Económica para América Latina y el Caribe). 1992. *Primer informe nacional sobre tipología de productores del sector social.* Mexico City: Subsecretaría de Política Social y Concertación and SARH.

SRA (Secretaría de la Reforma Agraria). 1987. *Sistema de inafectabilidad.* Mexico City: SRA Statistical Database.

———. Subdelegación de concertación agraria en zonas indígenas. 1989. *Acciones agrarias.* Mimeo. Tuxtla Gutiérrez, Chiapas.

———. Subsecretaría de Asuntos Agrarios. 1994. *Programa de abatimiento del rezago agrario. Estado de Chiapas.*

Secondary Sources

Books, Articles, Papers, and Dissertations

Aguayo, Sergio. 1987. "Chiapas: las amenazas a la seguridad nacional." Unpublished paper. Mexico: Centro Interamericano de Estudios Estratégicos.

———. 1988. *El éxodo Centroamericano.* Mexico City: Secretaría de Educación Pública.

Aguilar Zinser, Adolfo. 1983. "Mexico and the Guatemalan Crisis." Pp. 161–86 in *The Future of Central America: Policy Choices for the United States and Mexico,* edited by Richard Fagen and Olga Pellicer. Stanford, Calif.: Stanford University Press.

———. 1991. "Todo en Chiapas es Centroamérica." *El Financiero,* October 21, p. 56.

Amnesty International. 1986. *Mexico: Human Rights in Rural Areas. Exchange of Documents with the Mexican Government on Human Rights Violations in Oaxaca and Chiapas.* London: Amnesty International.

Arendt, Hannah. 1949. "The Rights of Man: What Are They?" *Modern Review* 3 (1) (Summer).

Ascencio Franco, Gabriel. 1995. "Milpa y ganadería en Ocosingo." Pp. 363–73 in *Chiapas: los rumbos de otra historia,* edited by Juan Pedro Viqueira and Mario Humberto Ruz. Mexico: Centro de Estudios Mayas del Instituto de Investigaciones Filológicas y Coordinación de Humanidades (UNAM), Centro de Investigaciones y Estudios Superiores en Antropología Social, Centro de

Estudios Mexicanos y Centroamericanos, and Universidad de Guadalajara.

Ascencio Franco, Gabriel, and Xochitl Leyva Solano. 1992. "Los municipios de la selva chiapaneca. Colonización y dinámica agropecuaria." Pp. 176–241 in *Anuario de cultura e investigación 1991*. Tuxtla Gutiérrez, Chiapas: Instituto Chiapaneco de Cultura.

Autonomedia. 1994. *Zapatistas! Documents of the New Mexican Revolution*. New York: Autonomedia.

Barry, Tom. 1995. *Zapata's Revenge*. Boston: South End.

Bartra, Armando. 1980. "Crisis agraria y movimiento campesino en los setentas." *Cuadernos Agrarios* 5 (10/11):15–64.

——. 1985. *Los herederos de Zapata*. Mexico City: Era.

——. 1991. "Pros, contras y asegunes de la apropiación del proceso productivo: organizaciones rurales de productores." *El Cotidiano* (39) (January–February): 46–52.

Bartra, Roger, ed. 1976. *Caciquismo y poder político en el México rural*. Mexico City: Siglo XXI Editores.

Bellinghausen, Hermann. 1992. "Xi'Nich y la cultura de la victoria." *La Jornada* April 27, p. 26.

——. 1995. "Causaron 'baja' en las pláticas las huestes del Instituto Nacional Indigenista." *La Jornada* November 15.

Benjamin, Tom. 1989. *A Rich Land, a Poor People: Politics and Society in Modern Chiapas*. Albuquerque: University of New Mexico Press.

Blom, Frans, and Gertrudis Duby. 1955. *La selva lacandona*. Mexico City: Editorial Cultura.

Bobbio, Norberto. 1989. *Democracy and Dictatorship*. Minneapolis: University of Minnesota Press.

Bonfil Batalla, Guillermo. 1990. *México profundo: una civilización negada*. Mexico City: Grijalbo and Consejo Nacional para las Ciencias y las Artes (CNCA).

Brading, David. 1980. "National Politics and the Populist Tradition." Pp. 1–16 in *Caudillo and Peasant in the Mexican Revolution*. Cambridge: Cambridge University Press.

Burbach, Roger. 1994. "Roots of Postmodern Rebellion in Chiapas." *New Left Review* 205:113–24.

Burguete Cal y Mayor, Araceli. 1987. *Chiapas, cronología de un etnocidio reciente: represión política a los indios, 1974–1987*. Mexico City: Academia Mexicana de los Derechos Humanos A.C.

——. 1995. "Autonomía indígena: un camino hacia la paz." *Revista Memoria* (175) (March):19–24.

Calva, José Luis. 1993. *La disputa por la tierra: la reforma del Artículo 27 y la nueva Ley Agraria*. Mexico City: Fontamara.

Camp, Roderic. 1993. *Politics in Mexico*. Oxford, N.Y.: Oxford University Press.

Canel, Eduardo. 1992. "Democratization and the Decline of Urban Social Movements in Uruguay: A Political-Institutional Account." Pp. 276–90 in *The Making of Social Movements in Latin America: Identity, Strategy and Democracy*, edited by Arturo Escobar and Sonia Alvarez. Boulder: Westview.

Cano, Arturo. 1994. "Lo más delgado del hilo: Pronasol en Chiapas." *Reforma* January 28, pp. 3–7.

Cardoso, Ruth. 1992. "Popular Movements in the Context of the Consolidation of Democracy in Brazil." Pp. 291–302 in *The Making of Social Movements in Latin America: Identity, Strategy and Democracy*, edited by Arturo Escobar and Sonia Alvarez. Boulder: Westview.

Carton de Grammont, Hubert. 1988a. "Jaramillo y las luchas campesinas en Morelos." Pp. 261–76 in *Historia de la cuestión agraria mexicana: los tiempos de la crisis*. Vol. 8, edited by Julio Moguel. Mexico City: Siglo XXI Editores and Centro de Estudios Históricos del Agrarismo en México.

———. 1988b. "La Unión General de Obreros Agrícolas y Campesinos." Pp. 222–60 in *Historia de la cuestión agraria mexicana: los tiempos de la crisis*. Vol. 8, edited by Julio Moguel. Mexico City: Siglo XXI Editores and Centro de Estudios Históricos del Agrarismo en México.

Casahonda Castillo, J. 1974. *Cincuenta años de revolución en Chiapas*. Tuxtla Gutiérrez: Instituto de Artes y Ciencias de Chiapas.

Castañeda, Jorge. 1993. *Utopia Unarmed*. New York: Knopf.

———. 1994. "The Chiapas Uprising." *Los Angeles Times*, January 3.

Castillo Burguete, M. T. 1985. "Revolución y contrarevolución en Chiapas." *Textual* (Universidad Autónoma de Chapingo), 5 (18/19) (March):76–92.

———. 1988. *Producción y comercialización de granos básicos: el movimiento de la Unión Estatal de Productores de Maíz de Chiapas*. Mexico: Universidad Autónoma Metropolitana (UAM)–Xochimilco.

Castillo, Carmen, and Tessa Brisac. 1995. Interview with Subcomandante Marcos. In appendix: "Historia de Marcos ye de los Hombres de la Noche." Pp. 129–42 in *Discusión sobre la historia*, by Adolfo Gilly, Subcomandante Marcos, and Carlo Ginzburg. Mexico City: Taurus.

Centro de Derechos Humanos Fray Bartolomé de Las Casas. 1996. *Ni Paz ni Justicia, o Informe general y amplio acerca de la guerra civil que sufren los Choles en la Zona Norte de Chiapas, diciembre de 1994 a octubre de 1996*. San Cristóbal de Las Casas, Chiapas: Centro de Derechos Humanos Fray Bartolomé de Las Casas.

CEPAL (Comisión Económica para América Latina y el Caribe). 1982. *Economía campesina y agricultura empresarial: tipología de agricultores del agro mexicano*. Mexico City: Siglo XXI Editores.

Cepeda Neri, Alvaro. 1992. "Chiapas: la lucha por los derechos humanos." *La Jornada*, April 21, p. 5.

"Chiapas: el ejército, solución a problemas agrarios." 1979. *Proceso*. (133) (May 21):22–27.

Coatsworth, John. 1988. "Patterns of Rural Rebellion in Latin America: Mexico in Comparative Perspective." Pp. 21–62 in *Riot, Rebellion and Revolution: Rural Social Conflict in Mexico*, edited by Friedrich Katz. Princeton, N.J.: Princeton University Press.

Colectivo. 1983. "Lucha laboral y sindicalismo en Simojovel." *Textual* (Universidad Autónoma de Chapingo), 4 (13) (September):77–80.

Collier, George A. 1987. "Peasants and the State in Highland Chiapas." *Mexican Studies/Estudios Mexicanos*. 3 (1) (Winter):71–98.

———. 1990. *Seeking Food and Seeking Money: Changing Productive Relations in a Highland Mexican Community*. Discussion Paper 10. Geneva: United Nations Research Institute for Social Development.

Collier, George A., and Elizabeth L. Quaratiello. 1994. *Basta! — Land and the Zapatista Rebellion in Chiapas*. Oakland, Calif.: Food First Books, Institute for Food and Development Policy.

Cook, Maria Lorena. 1990. "Organizing Opposition in the Teachers' Movement in Oaxaca." Pp. 199–212 in *Popular Movements and Political Change in Mexico*, edited by Joe Foweraker and Ann Craig. Boulder: Lynne Rienner.

———. 1996. *Organizing Dissent: The Teachers' Movement in Mexico*. University Park: Pennsylvania State University.

Córdova, Arnaldo. 1979. *La política de masas y el futuro de la izquierda en México*. Serie Popular 72. Mexico City: Era.

Cornelius, Wayne. 1996. *Mexican Politics in Transition: The Breakdown of a One-Party-Dominant Regime*. La Jolla: Center for U.S.-Mexican Studies, University of California, San Diego.

Cornelius, Wayne, Jonathan Fox, and Ann Craig, eds. 1994. *Transforming State-Society Relations in Mexico: The National Solidarity Strategy*. La Jolla: Center for U.S.-Mexican Studies, University of California, San Diego.

Costa, Nuria. 1989. *UNORCA: documentos para la Historia*. Mexico: Costa-Amic Editores.

Cruz, J. A. 1982. *Absalón Castellanos Domínguez y los terratenientes: un análisis coyuntural*. San Cristóbal de Las Casas: Universidad Autónoma de Chiapas.

de la Peña, Guillermo. 1986. "Poder local, poder regional." In *Poder regional en México*, edited by Jorge Zepeda Patterson. Mexico City: El Colegio de México.

"Denuncian PMS y CIOAC una campaña previa a violencias masivas." 1987. *Proceso* (565) (September 1):28–30.

de Vos, Jan. 1988a. *Oro verde: la conquista de la selva lacandona por los madereros tabasqueños, 1822–1949*. Mexico City: Fondo de Cultura Económica and Instituto de Cultura de Tabasco.

———. 1988b. *Viajes al desierto de la soledad: cuando la selva lacandona aún era selva*. Mexico City: Secretaría de Educación Pública (SEP) and Centro de Investigaciones y Estudios Superiores en Antropología Social (CIESAS).

———. 1993. *La paz de Dios y del rey: la conquista de la selva lacandona, 1525–1821*. Mexico City: Fondo de Cultura Económica.

———. 1995. "El lacandón: una introducción histórica." Pp. 331–61 in *Chiapas: Los rumbos de Otra Historia*, edited by Juan Pedro Viqueira and Mario Humberto Ruz. Mexico City: Centro de Estudios Mayas del Instituto de Investigaciones Filológicas y Coordinación de Humanidades (UNAM), Centro de Investigaciones y Estudios Superiores en Antropología Social, Centro de Estudios Mexicanos y Centroamericanos, and Universidad de Guadalajara.

Díaz Polanco, Héctor. 1992. "El estado y los indígenas." Pp. 145–70 in *El Nuevo Estado Mexicano*. Vol. 1. Mexico City and Guadalajara: Universidad de Guadalajara, Centro de Investigaciones y Estudios Superiores en Antropología Social, and Editorial Planeta.

Dichtl, Sigrid. 1987. *Cae una estrella: desarrollo y destrucción de la selva lacandona*. Mexico City: Secretaría de Educación Pública.

Dussel, Enrique. 1995. "Ethical Sense of the 1994 Maya Rebellion in Chiapas." *Journal of Hispanic/Latino Theology* 2 (3):41–56.

Eckstein, Susan. 1989. "Power and Popular Protest in Latin America." Pp. 1–60 in *Power and Popular Protest: Latin American Social Movements*, edited by Susan Eckstein. Berkeley and Los Angeles: University of California Press.

"El temor alcanza récords este sexenio. Chiapas: dos asesinatos políticos por mes." 1987. *Proceso* (580) (December 14):14–17.

Equipo Pueblo/Instituto Maya. 1988. "Desde Chihuahua hasta Chiapas . . . " Mexico City: Equipo Pueblo.

Escobar, Arturo. 1984. "Discourse and Power in Development: Michel Foucault and the Relevance of his Work to the Third World." *Alternatives* 10 (3):377–400.

———. 1992. "Culture, Politics and Economics in Latin American Social Movements Theory and Research." Pp. 62–85 in *The Making of Social Movements in Latin America: Identity, Strategy and Democracy,* edited by Arturo Escobar and Sonia Alvarez. Boulder: Westview.

Escobar, Arturo, and Sonia Alvarez. 1992a. "Conclusion: Theoretical and Political Horizons of Change in Contemporary Latin American Social Movements." Pp. 317–29 in *The Making of Social Movements in Latin America: Identity, Strategy and Democracy,* edited by Arturo Escobar and Sonia Alvarez. Boulder: Westview.

———, eds. 1992b. *The Making of Social Movements in Latin America: Identity, Strategy and Democracy.* Boulder: Westview.

Esteva, Gustavo. 1985. "The Archaeology of Development: Metaphor, Myth, Threat." Proposal presented before the 18th Conference of the Society for International Development (SID), Rome, July 1–4.

———. 1992. "Development." Pp. 6–25 in *The Development Dictionary: A Guide to Knowledge and Power,* edited by Wolfgang Sachs. London: Zed.

———. 1994. *El Secreto de Chiapas.* Mexico City: Era.

Ferguson, James. 1990. *The Anti-politics Machine: 'Development,' Depoliticization and Bureaucratic Power in Lesotho.* Cambridge: Cambridge University Press.

Fernández Ortiz, Luis M., and María Tarrío García. 1983. *Ganadería y estructura agraria en Chiapas.* Mexico City: Universidad Autónoma Metropolitana, Unidad Xochimilco.

Fernández Villegas, Manolo. 1991. "No queremos que nos den, nomás con que no nos quiten." Pp. 23–45 in *Cuadernos de Base 2. Los nuevos sujetos del desarrollo rural.* Mexico City: Interamerican Foundation.

Fiederlein, Suzanne L. 1996. "The 1994 Elections in Mexico: The Case of Chiapas." *Mexican Studies/Estudios Mexicanos* 12 (1) (Winter): 107–30.

Flores Lúa, Graciela, Luis Paré, and Sergio Sarmiento. 1988. *Voces del campo: movimiento campesino y política agraria, 1976–1984.* Mexico City: Siglo XXI Editores.

Floyd, Charlene. 1996. "A Theology of Insurrection? Religion and Politics in Mexico." *Journal of International Affairs* 50 (1):142–65.

Foucault, Michel. 1980. *History of Sexuality.* Vol. 1: *An Introduction.* New York: Vintage and Random House.

———. 1983. Afterword, "The Subject and Power." Pp. 208–26 in

Michel Foucault: Beyond Structuralism and Hermeneutics edited by P. Rabinow and H. L. Dreyfus. 2d ed. Chicago: University of Chicago Press.

Foweraker, Joe. 1990. "Popular Movements and Political Change in Mexico." Pp. 3–20 in *Popular Movements and Political Change in Mexico,* edited by Joe Foweraker and Ann Craig. Boulder: Lynne Rienner.

———. 1993. *Popular Mobilization in Mexico: The Teachers' Movement, 1977–87.* Cambridge: Cambridge University Press.

———. 1994. "Popular Political Organization and Democratization: A Comparison of Spain and Mexico." Pp. 218–231 in *Developing Democracy: Comparative Research in Honor of J. F. P. Blondel,* edited by Ian Budge and David McKay. London: Sage.

Foweraker, Joe, and Ann Craig, eds. 1990. *Popular Movements and Political Change in Mexico.* Boulder: Lynne Rienner.

Fox, Jonathan. 1992. *The Politics of Food in Mexico: State Power and Social Mobilization.* Ithaca, N.Y.: Cornell University Press.

———. 1994a. "The Difficult Transition from Clientelism to Citizenship." *World Politics* (46) (January):151–84.

———. 1994b. "Targeting the Poorest: The Role of the National Indigenous Institute in Mexico's Solidarity Program." Pp. 179–216 in *Transforming State-Society Relations in Mexico: The National Solidarity Strategy,* edited by Wayne A. Cornelius, Ann L. Craig, and Jonathan Fox. La Jolla: Center for U.S.-Mexican Studies, University of California, San Diego.

———. 1996. "National Electoral Choices in Rural Mexico." Pp. 185–209 in *Reforming Mexico's Agrarian Reform,* edited by Laura Randall. New York: M. E. Sharpe.

———, ed. 1990. *The Challenge of Rural Democratisation: Perspectives from Latin America and the Phillipines.* London: Frank Cass.

Fox, Jonathan, and Luis Hernández. 1989. "Offsetting the 'Iron Law of Oligarchy': The Ebb and Flow of Leadership Accountability in a Regional Peasant Organization." *Grassroots Development* 13 (2):8–15.

Friedrich, Paul. 1986. *The Princes of Naranja: An Essay in Anthro-Historical Method.* Austin: University of Texas Press.

Fuentes, Carlos. 1992. *The Buried Mirror: Reflections on Spain and the New World.* Boston, New York, and London: Houghton Mifflin.

———. 1995. *Nuevo Tiempo Mexicano.* Mexico City: Porrúa.

García de León, Antonio. 1979. "Lucha de clases y poder político en Chiapas." *Historia y Sociedad* 22:57–87.

———. 1985. *Resistencia y utopía*. 2 vols. Mexico City: Era.

———. 1989. "Encrucijada rural: el movimiento campesino ante las modernidades." *Cuadernos Políticos* (58) (September–December):29–40.

———. 1994. Prológo. Pp. 11–29 in *Documentos y Comunicados*, by EZLN. Vol. 1. Mexico City: Era.

———. 1995. "La vuelta del Katún (Chiapas: a veinte años del Primer Congreso Indígena)." *Chiapas* (Instituto de Investigaciones Económicas, UNAM, 1:127–47.

Gilly, Adolfo. 1980. "La guerra de clases en la Revolución Mexicana." Pp. 21–53 in *Interpretaciones de la Revolución Mexicana*, edited by Adolfo Gilly, Armando Bartra, Miguel Aguilar Mora, and Enrique Sema. Mexico City: Nueva Imagen.

———. 1989. *Cartas a Cuauhtémoc*. Mexico City: Era.

Gilly, Adolfo, Subcomandante Marcos, and Carlo Ginzburg. 1995. *Discusión sobre la historia*. Mexico City: Taurus.

Gledhill, John. 1988. "Agrarian Social Movements and Forms of Consciousness." *Bulletin of Latin American Research* 7 (2):275–76.

Gómez Cruz, M., and Cristina Kovic. 1994. *Conflictos agrarios y derechos humanos en Chiapas, 1989–93*. San Cristóbal de Las Casas, Chiapas: Centro de Derechos Humanos "Fray Bartolomé de Las Casas."

González Esponda, Juan. 1989. "Movimiento campesino chiapaneco, 1974–84." Undergraduate dissertation. 2 vols. School of Social Sciences, Universidad Autónoma de Chiapas, San Cristóbal de Las Casas.

González Esponda, Juan, and Elizabeth Pólito Barrios. 1995. "Notas para comprender el origen de la rebelión zapatista." *Chiapas* (Instituto de Investigaciones Económicas, UNAM, 1:101–23.

González Ponciano, Jorge Ramón. 1995. "Marqués de Comillas: cultura y sociedad en la selva fronteriza México-Guatemala." Pp. 425–44 in *Chiapas: los rumbos de otra historia*, edited by Juan Pedro Viqueira and Mario Humberto Ruz. Mexico City: Centro de Estudios Mayas del Instituto de Investigaciones Filológicas y Coordinación de Humanidades (UNAM), Centro de Investigaciones y Estudios Superiores en Antropología Social, Centro de Estudios Mexicanos y Centroamericanos, and Universidad de Guadalajara.

Gordillo, Gustavo. 1988. *Campesinos al asalto del cielo: de la expropiación a la apropiación campesina*. Mexico City: Siglo XXI Editores.

Gosner, Kevin. 1992. *Soldiers of the Virgin: The Moral Economy of a Colonial Maya Rebellion*. Tucson and London: University of Arizona Press.

Gracián, Jorge, and Jorge Sotomayor. 1981. "Tan lejos de Dios y tan cerca de Centroamérica." *Razones* 45 (September):14.

Haber, Paul. 1994. "Political Change in Durango: The Role of National Solidarity." Pp. 255–79 in *Transforming State-Society Relations in Mexico: The National Solidarity Strategy,* edited by Wayne A. Cornelius, Ann L. Craig, and Jonathan Fox. La Jolla: Center for U.S.-Mexican Studies, University of California, San Diego.

Halleck, Deedee. 1994. "Zapatistas On-Line" *NACLA Report on the Americas* 23 (2) (September–October):30–32.

Hamilton, Nora. 1982. *The Limits of State Autonomy: Post-revolutionary Mexico.* Princeton, N.J.: Princeton University Press.

Hardy, Clarissa. 1984. *El estado y los campesinos: la Confederación Nacional Campesina.* Mexico City: Nueva Imagen.

Harvey, Neil. 1990. "The New Agrarian Movement in Mexico, 1979–90." Research Paper 23. London: Institute of Latin American Studies, University of London.

———. 1992a. "Conservación a costa de la miseria." *Campo Uno,* supplement of *Uno Más Uno,* June 1 and 8, 1992.

———. 1992b. "La Unión de Uniones de Chiapas y los retos políticos del desarrollo de base." Pp. 219–32 in *Autonomía y nuevos sujetos sociales en el desarrollo rural,* edited by Julio Moguel, Carlota Botey, and Luis Hernández. Mexico City: Siglo XXI Editores and Centro de Estudios Históricos del Agrarismo en México.

———. 1994. "Rebellion in Chiapas: Rural Reforms, Campesino Radicalism and the Limits to Salinismo." Pp. 1–49 in *The Transformation of Rural Mexico,* No. 5. 2d ed. La Jolla: Center for U.S.-Mexican Studies, University of California, San Diego.

Hellman, Judith. 1988. *Mexico in Crisis.* 2d ed. New York: Holmes and Meier.

———. 1994. "Mexican Popular Movements, Clientelism and the Process of Democratization." *Latin American Perspectives* 21 (2): 124–42.

Hernández, Luis. 1991. "Nadando con los tiburones: la experiencia de la Coordinadora Nacional de Organizaciones Cafetaleras." *Cuadernos Agrarios* 1 (nueva época):52–75.

———. 1994a. "The Chiapas Uprising." Pp. 51–63 in *The Transformation of Rural Mexico,* No. 5. 2d ed. La Jolla: Center for U.S.-Mexican Studies, University of California, San Diego.

———. 1994b. "El café y la guerra." *La Jornada,* January 30, pp. 1 and 48.

———. 1995. "San Andrés: el ojo del huracán." *La Jornada,* November 21.

———. 1997. "Entre la memoria y el olvido: guerrillas, movimiento indígena y reformas legales en la hora del EZLN." *Chiapas* (4): 69–92.

Hernández Aguilar, Jorge E. 1986. *En nombre del maíz*. Mexico City: Equipo Pueblo.

Hernández Castillo, Aída Rosalva. 1994. "Reinventing Tradition: The Revolutionary Women's Law." *Akwe:kon. A Journal of Indigenous Issues* (Summer).

———. 1996. "Between Hope and Despair: The Struggle of Organized Women in Chiapas since the Zapatista Uprising." Unpublished paper presented at the 95th Annual Meeting of the American Anthropological Association.

Hernández Chávez, Alicia. 1979. "La defensa de los finqueros en Chiapas, 1914–20." *Historia Mexicana* 29 (3):299–312.

Hewitt de Alcántara, Cynthia. 1984. *Anthropological Perspectives on Rural Mexico*. London: Routledge and Kegan Paul.

———. 1992. *Economic Restructuring and Rural Subsistence in Mexico: Maize and the Crisis of the 1980s*. Discussion Paper 31. Geneva: UNRISD.

Hindley, Jane. 1996. "Towards a Pluricultural Nation: The Limits of Indigenismo and Article 4." Pp. 225–43 in *Dismantling the Mexican State?* edited by Rob Aitken, Nikki Craske, Gareth A. Jones, and David E. Stansfield. London: Macmillan and New York: St. Martin's.

Hughes, Sally. 1994. "You Can't Eat Basketball Courts." *El Financiero International,* January 24–30, p. 15.

Huizer, Gerrit. 1982. *La lucha campesina en México*. 3rd ed. Mexico City: Centro de Investigaciones Agrarias.

Instituto de Investigaciones Sociales. UNAM. 1985. "Interview with OCEZ Members." *Boletín Agro* 4:333–35.

Jaquette, Jane, ed. 1989. *The Women's Movement in Latin America: Feminism and the Transition to Democracy*. Boston: Unwin Hyman.

Jelin, Elizabeth. 1996. "Citizenship Revisited: Solidarity, Responsibility and Rights." Pp. 101–119 in *Constructing Democracy: Human Rights, Citizenship and Society in Latin America,* edited by Elizabeth Jelin and Eric Hershberg. Boulder: Westview.

Joseph, Gilbert M., and Daniel Nugent, eds. 1994. *Everday Forms of State Formation: Revolution and the Negotiation of Rule in Modern Mexico*. Durham, N.C.: Duke University Press.

Katz, Friedrich. 1988. "Rural Rebellion after 1810." Pp. 521–60 in *Riot, Rebellion and Revolution: Rural Social Conflict in Mexico,* edited by Friedrich Katz. Princeton, N.J.: Princeton University Press.

Knight, Alan. 1980. "Peasant and Caudillo in Revolutionary Mexico, 1910–17." Pp. 17–58 in *Caudillo and Peasant in the Mexican Revolution*. Cambridge: Cambridge University Press.

———. 1985. "The Mexican Revolution: Bourgeois? Nationalist? Or Just a 'Great Rebellion'?" *Bulletin of Latin American Research* 4 (2):1–37.

———. 1986. *The Mexican Revolution*. 2 vols. Cambridge: Cambridge University Press.

———. 1990. "Historical Continuities in Social Movements." Pp. 78–102 in *Popular Movements and Political Change in Mexico*, edited by Joe Foweraker and Ann Craig. Boulder: Lynne Rienner.

Laclau, Ernesto. 1985. "New Social Movements and the Plurality of the Social." Pp. 27–42 in *New Social Movements and the State in Latin America*, edited by David Slater. Amsterdam: CEDLA.

———. 1990. "New Reflections on the Revolution of Our Time." Pp. 3–85 in *New Reflections on the Revolution of Our Time*. London: Verso.

———. 1995. "Subject of Politics, Politics of the Subject." *Differences* 7 (1):146–64.

Laclau, Ernesto, and Chantal Mouffe. 1985. *Hegemony and Socialist Strategy: Towards a Radical Democratic Politics*. London: Verso.

Latapí, Pablo. 1994. "La democracia del EZLN." *Proceso* 905 (March 7):49–50.

Le Bot, Yvon. 1997. *Subcomandante Marcos. El sueño zapatista: entrevistas con el subcomandante Marcos, el mayor Moisés y el comandante Tacho, del Ejército Zapatista de Liberación Nacional*. Mexico City: Plaza y Janés.

Lehmann, David. 1990. *Democracy and Development in Latin America: Economics, Politics and Religion in the Post-war Period*. Philadelphia: Temple University Press.

Leyva Solano, Xochitl. 1995. "Catequistas, misioneros y tradiciones en las Cañadas." Pp. 375–405 in *Chiapas: los rumbos de otra historia*, edited by Juan Pedro Viqueira and Mario Humberto Ruz. Mexico: Centro de Estudios Mayas del Instituto de Investigaciones Filológicas y Coordinación de Humanidades (UNAM), Centro de Investigaciones y Estudios Superiores en Antropología Social, Centro de Estudios Mexicanos y Centroamericanos, and Universidad de Guadalajara.

Leyva Solano, Xochitl, and Gabriel Ascencio Franco. 1993. "Apuntes para el estudio de la ganaderización en la selva lacandona." Pp. 262–84 in *Anuario de Cultura e Investigación 1992*. Tuxtla Gutiérrez, Chiapas: Instituto Chiapaneco de Cultura.

López Arévalo, José. 1997. "Sobrelíneas." *Este Sur*, July 7, pp. 16–17.

López Astrain, Martha Patricia. 1996. *La Guerra de baja intensidad en México*. Mexico City: Universidad Iberoamericana and Plaza y Valdés Editores.

Lummis, C. Douglas. 1996. *Radical Democracy*. Ithaca, N.Y., and London: Cornell University Press.

MacEoin, Gary. 1995. *The People's Church: Bishop Samuel Ruiz and Why He Matters*. New York: Orbis.

Manjarrez, Froylán C. 1967. *Rubén Jaramillo: autobiografía y asesinato*. Mexico City: Editorial Nuestro Tiempo.

Marion Singer, Marie-Odile. 1984. *El movimiento campesino en Chiapas. 1983*. Mexico City: Centro de Estudios Históricos del Agrarismo en México.

———. 1988. *El Agrarismo en Chiapas (1524–1940)*. Mexico City: Instituto Nacional de Antropología e Historia.

Marshall, T. H. 1964. *Citizenship and Social Democracy*. New York: Doubleday.

McAdam, Doug, John D. McCarthy, and Mayer Zald, eds. 1996. *Comparative Perspectives on Social Movements: Political Opportunities, Mobilizing Structures, and Cultural Framings*. Cambridge Studies in Comparative Politics. Cambridge: Cambridge University Press.

McAdam, Doug, Sidney Tarrow, and Charles Tilly. 1997. "Toward an Integrated Perspective on Social Movements and Revolution." Pp. 142–73 in *Comparative Politics: Rationality, Culture and Structure*, edited by Mark Irving Lichbach and Alan S. Zuckerman. Cambridge Studies in Comparative Politics. Cambridge: Cambridge University Press.

McMichael, Philip, and David Myhre. 1991. "Global regulation vs. the nation-state: agro-food systems and the new politics of capital." *Capital and Class* 43:83–105.

Mejía Piñeros, M. C., and S. Sarmiento. 1987. *La lucha indígena: un reto a la ortodoxia*. Mexico City: Siglo XXI Editores.

Mestries, Francis. 1990. "Testimonios del Congreso Indígena de San Cristóbal de Las Casas. Octubre de 1974." Pp. 473–89 in *Historia de la cuestión agraria mexicana: los tiempos de la crisis*. Vol. 9, pt. 2, edited by Julio Moguel. Mexico City: Siglo XXI Editores and Centro de Estudios Históricos del Agrarismo en México.

Michels, Roberto. [1911] 1959. *Political Parties*. New York: Dover.

Moguel, Julio. 1988. "La cuestíon agraria en el periodo 1950–1970." Pp. 103–221 in *Historia de la cuestión agraria mexicana*. Vol. 8, edited by Julio Moguel. Mexico City: Siglo XXI Editores and Centro de Estudios Históricos del Agrarismo en México.

———. 1992a. "La lucha por la apropiación de la vida social en la economía cafetalera: la experiencia de la CNOC 1990–91." Pp. 98–118 in *Autonomía y nuevos sujetos sociales en el desarrollo rural,* edited by Julio Moguel, Carlota Botey, and Luis Hernández. Mexico City: Siglo XXI Editores and Centro de Estudios Históricos del Agrarismo en México.

———. 1992b. "Reforma constitucional y luchas agrarias en el marco de la transción salinista." Pp. 261–75 in *Autonomía y nuevos sujetos sociales en el desarrollo rural,* edited by Julio Moguel, Carlota Botey, and Luis Hernández. Mexico City: Siglo XXI Editores and Centro de Estudios Históricos del Agrarismo en México.

———. 1994. "Chiapas y el PRONASOL." *La Jornada del Campo,* supplement of *La Jornada,* January 25, pp. 7–8.

Moguel, Julio, and Pilar López Sierra. 1990. "Política agraria y modernización capitalista." Pp. 321–76 in *Historia de la cuestión agraria mexicana: los tiempos de la crisis.* Vol. 9, pt. 2, edited by Julio Moguel. Mexico City: Siglo XXI Editores and Centro de Estudios Históricos del Agrarismo en México.

Moguel, Julio, and Rosario Robles. 1990. "Los nuevos movimientos rurales, por la tierra y por la apropiación del ciclo productivo." Pp. 377–450 in *Historia de la cuestión agraria mexicana: Los tiempos de la crisis.* Vol. 9, pt. 2, edited by Julio Moguel. Mexico City: Siglo XXI Editores and Centro de Estudios Históricos del Agrarismo en México.

Molina, Virginia. 1976. *San Bartolomé de Los Llanos: una urbanización frenada.* Mexico City: Secretaría de Educación Pública and Instituto Nacional de Antropología e Historia.

Moncada, M. 1983. "Movimiento campesino y estructura de poder: Venustiano Carranza, Chiapas." *Textual* (Universidad Autónoma de Chapingo), 4 (13) (September):65–76.

Monsiváis, Carlos. 1987. *Entrada libre: crónicas de la sociedad que se organiza.* Mexico: Era.

Montes de Oca, M. E. 1977. "La cuestión agraria y el movimiento campesino: 1970–76." *Cuadernos Políticos* 14:57–71.

Morales Bermúdez, Jesús. 1992. "El Congreso Indígena de Chiapas: un testimonio." Pp. 242–370 in *Anuario de cultura e investigación 1991.* Tuxtla Gutiérrez, Chiapas: Instituto Chiapaneco de Cultura.

Morquecho, Gaspar. 1994. "Expulsiones en los altos de Chiapas." Pp. 57–77 in *Movimiento campesino en Chiapas: expulsiones, ideología y lucha por la tierra.* San Cristóbal de las Casas, Chiapas: DESMI, A.C.

Moscoso Pastrana, Prudencio. 1960. *El pinedismo en Chiapas, 1916–1920.* Mexico City: Cultura.

Mouffe, Chantal. 1993. *The Return of the Political.* London: Verso.

———, ed. 1992. *Dimensions of Radical Democracy.* London: Verso.

Narro, José. 1990. Interview. Pp. 261–83 in *Organizaciones campesinas: hablan diez dirigentes,* compiled by Guillermo Knochenhauer. Mexico City: PRI and El Día en Libros.

Nash, June. 1995. "The Reassertion of Indigenous Identity: Mayan Responses to State Intervention in Chiapas." *Latin American Research Review* 30 (3):7–41.

Olivera, Mercedes. 1979. "Sobre la explotación y opresión de las mujeres acasilladas en Chiapas." *Cuadernos Agrarios* 5 (9).

Otero, Gerardo. 1989. "The New Agrarian Movement: Self-Managed, Democratic Production." *Latin American Perspectives* 16 (4), (Fall):28–59.

———, ed. 1996. *Neoliberalism Revisited: Economic Restructuring and Mexico's Political Future.* Boulder: Westview.

Ovalle Múñoz, Pedro. 1984. "Movimientos campesinos en la zona tzeltal de Chiapas." *Textual* (Universidad Autónoma de Chapingo), 5 (17) (September):63–78.

Ovalle Múñoz, Pedro, and José Luis Pontigo Sánchez. 1983. *Movimientos campesinos en la Zona Norte y selva Lacandona de Chiapas.* San Cristóbal de Las Casas, Chiapas: Centro de Investigaciones Ecológicas del Sureste (CIES).

Paige, Jeffrey. 1975. *Agrarian Revolution: Social Movements and Export Agriculture in the Underdeveloped World.* New York: Free Press.

Paniagua, Alicia. 1983. "Chiapas en la coyuntura centroamericana." *Cuadernos Políticos* 38 (October–December):36–54.

Pansters, Wil. 1996. "Citizens with Dignity: Opposition and Government in San Luis Potosí, 1938–1993." Pp. 244–66 in *Dismantling the Mexican State?* edited by Rob Aitken, Nikki Craske, Gareth A. Jones, and David E. Stansfield. London: Macmillan and New York: St. Martin's.

Paré, Luisa. 1990. "The Challenge of Rural Democratisation in Mexico." Pp. 79–96 in *The Challenge of Rural Democratisation: Perspectives from Latin America and the Phillipines,* edited by Jonathan Fox. London: Frank Cass.

Pazos, Luis. 1994. *¿Por qué Chiapas?* Mexico: Editorial Diana.

Pérez, Matilde. 1995. "Resoluciones agrarias que datan de 1920; los cambios al 27 truncaron esperanzas." *La Jornada,* August 10.

Pérez Castro, Ana Bella. 1981. "Estructura agraria y movimientos campesinos en Simojovel, Chiapas." Undergraduate thesis, Escuela Nacional de Antropología e Historia, Mexico City.

——. 1982. "Movimiento campesino en Simojovel, Chiapas, 1936–1978: ¿Problema étnico o de clases sociales?" *Anales de Antropología* 2 (19):207–29.

——. 1995. "Bajo el símbolo de la ceiba: la lucha de los indígenas cafeticultores de las tierras de Simojovel." Pp. 301–17 in *Chiapas: los rumbos de otra historia,* edited by Juan Pedro Viqueira and Mario Humberto Ruz. Mexico City: Centro de Estudios Mayas del Instituto de Investigaciones Filológicas y Coordinación de Humanidades (UNAM, Centro de Investigaciones y Estudios Superiores en Antropología Social, Centro de Estudios Mexicanos y Centroamericanos, and Universidad de Guadalajara.

Pontigo Sánchez, José Luis. 1985. "Dinámica social y movimientos campesinos en Simojovel y Huitiupán, Chiapas." Thesis in economics, Area of Social Sciences, Autonomous University of Chiapas.

Popkin, Samuel. 1979. *The Rational Peasant: The Political Economy of Rural Society in Vietnam.* Berkeley and Los Angeles: University of California Press.

Proceso. 1994. (897) (January):28–31.

Punto Crítico. 1981. (116) (March):22.

Ramos Hernández, L. E. F. 1978. "La colonización campesina en la selva lacandona (análisis y perspectivas)." Undergraduate dissertation, Instituto Politécnico Nacional, Mexico City.

Ravelo, Renato. 1978. *Los jaramillistas.* Mexico City: Editorial Nuestro Tiempo.

Reis, Fábio Wanderley. 1996. "The State, the Market and Democratic Citizenship." Pp. 121–37 in *Constructing Democracy: Human Rights, Citizenship and Society in Latin America,* edited by Elizabeth Jelin and Eric Hershberg. Boulder: Westview.

Rello, Fernando, ed. 1990. *Las organizaciones de los productores rurales en México.* Mexico City: Facultad de Economía, UNAM.

Renard, María Cristina. 1985. "Historia de la comunidad de San Bartolomé de los Llanos, Chiapas." 2 vols. Master's thesis in social anthropology. UNAM, Mexico City.

Reyes Heroles, Federico. 1992. "Esa vergüenza nacional." *La Jornada,* April 22, p. 19.

Reyes Ramos, María Eugenia. 1992. *El reparto de tierras y la política agraria en Chiapas, 1914–1988.* Mexico City: UNAM and Centro de Investigaciones Humanísticas de Mesoamérica y del Estado de Chiapas.

Reygadas, Pedro, Iván Gómezcesar, and Esther Kravsov. 1994. *La guerra de año nuevo: crónicas de Chiapas y México.* Mexico City: Editorial Praxis.

Reyna, José Luis, and Richard S. Weinert, eds. 1977. *Authoritarianism in Mexico.* Philadelphia: Institute for the Study of Human Issues.

Robles, Rosario. 1988. "El campo y el pacto." *El Cotidiano* 23:65–72.

———. 1992. "Xi'Nich: la marcha por la paz y la dignidad." *Campo Uno,* supplement of *Uno Más Uno,* April 27, p. 5.

Robles, Rosario, and Julio Moguel. 1990. "Agricultura y proyecto neoliberal." *El Cotidiano* 34:3–12.

Rojas, Rosa. 1995. Chiapas: *¿Y Las mujeres, qué?* Vol. 1. Mexico City: La Jornada Ediciones.

———. 1996. Chiapas: *¿Y Las mujeres, qué?* Vol. 2. Mexico City: La Jornada Ediciones.

Ross, John. 1995. *Rebellion from the Roots: Indian Uprising in Chiapas.* Monroe: Common Courage Press.

Rovira, Guiomar. 1997. *Mujeres de maíz.* Mexico City: Ediciones Era.

Rubin, Jeffrey. 1990. "Popular Mobilization and the Myth of State Corporatism." In *Popular Movements and Political Change in Mexico,* edited by Joe Foweraker and Ann Craig. Boulder: Lynne Rienner.

———. 1994. "COCEI in Juchitán: Grassroots Radicalism and Regional History." *Journal of Latin American Studies* 26 (1) (February).

———. 1996. *Decentering the Regime: History, Culture and Radical Politics in Juchitán, Mexico.* Durham, N.C.: Duke University Press.

Rubio, Blanca. 1987. *Resistencia campesina y explotación rural en México.* Mexico City: Era.

Rubio López, Marín. 1985. "Formas de organización campesina y conciencia de clase: el caso de la Unión de Uniones 'Quiptic Ta Lecubtesel' del municipio de Ocosingo, Chiapas." Dissertation in rural sociology, Universidad Autónoma de Chapingo, Mexico City.

Ruiz Hernández, Margarito. 1993. "Todo indigenismo es lo mismo." *Ojarasca* (17) (February):30–36.

Rus, Jan. 1983. "Whose Caste War? Indians, Ladinos, and the Chiapas 'Caste War' of 1869." Pp. 129–40 in *Spaniards and Indians in Southeastern Mesoamerica: Essays on the History of Ethnic Relations,* edited by Murdo J. MacLeod and Robert Wasserstrom. Lincoln and London: University of Nebraska Press.

———. 1994. "The 'Comunidad Revolucionaria Institucional': The Subversion of Native Government in Highland Chiapas, 1936–1968." In *Everyday Forms of State Formation: Revolution and the Negotiation of Rule in Modern Mexico,* edited by Gilbert Joseph and Daniel Nugent. Durham, N.C.: Duke University Press.

———. n.d. "Contained Revolutions: Indians and the Struggle for Control of Highland Chiapas, 1910–1925." Manuscript.

Russell, Philip. 1995. *The Chiapas Rebellion*. Austin, Tex.: Mexico Resource Center.

Sachs, Wolfgang, ed. 1992. *The Development Dictionary: A Guide to Knowledge and Power*. London: Zed.

Sanderson, Steven. 1981. *Agrarian Populism and the Mexican State: The Struggle for Land in Sonora*. Berkeley and Los Angeles: University of California Press.

Sarmiento, Sergio. 1991. "Movimiento indio y modernización." *Cuadernos Agrarios* (nueva época) (2):90–113.

Schmitter, Philippe. 1974. "Still the Century of Corporatism?" Pp. 85–131 in *The New Corporatism*, edited by Fredrick B. Pike and Thomas Stritch. Notre Dame, Ind.: University of Notre Dame.

Schneider, Cathy. 1992. "Radical Opposition Parties and Squatters' Movements in Pinochet's Chile." Pp. 260–75 in *The Making of Social Movements in Latin America: Identity, Strategy and Democracy*, edited by Arturo Escobar and Sonia Alvarez. Boulder: Westview.

Schryer, Frans. 1990. *Ethnicity and Class Conflict in Rural Mexico*. Princeton, N.J.: Princeton University Press.

Scott, James C. 1985. *Weapons of the Weak: Everyday Forms of Peasant Resistance*. New Haven, Conn.: Yale University Press.

———. 1990. *Domination and the Arts of Resistance: Hidden Transcripts*. New Haven, Conn.: Yale University Press.

Semo, Enrique. 1986. "The Mexican Left and the Economic Crisis." Pp. 19–32 in *The Mexican Left, the Popular Movements and the Politics of Austerity*, edited by Barry Carr and Raúl Anzaldúa Montoya. La Jolla: Center for U.S.-Mexican Studies, University of California, San Diego.

Sereseres, C. 1984. "The Mexican Military Looks South." In *The Modern Mexican Military: A Reassessment*, edited by David Ronfeldt. La Jolla: Center for U.S.-Mexican Studies, University of California, San Diego.

Slater, David. 1985a. "Social Movements and a Recasting of the Political." Pp. 1–26 in *New Social Movements and the State in Latin America*, edited by David Slater. Amsterdam: CEDLA.

———, ed. 1985b. *New Social Movements and the State in Latin America*. Amsterdam: CEDLA.

Spenser, Daniela. 1988. *El Partido Socialista Chiapaneco: rescate y reconstrucción de su historia*. Mexico City: Centro de Investigaciones y Estudios Superiores en Antropología Social (CIESAS).

Stavenhagen, Rodolfo. 1996. "Indigenous Rights: Some Conceptual

Problems." Pp. 141–59 in *Constructing Democracy: Human Rights, Citizenship and Society in Latin America,* edited by Elizabeth Jelin and Eric Hershberg. Boulder: Westview.

Stephen, Lynn. 1995. "The Zapatista Army of National Liberation and the National Democratic Convention." *Latin American Perspectives* 22 (4):88–100.

———. 1996. "Democracy for Whom? Women's Grassroots Political Activism in the 1990s, Mexico City and Chiapas." Pp. 167–85 in *Neoliberalism Revisited: Economic Restructuring and Mexico's Political Future.* Boulder: Westview.

Stern, Steven. 1987. "New Approaches to the Study of Peasant Rebellion and Consciousness: Implications of the Andean Experience." Pp. 3–25 in *Resistance, Rebellion and Consciousness in the Andean Peasant World, 18th to 20th Centuries.* Madison: University of Wisconsin Press.

Tangeman, Michael. 1995. *Mexico at the Crossroads: Politics, the Church and the Poor.* New York: Orbis.

Tannenbaum, Frank. 1929. *The Mexican Agrarian Revolution.* New York: Macmillan.

Tarrow, Sidney. 1994. *Power in Movement: Social Movements, Collective Action and Politics.* Cambridge Studies in Comparative Politics. Cambridge: Cambridge University Press.

Tello, Carlos. 1995. *La rebelión de las Cañadas.* Mexico City: Cal y Arena.

Thompson González, Roberto, Ma. del Carmen García Aguilar, and Mario M. Castillo Huerta. 1988 *Crecimiento y desarrollo económico en Chiapas, 1982–1988.* Tuxtla Gutiérrez: Universidad Autónoma de Chiapas.

Tilly, Charles. 1995. "Citizenship, Identity and Social History." *International Review of Social History* 40, supplement, 3:1–17.

Tironi, Eugenio. 1988. "Pobladores e Integración Social." In *Proposiciones: pobladores, marginalidad y democracia,* edited by Eugenio Tironi. Santiago: Sur.

Touraine, Alain. 1988. *The Return of the Actor.* Minneapolis: University of Minnesota Press.

van Gunsteren, Herman. 1978. "Notes on a Theory of Citizenship." In *Democracy, Consensus and Social Contract,* edited by Pierre Birnbaum, Jack Lively, and Geraint Parry. London: Sage.

Viqueira, Juan Pedro. 1995. "Las causas de una rebelión india: Chiapas, 1712." Pp. 103–43 in *Chiapas: los rumbos de otra historia,* edited by Juan Pedro Viqueira and Mario Humberto Ruz. Mexico: Centro de Estudios Mayas del Instituto de Investigaciones Filológicas y

Coordinación de Humanidades (UNAM), Centro de Investigaciones y Estudios Superiores en Antropología Social, Centro de Estudios Mexicanos y Centroamericanos, and Universidad de Guadalajara.

Warman, Arturo. 1980. *Ensayos sobre el campesinado en México.* Mexico City: Nueva Imagen.

———. 1988. "The political project of Zapatismo." Pp. 321–37 in *Riot, Rebellion and Revolution: Rural Social Conflict in Mexico,* edited by Friedrich Katz. Princeton, N.J.: Princeton University Press.

———. 1994. "Chiapas hoy." *La Jornada,* January 16, p. 1.

Wasserstrom, Robert. 1983. *Class and Society in Central Chiapas.* Berkeley and Los Angeles: University of California Press.

Wolf, Eric R. 1957. "Closed Corporate Peasant Communities in Mesoamerica and Central Java." *Southwestern Journal of Anthropology* 13 (1):1–18.

———. 1969. *Peasant Wars of the Twentieth Century.* New York: Harper and Row.

Womack, John. 1969. *Zapata and the Mexican Revolution.* New York: Alfred Knopf.

Zámosc, Leon. 1986. *The Agrarian Question and the Peasant Movement in Colombia: Struggles of the National Peasant Association, 1967–1981.* Cambridge: Cambridge University Press.

Zepeda Patterson, Jorge. 1986. "No es lo mismo agrario que agrio, ni comuneros que comunistas, pero se parecen." Pp. 323–78 in *Perspectivas de los movimientos sociales en la Región Centro-Occidente,* edited by Jaime Tamayo. Guadalajara: Editorial Línea.

Zermeño, Sergio. 1985. "Los referentes históricos y sociológicos de la hegemonía." Pp. 251–78 in *Hegemonía y alternativas políticas en América Latina,* edited by Julio Labastida Martín del Campo. Mexico City: Siglo XXI Editores.

———. 1987. "La democracia como identidad restringida." *Revista Mexicana de Sociología* 49 (4) (October–December):3–7.

———. 1990. "Crisis, Neoliberalism and Disorder." Pp. 160–80 in *Popular Movements and Political Change in Mexico,* edited by Joe Foweraker and Ann Craig. Boulder: Lynne Rienner.

Zúñiga, Juan. 1995. "Los lazos de sangre, tierra, dinero y poder en Chiapas," *Perfil de La Jornada,* supplement of *La Jornada,* June 2.

INDEX

Neil Harvey is Assistant Professor in the Department of Government at New Mexico State University. He is the editor of *Mexico: Dilemmas of Transition* (1993) and author of "The New Agrarian Movement in Mexico, 1979–1990" (1990), in London's Institute of Latin American Studies research paper series.

Library of Congress Cataloging-in-Publication Data

Harvey, Neil

The Chiapas Rebellion : the struggle for land and democracy / Neil Harvey.

p.   cm.

Includes bibliographical references and index.

ISBN 0-8223-2209-9 (cloth : alk. paper). —

ISBN 0-8223-2238-2 (pbk. : alk. paper)

1. Mexico — Politics and government — 1988–   .   2. Chiapas (Mexico) — History — Peasant Uprising, 1994–   .   3. Social movements — Mexico — Chiapas — History.   4. Peasants — Mexico — Chiapas — Political activity — History.   5. Indians of Mexico — Mexico — Chiapas — Government relations.   6. Land reform — Mexico — Chiapas — History.   7. Representative government and representation — Mexico — History.   I. Title.

F1236.H37   1998

972'.750835 — dc21   98-16066